The Autonomous Animal

The Autonomous Animal

SELF-GOVERNANCE AND THE MODERN SUBJECT

Claire E. Rasmussen

University of Minnesota Press

Minneapolis

London

Published by the University of Minnesota Press
111 Third Avenue South, Suite 290
Minneapolis, MN 55401-2520
http://www.upress.umn.edu

Printed in the United States of America on acid-free paper

Library of Congress Cataloging-in-Publication Data
Rasmussen, Claire Elaine.
    The autonomous animal : self-governance and the modern subject /
Claire E. Rasmussen.
        p.   cm.
    Includes bibliographical references and index.
    ISBN 978-0-8166-6956-1 (hc : alk. paper)
    ISBN 978-9-8166-6957-8 (pb : alk paper)
    1. Autonomy. 2. Self-determination, National. I. Title.
JC327.R33 2011
320.1'5–dc22   2010048758

Printed in the United States of America on acid-free paper

The University of Minnesota is an equal-opportunity educator and employer.

18 17 16 15 14 13 12 11   10 9 8 7 6 5 4 3 2 1

Contents

Acknowledgments

During the long process of writing this book, I have been fortunate to have friends and critics contribute to my thinking. At the University of Washington I was privileged to work with Christine Di Stefano, Michael McCann, Nancy Hartsock, and Mika LaVaque-Manty, all of whom left an impression on the final product. I owe a particular debt of gratitude to Stuart Scheingold and Michael Brown, who were instrumental not just in shaping this project but also in influencing my ideas about how to be a scholar.

Many readers of the manuscript deserve recognition, including Glenn Mackin, Matthew Sothern, David Watkins, Jamie Mayerfeld, Eric Rasmussen, my anonymous reviewers, and hapless panel and audience members at conferences.

This book would not be possible without the enormous help I received from the University of Minnesota Press, especially from Pieter Martin. I appreciate his patience.

Finally, I acknowledge the support and kindness extended to me by friends and family in this process, especially my parents. And, of course, thank you to Wally, the dog who inspired this project by defying the human/animal boundary.

Introduction

CONCEIVING A HUMAN BEING

> Two things fill the mind with ever
> new and increasing admiration and
> reverence . . . the starry heavens above
> me and the moral law within me.
>
> —Immanuel Kant,
> *Practical Philosophy*

According to biographers, Immanuel Kant was fond of exclaiming, "Is it possible to conceive a human being with more perfect health than myself?" (Youngquist 1999, 347). Waking every morning at exactly 4:55, he ate only foods he considered conducive to thinking, carefully measured out an exact dosage of sleep, and, famously, claimed he did not sweat. The careful precision with which he constructed his texts on epistemology, morality, and politics was exceeded only by the care with which he tended his body. By all accounts, this guiding mind of the Enlightenment, the representative of reason, was also a bit of a health nut.

While we may never know what the relevance was for Kant between his highly influential account of moral autonomy and his private self-management, speculating on a relationship between the corporeal subject and the nature of autonomy may help illuminate the starry heavens of the self that preoccupied so much of Kant's work. Kant's giddy reflections on both the moral law and his own body reflect his modern sensibility, a humanist standing in awe before the capabilities of humanity, celebrating his individual uniqueness beneath the starry heavens. Critics of postmodern critiques of the humanist subject have often accused postmodernism of killing not only the contemplative subject but also the sense of Kantian wonder and optimism. In their rush to challenge the sovereign, reasoning subject, critics worry, post-foundationalists have also lost sight of the accomplishments and possibilities that remain within the self-reflexive subject posited in the works of theorists like Kant.

Most troubling to those who argue for the sanctity of the subject is the rejection of the possibility of autonomy, or self-rule. A central concept at work in much of modern theory, autonomy is critical to political subjectivity as it defines the subject capable of self-governance, able to turn inward and make reasonable decisions and engage in self-management. Perhaps most critically, autonomy is an important concept at work in democratic theory that provides both justification for participatory government and the normative end of democratic governance, to protect the ability of the individual to self-govern. To deny the subject intentionality and agency appears to undermine the entire history of modern thought, which endows the self with free will, justifies democratic self-rule, and leaves the political subject to a free-fall of heteronomous forces that determine the self from outside.

The concept of autonomy has an extensive biography, tracing back to the Greek origins of the term *autos* (self) and *nomos* (law), originally referring to a collective that ruled itself or generated its own laws without outside imposition. The idea of autonomy became linked with sovereignty or the idea of, to borrow Aristotle's terminology, the "unmoved mover" or the ultimate origin or ground of decision and the law. The sovereign undivided subject could serve as the guarantor of order. As a consequence, autonomy and sovereignty have been at the heart of much Western political thought, seeking to define the center of political order. In Roman thought, the *patria potestas*, or law of the father, granted the male head of household sovereign power over the members of the household who were incapable of rule and thus required a single power to govern. In Hobbes's *Leviathan*, the sovereign serves as the "head" of the political order, which can hold together its heterogeneous elements through the invocation of fear. In much modern political thought, especially liberal theory, the concept of autonomy has shifted from being used to describe governance at a collective level to being an individual characteristic that determines the parameters of legitimate political authority. The normative ideal of individual autonomy introduced a profound shift in thinking about human subjectivity and good government, changes that were linked to processes of democratization and the rise of liberal theory and its critics. Mill's declaration that "man, over himself, over his body, is sovereign" embodied the view that autonomy was to be found not in external executors of power but in the subject itself as legislator (1859, 22). The autonomy of the subject defined its capability for self-governance and the limits of the government, which could not impinge on the individual's right to self-management. Political order was to be secured through the proper self-regulation of individual subjects, reconfiguring the relationship between autonomy and sovereignty that shifted focus at least partially away from institutional sources of power and onto thinking about the practical and normative dimensions of self-governance. Order was less a matter of centralized power and more a matter of balancing the varying interests of individual subjects.

Consequently, much thinking about the maintenance of political order has focused on securing the autonomy of subjects against heteronomy, or perceived threats to the ability of the subject to govern itself. Emily Gill describes the features of this bounded self and the various threats to the autonomous self:

> First the individual must be free to act without compulsion or threat from external forces. Second, the individual must be a "rational free chooser," undriven by mind-altering substances or irresistible urges that would color his or her choices. Finally, the individual must prescribe for himself or herself the law to be followed, rather than allowing his or her will to be determined by customs, practices, or the will of other individuals. (2001, 17)

Personal autonomy requires a sense of self that can be clearly distinguished from external forces, whether the threat of actual, physical external force, a freedom from physical or material compulsion, and, finally, a freedom of conscience or lack of cultural determination. The definition of individual autonomy differs from the Greek deployment of "autonomy" applied to a territory. The individual is threatened not just by state power but also by a range of social and cultural pressures that may coerce—with or without force—individuals and prevent them from freely reflecting on their actions. Even more significantly, the individual's autonomy is threatened not only by forces without, but also by forces within, the irrational and "irresistible urges" that prevent rational reflection.

The focus on the autonomous subject as the means and ends of political action has important consequences for thinking about politics and the nature of freedom. If autonomy is both the condition of boundaries and the process by which boundaries are drawn between the self and the world, it also implies the necessary boundaries of the political sphere. Autonomy becomes the precondition for participation in the democratic polity since the right to self-governance is dependent on the judged capacity of that individual to govern herself. Or, as Joel Feinberg puts it, "Persons have the right to self-government if and only if they have the capacity for self-government,... the ability to make rational choices, a qualification usually so interpreted as to exclude infants, insane persons, the severely retarded, the senile, and the comatose, and to include virtually anyone else" (1989, 28).

In spite of the ubiquity of autonomy in the philosophical and cultural milieu, the concept itself has gotten relatively little attention among scholars associated with postmodernism or postfoundationalist thought. Debates about autonomy remain primarily between political philosophers attempting to pin down a coherent concept or liberal theorists who take autonomy as a normative ideal that underpins liberal practices. The concept of autonomy is rarely discussed except as it emerges in genealogies of liberal thinking in Foucault's later lectures, or in the work of governmentality scholars who have sketched the development of liberal and neoliberal thought. On the one hand, the image of Kant as the sovereign subject mastering his corporeal body through the rigorous application of rational planning is prototypically modern and an affront to challenges to the unitary subject posed by postmodern thought. Yet Kant, deriving pleasure from his subjectification, may also be seen as illustrating Deleuze's description of the Foucauldian definition of subjectification:

> [T]he man fit to govern others is the man who's completely mastered himself. . . . We're no longer in the domain of codified rules of knowledge. . . and constraining rules of power . . . but in one of rules that are in some sense *optional:* the best thing is to exert power over yourself. (Deleuze 1997, 113)

The overlap between the philosophical descriptions of autonomy and the Foucauldian understanding of subjectification suggests that the theoretical impasse between those who retain the autonomous subject as an ontological and normative concept and those who would abandon the modern subject altogether may not be insurmountable. The paradox of self-governance is that freedom is found in self-limitation, creating a compulsion to exercise power over oneself. This paradox is well clarified in works by Foucault (1971), Butler (2005), Connolly (1991), and others. However, the consequences of this paradox of the interrelationship between autonomy and heteronomy remain to be explained.

This text analyzes autonomy from a postfoundationalist perspective, one sympathetic to the critique of sovereignty and the unified subject. However, rather than further elucidate the theoretical argument about the concept of autonomy, this text instead examines how autonomy is experienced with particular attention to the practices of the self that are required of us in order to be seen by others—and our self—as autonomous. The approach is influenced by Rose's genealogy of freedom, in which he argues that "concepts are more important for what they do than for what they mean. Their value lies in the way in which they are able to provide a purchase for critical thought upon particular problems in the present" (Rose 1999, 9). Thus rather than reconstructing or repudiating the concept of autonomy, I elucidate the multiple and contingent effects of the concept of autonomy by looking at very different examples where the ideal of self-governance has shaped social practices: adolescent sexuality, the drug war, the animal rights movement, and fitness culture. Attention to the everyday life of autonomy in shaping various practices can clarify the way that autonomy is linked with the Foucauldian idea of subjectification as a modality of power that operates to establish limits on subject formation and, in doing so, creates new forms of subjectivity. Exploring autonomy as practice can reveal "the humble, the mundane, the little shifts in our ways of thinking and understanding, the small and contingent struggles, tensions and negotiations that give rise to something new and unexpected" (Rose 1999, 11).

The following chapters trace autonomy and its paradoxical linkage with heteronomy through the various ways autonomy is not merely an idea but also a set of practices. The purpose is to further understand the ways that autonomy as the ability to self-govern remains a powerful way to determine who may occupy the status of political subject. Further, I argue that autonomy and the compulsion to self-legislate may continue to have political use as a creative force that produces new and different forms of political subjectivity. The chapters consider multiple sites in which the ideal of autonomy shapes specific practices in different ways. These examples demonstrate the ways in which autonomy binds the subject to the compulsion to be autonomous, while simultaneously unfolding the creative potential remaining in the conceptualization of autonomy as a process of self-reflection and action.

The first chapter explores the theoretical terrain of autonomy by laying out key debates within theorists of autonomy with a brief overview of a few key debates and tensions within approaches sympathetic to autonomy. Rather than attempting a thorough account of autonomy I explore the Kantian ideal of autonomy and its influence on Habermas and Castoriadis to trace the key tensions between autonomy and heteronomy and between a conceptualization of autonomy as law and a conceptualization of autonomy as creation. This distinction frames an apparent tension within Foucault between his characterization of self-governance as a form of power relations in his work on governmentality and his characterization of self-governance as an ethical strategy of freedom in his work on the ethics of care. Examining this tension highlights the continued political importance of autonomy and the necessity of examining the practices of autonomy in context.

This tension between autonomy as a discourse of law whereby the self must limit or constrain itself or risk becoming a nonsubject and autonomy as creativity in which the compulsion to self-regulate can produce new and unexpected forms of subjectivity frames the following four chapters. Chapters 2 and 3 explore ways in which the requirement to self-regulate has privileged certain forms of subjectivity and excluded others primarily based on the ability to appropriately regulate the body. The examination of the emergence of the idea of adolescence in chapter 2 highlights the ways that the ideal of self-governance generates practices intended to cultivate autonomy by shaping individuals' relationships to their own bodies. The need to shape the development of subjects to ensure that they become productive citizens allows intervention into the lives of subjects deemed not-yet-autonomous. Chapter 3 focuses on the drug war and the perception that drug addicts, unable to regulate their own physical desires, are the antithesis of autonomy and thus must be regulated for their own good. Both chapters trace the way that our perceptions of autonomy, who or what constitutes autonomy, is profoundly shaped by context-specific power relationships.

Chapters 4 and 5 examine the creative potential of autonomy by exploring ways that the impulse for self-governance can produce new forms of subjectivity and ethical challenges to the power relationships that shape the present. I argue that the self-critical impulse encouraged by the discourse of autonomy can have effects that challenge as well as enforce existing relationships of power. Critique may reveal the contingency of current relationships and thus open up the possibility of choosing to act differently. Animal rights provide one opportunity for this analysis as the distinction between human and animal has been one of the most important means of measuring the autonomy of human subjects. However, animal rights may challenge human sovereignty only if it challenges the assumption that human and animal are so easily distinguished. Chapter 5 looks at fitness culture, where self-management of the body is the exemplar of autonomous subjectivity. However, the endurance athlete challenges the clear differentiation between autonomy and heteronomy when the addiction to self-regulation challenges the integrity of the self.

The purpose of exploring such disparate examples is to challenge how we think about autonomy as self-governance, an idea so ubiquitous we often do not realize how thoroughly it influences how we think about politics and about ourselves. The demand that we be allowed to self-govern is also a command that we do so. The effects of

this compulsion to autonomy must be articulated to give a more careful account of our freedom. In this light, Kant's meticulous accounting
of his body is a political and ethical choice saturated by power and
pleasure. This text analyzes this relationship not in order to judge Kant
but to help us think differently about him and ourselves.

1

The Choice of Law

AUTONOMY BETWEEN NORM AND CREATION

This means nothing less than
that he will be forced to be free.

—Jean-Jacques Rousseau,
The Social Contract

Rousseau's *Confessions* includes a salacious passage describing a spanking at the hands of his caregiver, Mademoiselle de Lambercier, and his subsequent sexual arousal. He spends several pages describing his erotic response to the act of physical discipline and the profound impact it had on his relationships with women, his sexuality, and his sense of self. Ultimately he articulates how this sexual experience enables his sexual chastity by generating the fantasy of being able "to lie at the feet of an imperious mistress, to obey her commands, to be obliged to beg for her forgiveness, these were sweet pleasures, and the more my inflamed imagination roused my blood, the more I played the bashful lover" (Rousseau 2000, 17). This ribald confession from Rousseau is a more titillating formulation of his famous paradoxical statement of the complementary nature of force and freedom. Ironically, the act of disciplining induces Rousseau to control his physical impulses, not through suppressing those impulses but by making self-control the source of pleasure. The experience creates a desire for submission, a will to control one's self and to be controlled.

While Rousseau's tale of spanking may be a less famous formulation of modern subjectivity than *The Social Contract*, it may be a more provocative illustration of the tensions within the concept of autonomy. As the exercise of self-governance, autonomy is fundamentally also a practice of self-limitation. While this process of self-limitation is often understood as oppressive, it can also be a source of pleasure and self-creation. As a young child being punished for misbehaving, he unwittingly stumbled on the conceptual puzzle of autonomy at the heart of modern subjectivity and democratic theory.

Autonomy as a defining characteristic of individuals has been central in shaping modern political thought, whether in affirming or challenging that centrality. The idea of self-governance has been instrumental on a practical level in the development of modern democracy, which affirms the right and ability of individuals to participate in their own governance. The norm of autonomy underpins, among other things, the possibility of the rights-bearing subject, theories of individualism, and conceptions of unitary identity. While autonomy as a concept has a long history spanning different philosophical orientations, the current debate over its definition and value has been monopolized by political philosophy, which has sought a clearer definition of the term in the abstract, and liberal political theory, which has sought to determine the parameters of autonomy in more practical or concrete terms. This chapter seeks to bring the idea of autonomy into dialogue with postfoundationalist political thought—especially that of governmentality scholars and deconstructionist literature—by noting the ways that many of the crucial paradoxes within the category of autonomy are also at work in challenges to the modern subject.

In order to bring more sympathetic accounts of autonomy into dialogue with critics of the concept, this chapter traces a tension within scholarship examining later works of Foucault between the critique of self-governance in his genealogy of liberalism and his embrace of self-governance in literature on the care of the self. My argument is not that the concept of autonomy can provide a bridge between disparate bodies of literature but that thinking through the paradoxes of autonomy is useful for thinking about politics in the absence of the sovereign subject at the center of modern political thought. I lay out the ways the tension between the juridical and creative dimensions of autonomy that is present in the thought of theorists of self-governance mirrors tensions within the idea of the technology of the self within Foucault, who at times seems to both critique and embrace the norm of self-governance.

My brief examination of the autonomy literature is focused primarily on Kantian formulations of autonomy in order to emphasize a few important concepts. As a genealogy it is necessarily incomplete and is not intended as a thorough survey of the vast literature on autonomy. Instead I focus on three authors, Kant, Habermas, and Castoriadis, to provide a map of some of the most theoretically useful puzzles with regard to the idea of autonomy. My goal is to highlight several shared themes or tensions within the concept of autonomy. The first is the understanding of the *autos*, or self, within the category of autonomy. How does the autonomous subject relate to itself in terms of reflecting on and managing potential sources of nonautonomous action from within, such as impulse, desire, or instinct? How does the subject learn the processes of self-reflection, which presumably free her from mere instinct? How do we learn to judge whether or not the autonomous subject has been successful in doing so? The second is a tension between the normative or lawmaking portion of the concept—the *nomos*—which encourages self-legislation, and the more creative compulsion of self-invention generated by the idea of autonomy.

The goal of exploring these tensions is to frame a discussion of the later Foucault, focusing on two major strands in his thinking. The first is the governmentality literature, which includes Foucault's own theorization of the rise of liberalism and the development of the norm of self-governance. In this literature Foucault famously argues that the "self" that governs itself is not outside of power but is in fact a product of power, noting the ways that self-governance operates as a form of disciplinary power. The second strand comes from the care-of-the-self literature, in which Foucault argues that processes of self-critique can in fact be politically and ethically productive as a form of resistance to power. This debate highlights the conflictual view of the Enlightenment discussed in Foucault's "What Is Enlightenment?" one: Enlightenment emphasizing universality, rationality, and conformity and the second embracing self-questioning (Gordon 1986, 71–73). I argue that Foucault is in fact articulating a relationship between the juridical and ethical components of autonomy that can be useful in imagining a postfoundationalist politics. This chapter lays out this theoretical discussion and makes a case for the importance of autonomy even in light of the critique of the subject, though not as a reconstructed, abstract concept. Instead, I suggest, that rather than viewing autonomy as a trait inherent in the transcendental subject of the Enlightenment, it must instead be viewed as a practice or, in Nancy's terms (1988), as a part of the experience of freedom that necessarily vacillates between the juridical and ethical to create contingent spaces of freedom. In laying out this account my goal is to suggest that autonomy ought to be a central category for discussion within postfoundationalist politics and between modern and postmodern thinkers. Finally, I propose that thinking through the concept of autonomy in a manner sympathetic to Foucault's project of the ethic of care can render a different way of looking at the concept of autonomy, which grounds it in concrete practices through which autonomous subjects are constituted.

Laying Down the Law

The modern subject of autonomy is unquestionably an individual but rarely appears as a solipsistic individual or as, in Feinberg's (1989) formulation, an "inner citadel" disconnected from or even threatened by social ties. Modern political thought has grappled with the autonomous subject as a member of a political community and with the implications of living with others. One example of this tension emerges in Rousseau, who gives two different visions of autonomy in the *Second Discourse* and *The Social Contract*. In the former, he envisions a form of autonomy that involves an independent and fetterless subject completely unencumbered by social ties or outward forces and thus who responds merely to internal or physical demands.[1] In the latter, Rousseau finds autonomy within sociality only in submission to a general will or a will formulated by a democratic collective. In identification with a collective subject, autonomy could be achieved through willing the terms of one's own restriction.

The work of Kant can be seen as grappling with the unsatisfactory alternatives proposed by Rousseau. Kant is not satisfied with a choice of autonomy personified by the subject of pure will who is (almost) completely independent of external forces or based on pure inter-dependence, self-governance through a collective will. If the first version is a pure philosophical fantasy of a presocial self, then the second is in danger of becoming a totalitarian nightmare in which individual choice and responsibility were subsumed into the general will. In submitting to a foreign will, the individual would abandon independent rational capacity in favor of a unitary collective will. True autonomy would require a more rigorous conceptualization of the autonomy of the individual will that could on the one hand preserve the independent self while, on the other, acknowledging the responsibility of living with others.

Kant's moral law negotiates this space carved out by Rousseau with the deceptively simple formulation that "I ought never to act except in a way that I could also will that my maxim become a universal law" (Kant 1996, 57). This brief summary captures several important elements of Kant's overall theory. First, morality requires autonomy of the will, or the ability of the individual to formulate and act on its own reasons that it could, in turn, formulate as universal (Dodson 1997, 97). This is a more complex concept than simply an unfettered will that acts; it is also a will that acts according to reasons. For Kant, these reasons are not arbitrary or subjectively determined but ought to be according to a universal rationality. Thus the subject is "doubled," or is both author and subject of the moral law: "We're indeed legislative members of a moral realm…yet we are at the same time subjects in it, not sovereigns" (1989, 86). The moral law is the product of individual choice or a form of self-limitation stemming from the moral agents' rational reflection on their choices. At the same time, the moral law is also the product of a universal rationality that exists external to any individual rational will. Thus for Kant autonomy is not merely a will capable of choice but also a will capable of generating its own principles and holding itself accountable to those principles in legislating and executing its own moral law (Bielefeldt 1997, 529).

Thus Kant believes he has preserved the autonomy of the subject in a more sophisticated way than Rousseau by preserving the principle of self-government and retaining subjective judgment. Autonomy therefore lies in the process of utilizing universal reason free from heteronomous influences in a more thorough fashion than proposed by Rousseau. His account "frees" the subject in two ways. First, in "What Is Enlightenment?" Kant is quick to castigate those willing to uncritically "follow orders" from others, substituting their judgment for one's own. In this he includes the explication of a single set of rules that may be blindly followed. To be truly autonomous, the individual must create the law for herself, as the act of critical self-reflection is at the heart of autonomy. The law must remain abstract and universal, created by individual, autonomous wills without imposition from the outside.

Yet Kant also posits that threats to autonomy may be internal to the subject, stemming from any source that might interfere with the process of reason, including physical sensations or personal desires.[2] For a subject to be autonomous, reason must be sovereign to guarantee the objective distance from one's own position necessary for moral reflection. An autonomous subject "has the capacity to exempt oneself from the influence of all sensible and empirical causes—psychological, social, or cultural.... An autonomous will is therefore not beholden to the ... desires ... that animate the subject since, in that case, the subject would be dependent on an empirical coefficient of pleasure or pain that is unrelated to morality" (Chalier 2002, 63). The subject's limited control over bodily impulses exempts the body from consideration as a source of autonomous action; only contemplation can provide a template for reasoned action. The autonomous subject must be able to distance herself from her own empirical conditions (including the body) and self-legislate. Autonomy is thus not an attribute of human beings but an activity that transforms the self into the subject of contemplation and author of the decision. Thus subject is ultimately determined by the universality of rationality.

Kant's account of autonomy is useful in highlighting fundamental paradoxes within the very idea of autonomy. He emphasizes that autonomy does not exist in a lawless freedom of the will but in tying our will to the law that must, as a moral law regulating our relationships with others, be universal. Kant's solution to the problem of autonomy and sociality produces the conclusion that "you are free to choose as long as you make the right choice, as long as you choose universal moral maxims.... Although adherence to moral laws is a duty and an absolute imperative, it is still a duty that is freely chosen by the individual" (Newman 2003, 3). Kant's account of autonomy differentiates autonomy from a will to anything. The autonomous subject is defined not only by the absence of external determination but by a willingness to engage in self-limitation based on reflection or the ability to make oneself the object of analysis. Autonomy is not anything goes, but rather it is constituted by the act of making the law.

Kant's influential account was critiqued by Hegel, who viewed his version of autonomy as ahistorical and based in purely subjective reason. These critiques have influenced even those sympathetic to the Kantian account. In examining just two of the post-Kantian accounts of autonomy in Habermas and Castoriadis, we can see an emergent tension regarding the relationship between the auto and the *nomos*, or between an emphasis on self-creation (Castoriadis) and the law (Habermas). Unpacking this distinction can provide a framework for discussing the two apparently contradictory positions taken in Foucault toward processes of self-governance.

Habermas's account of autonomy seeks to privilege political autonomy over moral autonomy by emphasizing the role of public debate in human rationality. He utilizes a distinction between types of autonomy as a difference between subject-centered reason in which an isolated subject independently reflects on the moral law, and communicative reason reliant on participation in a public discussion of normative issues (1990, 294–326). Therefore, autonomy is located not in the private generation of a moral law but in the political process of generating public laws, endorsing a robust democratic polity as the means through which autonomy can be achieved: "It is only participation in the practice of politically autonomous lawmaking that makes it possible for the addressees of law to have a correct understanding of the legal order as created by themselves" (1996, 121).

Habermas identifies the law as the critical location of autonomy because it can link public and private forms of autonomy through the internal relationship between democracy and power.[3] Habermas's understanding of autonomy can be explicated by unpacking these relationships he sees as intrinsic to the law. First, he establishes a relationship between private and public (or civic) autonomy, both of which he sees as critical to the subject's overall autonomy. Private autonomy is usually understood as rights and liberties possessed by individuals that are then enacted or protected by public authority. This understanding of private autonomy is antithetical to Habermas's own construction of autonomy since individuals would not have deliberated on and constructed these rights as their own; they would simply have been attributed to them. Therefore, he argues, we may assume that individuals have private autonomy, but it takes on content and meaning only within public autonomy, defined as the right to participate in the intersubjective practice of self-legislation in the medium of positive law (1996, 129).

Through the process of democratic law making, subjects may then grant themselves the specific rights and liberties they see as necessary to secure private autonomy. As Habermas describes it:

> The scope of citizens' public autonomy is not restricted by natural or moral rights just waiting to be put into effect, nor is the individual's private autonomy merely instrumentalized for the purposes of popular sovereignty. Nothing is given prior to the citizen's practice of self-determination other than the discourse principle. (1996, 127–28)

In other words, he believes he has secured the autonomy of the subject not by simply granting her protection but by enabling her to determine the very meaning of her own autonomy through the formulation of her rights through the medium of the law. The autonomous subject is *self-determining* in an ultimate sense in giving shape to her own autonomy.

In addition to acting as the mediator between public and private autonomy, the law is privileged because it is a more effective means of securing autonomy for individual subjects. Habermas draws this conclusion through a consideration of the relationship between the law's democratic features and its coercive power. On the one hand, the law is democratic in providing a medium for the stabilization of expectations, or a way of coordinating social action through a shared language. The law provides a structure through which the democratic process may be enacted. Habermas also values the coercive power of the law that makes it a more powerful tool for social coordination than the moral law. Morality requires that the actor's motives be transformed into effective action and are dependent on "the moral actor's precarious, highly abstract system of self-control, and in general on accounts of the vicissitudes of socialization processes that promote such demanding competences" (1996, 114). Combining knowledge and action requires the subject first to be able to formulate a rule that accords with the moral law and then determine what action is appropriate. The law, on the other hand, is designed as a system of action and moves the interpretation of morality from a private, cognitive act to a public moment of deliberation on what norms may be established in law and how they ought to be applied (1996, 115). Further, the law may coerce appropriate action in accordance with autonomous deliberation. Since the process of lawmaking is also a moment of self-reflection and self-formation, the subject is formed through participation in the language of the law—external to the self—and comes to self-understanding as a *legal* subject. As with Kant, Habermas's vision of autonomy is grounded in a view of autonomy as an action, specifically the act of creating and enforcing a law. The difference lies in the move from the subjective realm of moral lawmaking to the political realm of public lawmaking. And, as with Kant, the activity of autonomy is not arbitrary but determined by the limits of rationality. Habermas gives these limits very specific terms, tying them to liberal democracy; he clearly believes that this requires a particular type of subject and society: "Democratic institutions of freedom disintegrate without the initiatives of a population accustomed to freedom. Their spontaneity cannot be compelled simply through law; it is regenerated from traditions and preserved in the associations of a liberal political culture" (1996, 131). The idea of political culture is critical in Habermas, establishing the external conditions necessary for individual subjects to achieve their autonomy, conditions that must include the coercive force of the law to bind subjects to the laws that they have generated.

If Habermas is chiefly concerned with the linkage between autonomy and the law, Castoriadis, who also casts himself as an inheritor of Kant, is more concerned with a determination of the "self" in self-governance. As with Habermas, he rejects the possibility of grounding autonomy in an individual will that reflects on its contents and acts in accordance to its subjectively determined but transcendental rule. Instead he suggests that autonomy has sociohistorical dimensions and must be viewed as a process of collective reflection, action, and change. Unlike Habermas, who places importance on collective

processes of positing the law, Castoriadis emphasizes collective processes of self-formation. He argues that autonomy is not found merely
in the process of a subject (individual or collective) generating laws
but in the production of the subject itself.

Castoriadis casts his argument in sweeping terms: "The very history
of the Greco-Western world can be viewed as the history of the struggle
between autonomy and heteronomy" (1991, 88).[4] The first step toward
autonomy, he argues, is recognition of the "ultimate responsibility" of
human existence, or recognition of a fundamental contingency of all
sociohistorical formations. History lacks any explanatory narrative or
causality that makes any particular social arrangement or way of being
necessary (1991, 1998). Society must recognize itself as the origins
of its own norms and, in doing so, open them up to questioning and
change. Unlike Kant, who argues that the autonomous will must be
distinguished from empirical referent, Castoriadis believes autonomy
must be embedded within the particular sociohistorical context in
which reflection and change is to take place.

A specific sociohistorical formation is described as an instituted
society, or a society with a relatively stable set of norms or values that
coordinate social action. The social institution is not to be mistaken
for empirical institutions such as the state or the positive law. The
important "institutions" are the "magma of meanings" that underpin
and enable the creation of these "second order" institutions. Castoriadis calls the relative sedimentation of meaning in any given society the
imaginary institution of society because any particular set of meanings is a function of a social imaginary. All societies have a constructed
understanding of the world—the imaginary—that enables a particular
way of life but is not necessary and therefore may also be imagined differently. A society is heteronomous when it imagines any given institution as externally imposed or a necessary way of life that cannot be
changed. Autonomy is located in the notion of an *instituting* society,
or the society that reflects on why it has chosen a particular imaginary,
and is capable of imagining and constructing other institutions.

Autonomy is comprised of two subsets of activity in relationship
to the imaginary institution. The subjective dimension is philosophy,
or the reflection on a particular social imaginary. The recognition that
"we posit our own laws" absent any external necessity—the essence of

autonomy—enables questioning present conditions, including the conditions under which we claim to be autonomous (1991, 105). Autonomous reflection may then question who the "we" is who has chosen these laws, why any particular set of laws has been chosen, and how we judge both the construction of the "we" and the particular content of the social imaginary. The second element of autonomy lies in politics, or the public activities of instituting society. For Castoriadis, autonomy is conceptually linked with democracy as the collective process of putting society into question and producing social change. Autonomy is achieved only through the successful combination of reflection and action.

Unlike the previous authors, Castoriadis begins with a notion of autonomy as a social phenomenon that occurs on a collective level as the critical reflection on the instituted society and the continual process of instituting society. The collective recognition that any given society's institutions are in fact contingent and not predetermined allows that society to realize that those institutions are subject to critique and change. "The individual" as a form of subjectivity is the product of a particular social imaginary that institutionalizes the individual through secondary institutions such as the economy, a system of rights, and so on. Therefore, the notion of autonomy may be applied to the individual subject only through a *particular* social imaginary that privileges autonomy.[5] He describes the process of subject formation beginning with the "monadal psyche," which, through a process of socialization, internalizes social institutions in order to become a subject. The subject is a dynamic interaction between psychical impulses and socialization.

Through the tensions within the subject, creativity emerges. The self becomes autonomous in both reflecting on itself as a subject and on its sociohistorical position in a critical manner. While the social imaginary leaves its "violent imprint," the impulses of the psyche are never eradicated and therefore subjects are open to creative impulses, in imagining themselves and their society to be other than they are. For Castoriadis, the process of political change is not fully rational—though it is in part guided by the rational process of self-reflection—but is produced by the creative and irrational force of the psyche.

Castoriadis captures an element of autonomy and a particular notion of social and individual change. As Zerilli (2002) describes it, Castoriadis requires truly autonomous political action to be "completely new," in a sense similar to Arendt's description of spontaneity. Truly autonomous creation cannot be determined by or derived from any external force or it becomes heteronomous. Therefore, creativity must be a rupture with the past and the birth of something new. Politics, if it is autonomous, is revolutionary, provoking an overhaul of the very institutions of society and heroically emerging from a space outside of power (i.e., the existing institutions). Autonomy may be grounded within a particular sociohistorical framework within which *reflection* takes place, but autonomous *action* must break with the particular context to imagine and generate something new. Autonomy ultimately exists in the capacity of the imagination to break with the given and overhaul the structures of power. Political action is identifiable in a clear and conscious challenge to the instituted society. In this political vision only two forces exist, the sedimented institutions of power and the creative forces of change. Castoriadis's autonomous subject is compelled toward the new, bound by the continual drive to overcome the present and invent, she is a slave to the need for spontaneity.

Autonomy, in these accounts, is found in the activity of the generation of laws, but tension exists between the varying emphases on autonomy as law and autonomy as creation. If Kant and Habermas emphasize the processes of self-limitation, Castoriadis in turn is interested in the self that is limited. These tensions suggest that autonomy as a concept contains potential productive paradoxes that link autonomy with limitation and coercion on the one hand, while on the other hand compelling creativity. The emergent image of autonomy is of a form of freedom that is simultaneously restrictive and spontaneous. Individual freedom justifies the dismantling of systems of domination that restrict autonomous action, but that same autonomous subject is presumed to be governed by reason that always already shapes the subject's will, ensuring the preservation of public order. Bell identifies this tension as at the heart of liberalism, which is premised on the subject of calculated reason while resting on a vision of freedom that gestures toward newness and creativity. Drawing from Arendt she describes the tension: "Truly beginning anew—the true performance of freedom—is arguably incompatible with the notion of calculable man upon which the ability to promise rests" (Bell 1996, 82). This inherent contradiction within autonomy and, especially, in how the discourse of autonomy manifests itself within the liberal polity, does not necessarily mean that the concept is incoherent or without value. Instead, examining a similar tension within Foucault's work between his critique of the self-governing subject of liberalism and his embrace of self-critique in the care of the self point toward a more productive way to conceptualize and critique autonomy.

Self-Governance in Another Light

The term "autonomy" does not appear frequently in the work of Foucault, but the general concept of self-governance is ubiquitous. While not intervening directly into the debates over autonomy, Foucault's work can be read as a general critique of the very possibility of the autonomous subject. In suggesting that society is thoroughly saturated by power relations that constitute the subject, he suggests that autonomy is an impossible fantasy wedded to the unitary subject who can step outside of power in order to rationally reflect on itself. Indeed, in the literature on governmentality, Foucault and his inheritors lay out a brutal genealogy of liberalism and its underlying conceits of individual liberty, limited government, and personal freedoms. In this account the norm of self-governance is itself an instrument of power through which the liberal subject is constructed. On the other hand, Foucault embraces a self-critical form of subjectivity in which the self makes itself the object in *The Care of the Self* and much of his later work. This section lays out this tension in Foucault suggesting it can be framed in terms similar to the distinction between autonomy as lawmaking and autonomy as self-making, bringing Foucault into dialog with some of the purveyors of the modern subject.

Foucault's work on governmentality undermines the premise that autonomy or self-governance represents a freedom from relationships of power. The political rationality of liberalism instrumentalizes the autonomous subject as a means of governance. The emphasis on self-governance or the ability of individuals to delimit their own actions enables the minimization of juridical power, or the coercive power of the state, but cannot be interpreted as a decline in the role of power. Instead, responsibility shifts to individual subjects who are expected to govern themselves without external intervention. Self-governance represents a displacement but not disposal of relationships of power. State power may decrease when subjects voluntarily limit their own actions: "Liberalism... constructs a relationship between government and governed that increasingly depends on ways in which individuals are equipped to assume the status of being subjects of their lives" (Burchell 1996, 29).

Burchell traces a distinction between liberal and neoliberal (or liberal and advanced liberal) practices. While liberalism grounds the view of the subject in a natural order, "the rationality of the free conduct of governed individuals" (1996, 24), liberalism forwards a constructivist view of governance in which the role of government is not merely to protect/avoid interfering with natural liberty but to actually cultivate the capacity for self-governance. Whether the demarcation between two distinct modes of liberalism is necessary,[6] he is correct in noting that the ideal of autonomy functions as both "the basis of government in some contexts and as artefact of government practices in others" (Hindess 1996, 73). Autonomy on the one hand serves to justify the liberal mode of governance as appropriate to subjects who are capable of governing themselves, but it also generates particular practices intended to maximize autonomy, creating the very subject it claims as its foundation. Liberalism exists to act "on subjects from a distance in so far as they could reasonably be regarded as already autonomous, and acts on them more directly in so far as their autonomy is seen as something that has yet to be realized" (Hindess 1996, 73).

The work of Foucault and others has traced the emergence of a variety of "technologies of the self," or practices by which individuals are intended to learn how to govern themselves. From the social sciences to psychiatry a gamut of emergent discourses teach individuals how to maximize their mental and physical health, improve their productivity, and manage their lives. Proper subjects are trained in how to be appropriately self-governing according to shifting norms and expectations. The compulsion to be autonomous includes not only breaking with external influences and dependence on others but also acute attention to the ways that one's own internal desires, whether physical, sexual, or emotional, must be governed or channeled. Thus emerges the ubiquity of biopower, the governance of life itself, often governing on or through the individual body (Foucault 1986, 2003).

The governmentality literature suggests that autonomy is not a transcendental category but a historically located conception of freedom tied with particular forms of governance. Autonomous subjectivity is a contingent way of understanding human subjectivity that generates and is generated by a political rationality. The goal of governmentality literature, however, is not merely to note the historically contingent rather than transcendental nature of autonomy, but also to analyze the consequences of the discourse of autonomy.

The first consequence is that autonomy serves as a way of differentiating between populations and adopting governance strategies appropriate to each, examining how "individuals are privileged as self-regulating agents or are marginalized, disciplined, or subordinated as invisible and dangerous" (Nadesan 2008, 1). The emergence of autonomy as the predominant mode of self-understanding has consequences described by Dean as "division between those capable of bearing the freedoms and responsibilities of mature subjectivity and those who are not" (2009, 157). In other words, just as Kant suggests, autonomy is a discourse that compels obedience to the law with the underlying danger of being deemed to be a nonautonomous or heteronomous subject for failing to exercise appropriate self-governance. This generates relationships of exclusion for those who then fail to be viewed as autonomous subjects and thus are not given the same regard, rights, or freedoms as those who have been adequately forced to be free. These processes of exclusion can have dire consequences for those viewed as incapable of self-governance. While Kant imagined the autonomous subject would conform to universal rules of rationality, the political norm of autonomy requires that autonomous subjects conform to socially defined expectations of autonomous subjects, a benchmark that may be unstable and shifting.

At the same time, the compulsion to self-regulate generates an entire regime of technologies of the self whereby the ways in which the self is expected to self-legislate are continually proliferating. Cruickshank argues that the self is the site of the intensification of power relations:

"Democratic modes of governance and social scientific ways of knowing (re)produce citizens who are capable of governing themselves, of acting in their own interests, and in solidarity with others. Citizens are not born; they are made" (Cruickshank 1999, 3). Thus liberal democracy is not merely a space for the exercise of self-governance; it must also be a space for the production of subjects capable of self-governance. Autonomy is not an achievement but requires constant vigilance to continually demonstrate one's capacity for self-governance. The distinction between autonomy as law and autonomy as creation is blurred as the need to continually self-govern is transformed into a need to continually improve and even create one's self. Deleuze (1997) describes the transformation into a control society in which self-legislation necessarily entails more than internalizing existing norms but in being the actual origin of new laws and norms by which the self is crafted. In Foucault's own terms, "This modernity does not liberate man into his own being; it compels him to face the task of producing himself" (1986, 42).

The analysis of the political rationality of liberalism that describes the ways in which autonomy is itself a discourse of power, or as Rose puts it, instrumentalizes the "powers of freedom," certainly casts doubt on the depiction of autonomy as the definitive understanding of liberation. The acts of the subject are themselves exercises in power, indeed heteronomous forms of power, that represent sociohistorical forces beyond the individual, who is himself or herself a product of power. In this account, even the creative act of self-creation is invested with power relationships. As Butler writes:

> The work on the self, this act of delimiting, takes place within the context of a set of norms that precede and exceed the subject. They are invested with power and recalcitrance, setting the limits to what will be considered to be an intelligible formation of the subject within a given historical scheme of things. There is no making of oneself (poiesis) outside of a mode of subjectification and, hence, no self-making outside of the norms that orchestrate the possible forms that a subject may place (Butler 2005, 17).

It would seem, then, that Foucault would see his project as fundamentally at odds with that of Kant, Habermas, or even Castoriadis, all of whom conceptualized autonomy as liberation from power, as a space in which the reflective subject could act freely.

However, Foucault described himself as an inheritor of the Kantian legacy, borrowing Kant's title "What Is Enlightenment?" and arguing that he belonged to the tradition of self-reflection and critique opened up by Kant's view of autonomy. Kant's failing, however, was failing to heed the warning that enlightenment is a process rather than the achievement of the enlightened: "The problem with Kant is that he opens up a space for individual autonomy and critical reflection on the limits of oneself, only to close the space down by reinscribing it in transcendental notions of rationality and morality" (Newman 2003, 26).

Thus Foucault sought to retain the autonomous subject as the subject who, to borrow Deleuze's terminology, folds in on itself, questioning its own limits, boundaries, and constitution in order to seek out other ways of being. Foucault seems to endorse a political project of self-critique in describing his project as

> an aesthetics of existence . . . as the search for an ethics of existence . . . to give to one's own life a certain form in which one could recognize oneself, be recognized by others . . . the subject is constituted through practices of subjection or, rather, through practices of liberation. . . starting of course from a certain number of rules, styles, and conventions that are found in the culture. (1989, 311–12)

Without the moral (or political) certainty of rational universality, the process of self-critique leads not to a unified subject able to will the law but to a divided subject who recognizes the contingency of one's current existence by challenging us "to imagine ourselves as having different features from those we normally take for granted both in ourselves and in others" (Hoy 1994, 84). Foucault thus sees the process of self-governance as having two potential sides. One element is the Kantian accountant who takes stock of the self and brings it into line with the law. The other is a creative subject who takes stock of the self in order to understand and resist the imposition of power on the self, though in the process generating a new law that governs the self. Patton describes this process:

> In the attempt to exercise their capacity for autonomous action, those subject to relations of domination will inevitably be led to oppose them. It is not a question of advocating such resistance, of praising autonomy, or blaming domination as respective exemplars of good and evil for all, but simply of understanding why such resistance does occur. . . . Resistance follows from the nature of particular human beings. It is an effect of human freedom. (1998, 73)

Thus for Foucault autonomy as self-governance is a double-edged sword that on the one hand compels the self to exercise power over itself (and others) while at the same time provoking resistance to that power in selves that, using the compulsion to self-legislate, may always legislate in different ways. Autonomy as law is also autonomy as self-creation, a paradox that requires the continual "folding of the self" onto itself to critically reflect on and manage its self-limitations. Thus Foucault captures a kind of political agency that is not the authentic action of a self that is liberated from power relationships to act on its own interests or desires but a self that acts with and through the process of subjectification. Foucault has historicized debates over autonomy by placing them in the context of developing political rationalities and thereby indicates a way that the concept of autonomy may continue to have use for postfoundationalist political theory even as the idea of the unitary subject loses its cache. The final section of this chapter connects Foucault's "ethics of care" with the ethical turn in deconstruction to suggest an overlapping concern with the political import of undecidability that may help elucidate the connection Foucault sees between his critique of self-governance within liberalism and his embrace of self-critique as a political strategy.

A Politics of Undecidability

Foucault's embrace of subjectification as a strategy of resistance is most evident in *The Care of the Self* and in later essays on the technologies of the self. In these texts Foucault clearly differentiates his ethic of care from moral autonomy as posited by Kant. While both require an accounting of the self, or a continual monitoring and evaluation of the self, Kant turns to universal and transcendental rationality to provide a benchmark of judgment against which the self may be measured. In reflecting on the universal rules of rationality, the subject may be secure in its moral actions. Foucault holds that an ethical, not moral, relationship to the self is based on a scrutiny of the self and of the rules or norms against which the self is judged. Consequently he argues for greater attention to everyday practices and relationships within which our actions have meaning, scrutiny that must be undertaken without a set of universal rules by which to judge these actions. The removal of the certain ground of universal rationality is, for Foucault, a move that makes the subject ultimately responsible, ethically responsible, for its actions: "The celebration of the risk of non-identity, of what it might mean to occupy that ontologically insecure position which poses the question anew: who will be a subject here and what will count as a life" (Golder 2008, 755).

Foucault's emphasis on ethics in the face of uncertainty and privileging of everyday practices over transcendental categories overlaps with concerns in deconstructive analyses, particularly work by Derrida and Nancy emphasizing the role of ethics in politics. Reading these accounts with Foucault may elucidate the distinction Foucault wishes to make between techniques of self-government that reinforce existing power relationships and those that resist them. In turn, reading Foucault with these texts may also help uncover the political content in the ethical turn within deconstruction. Like Foucault, Derrida's work on ethics emphasizes a post-Kantian view that eschews the transcendental, universal and fixed notion of the moral law for the everyday, contingent, and shifting arena of ethics. For Derrida, all attempts to ground the law in a single, sovereign foundation such as rationality demonstrate the impossibility of identifying a unitary ground that can serve as the singular foundation of a moral or political order. Derrida's argument about the insecurity of foundations relies in part on his philosophical claims about the impossibility of locating the "unmoved mover," or a sovereign subject, rationality, or rule that is not heteronomous or haunted by an other that disrupts its unity (2005, 100). His argument is also, however, a claim that deconstructive ethics are *more responsible* than the moral certainty of a thinker like Kant, who believes we can understand and elucidate the universal moral law. Following Nietzsche he argues that the subject unmoored from a fixed, universal law who has nothing outside of itself to which to refer is truly autonomous and fully responsible. Without a law outside of itself to justify its actions, the self must make the decision without reference to a predetermined rule.

For Derrida, the absence of a singular ground enables rather than undermines the possibility of ethical engagement. In the absence of a categorical imperative or a single set of rules, he argues, we must confront the Other on its own terms without a prior rule that determines how we act. Such ethical action requires the sort of continual self-critique called for in Foucault's ethics of care, without a fixed point of reference, the law must continually be revised to be adequate to the situation at hand. The absence of a fixed rule opens up the possibility of ethical thinking (La Caze 2007, 784). The Kantian impulse of self-critique is radicalized and put to work under conditions in which the self is not accessing a transcendental moral law but must continually make the law, and the self, anew. For Derrida the uncertainty generated by decision making in the absence of a law by which to judge our actions is the impetus for further self-scrutiny. Just as the Foucauldian subject turns in on itself, so too does Derrida's ethical subject continually scrutinize the act of decision. He refers to this as the call of the Other, the way in which the ethics of action is not based on conformity to an abstract rule but on the analysis of the concrete relationships to Others to whom we are responsible.

The deconstructive turn to ethics is not uncontroversial even among postfoundationalist thinkers. Critchley (1996) and Laclau (1996), for example, argue that the emphasis on ethics obfuscates the role of politics, which, ultimately, requires the act of decision. Ethical self-critique and uncertainty cannot provide an adequate account of decision, leading either to political quietism in the inability to act or to political indifference in an inability to choose between political possibilities (La Caze 2007, 785). These concerns may be addressed through an analysis of Nancy's discussion of freedom and, finally, a return to Foucault.

Nancy's similar conceptualization of action under conditions of uncertainty explicitly links ethics with a discourse of freedom to be found in actions taken under conditions not entirely within the control of the subject and without a moral law. These conditions embody, for Nancy, a more thorough conceptualization of freedom in which the freedom of the self must be understood in its existence:

> Thus it is no longer a question of winning or defending the freedom of man, or human freedoms, as if these were goods that one could secure as possession or property, and whose essential virtue would be to allow human beings to be what they are. . . . Instead, it is a question of offering human beings to a freedom of being, it is a question of presenting the humanity of the human being to a freedom as being by which existence absolutely transcends, that is, ex-ists. (1988, 13)

Nancy calls the experience of freedom, the uncertainty in which the subject acts, not individuality but singularity. The subject is neither independent from nor determined by the set of conditions, or power relationships, in which the subject is embedded. The singularity of those conditions creates the possibility of acting in a manner that is not determined by circumstances. Nancy argues that the analysis of freedom must focus not on freedom as an abstract transcendental quality that can be determined in advanced, but in relationship to existence. He calls, therefore, for an empirical rather than philosophical relationship to freedom that is attentive to singularity, or the conditions of the emergence of freedom in human action.

In this discussion Nancy also argues that freedom of action is not reliant on the sovereign, autonomous agent. Change does not emerge from fully conscious action but from what he calls *surprise*: "History is perhaps not so much that which unwinds and links itself, like the time of causality, as that which surprises itself. 'Surprising itself,' we will see, is a mark proper to freedom" (1988, 15). This account of surprise echoes the Foucauldian notion that power produces resistance and thus produces change. Here we see the linkage between the normative and creative dimensions of autonomy in which power is never able to fully determine relationships, and the singularity of those power relations always has the possibility of producing a surprise. The ethical call to self-critique can produce political change through the emergence of resistance to the sedimentation of any particular set of power relationships. Foucault recognizes the normative, lawmaking and creative, self-making dimensions of autonomy and their necessary and paradoxical interconnection.

Unquestionably, this account of political autonomy would be unsatisfactory for critics of Foucault (and others) who argue that without a normative foundation against which to judge political action, Foucault cannot and does not provide an account of liberation. This analysis is correct but it is not the case that a Foucauldian account of autonomy is not political. Instead, it calls for the continual practice of self-critique in order to generate different ways of relating to one's self, undermining any attempts to present any particular set of power relationships "as permanent and invariable" and instead revealing their contingency and, thus, reversibility (Phillips 2002, 335–36). To be an adequate political account, however, it must continually move between a persistent critique of political conditions to emphasize their contingency while also considering the ethical, keeping open the possibility of change.

Conclusion

Viewing autonomy as a normative *and* creative concept opens the term up to a new political analysis that emphasizes singularity, or the ways in which particular practices of autonomy generate the sedimentation of or resistance to existing power relationships. The paradoxical conclusion of many theorists of autonomy that freedom exists in self-limitation is appropriated in Foucauldian accounts as a productive contradiction that recognizes the inescapability of power. Yet Foucault embraces this paradox in the ethic of care, in which self-analysis is central to the production of political change. Subsequent chapters explore the tension between these two dimensions, emphasizing the ways in which the juridical function of autonomy produces relationships of exclusion and creates new ways of being.

The deconstructive analysis of ethics emphasizes the ways in which the uncertain ground of autonomous action that frees the subject from transcendental categories (and categorical imperatives) also calls for a different approach to the analysis of autonomy. Nancy calls for an empirical analysis of freedom or examination of the singular conditions of the emergence of particular practices of autonomy. Each of the chapters that follows examines particular instantiations of the norm of autonomy with attention to the ways in which these practices embody the theoretical paradoxes laid out in this chapter. However, the examination of practices is done not to generate a more thorough or perfect account of autonomy but to emphasize the ways that autonomy is itself an activity or, in Nancy's terms, the *experience* of freedom. These chapters will highlight Nancy's theorization of the surprise or the ways in which political change is possible in the absence of a center or a sovereign, how the law of autonomy is not determinate but is itself uncertain.

2

Mature Subjects

PHYSICAL EDUCATION AND THE POLITICAL CHILD

> What can the child do that even the
> lion could not do? [. . .] The child
> is innocence and forgetting, a new
> beginning, a game, a self-propelled
> wheel, a first movement, a sacred "yes".
>
> —Friedrich Nietzsche,
> *Thus Spoke Zarathustra*

The following is an exchange between Whitney, a fifteen-year-old girl, and Dr. Phil McGraw (Dr. Phil), a self-described "Life Strategist" and well-known pop psychologist appearing on the *Oprah Winfrey* show:

WHITNEY: You don't have to be depressed or have low self-esteem to want to do anything sexual. I think it's more fun than people realize. I feel that it's my choice what I do with my body and my friends.

DR. PHIL: And you said something a minute ago. You said, "It's my body, and I have the right to do with it what I want." Let me tell you, I have to take issue with that. I think self-determination is a privilege. I think it is a privilege that is earned by mature decision making and sound problem-solving, and if you're making bad decisions and you're not solving problems well, I don't think self-determination is something that should be given to a fourteen-year-old kid, to say, "It's my body and I have the right to do what I want to with it." That's not true unless and until they've earned the right to make those decisions.

Whitney's statements, a common expression of selfhood by a teenager, brought shock and horror from the crowd of mostly middle-aged women. In contrast, Dr. Phil's admonition of the girl, emphasizing her age and minimizing her maturity, brought applause from the crowd. Whitney tries to use a familiar language of choice and bodily autonomy while Dr. Phil and the audience deny her these capacities on the basis of her age and their perceptions of her behavior. Later the audience further applauded his claims that, because teenage boys have nothing to gain by refusing oral sex, the onus is placed on teenage girls to refuse male advances. Demonstrating self-determination for young women like Whitney entails a single choice; she must learn to say no.

This exchange between the teenager and the doctor captures the stereotypical struggles between parents and children over their behavior and the privileges appropriate to their age, but it also captures a deeper level of discourse about the meaning and granting of autonomy in relationship to "maturity," the presumed process of acquiring autonomy. "Kids" may not practice self-determination because of their inability to adequately control themselves; they must be forced to be free, to learn autonomy through submission to external authority. Autonomy is the right of those who have learned to exercise it properly and demonstrate the ability to make the decisions. The paternalist refutation of Whitney's autonomy by the good doctor represents the paradoxical law of autonomy whereby only certain choices are considered authentically autonomous, while Whitney's own sexual desire is viewed as immature and improper. Acting on her own desires renders Whitney a nonautonomous subject.

Autonomy as self-governance dictates that subjects must demonstrate their capacity for and willingness to limit their actions. This paradoxical dimension of autonomy enables the exclusion or disciplining of certain subjects who fail to live up to the perceived standards of self-governance. This normalizing dimension of autonomy that determines who does and does not count as an autonomous subject also produces mechanisms whereby subjects may learn to behave autonomously: "Subjection is also a condition of freedom; in order to act freely, the subject must first be shaped, guided, and molded into one capable of responsibly exercising that freedom through systems of domination" (Dean 2009, 193).

Few subjects demonstrate the school of autonomy better than kids who are constantly described as lacking mature subjectivity and thus may be denied full control over their lives and bodies. At the same time, they are the focus of intense attention in order to push them toward becoming productive adult citizens. The discourses that circulate around kids, especially adolescents about to enter into adulthood, demonstrate the conclusion that autonomy is a discourse of exclusion, sorting out who does and does not constitute a subject. Further, the processes by which adolescents are trained to be autonomous show how autonomy is a conditioned characteristic, a learned set of practices whereby subjects take on norms that show they are appropriately self-governing (Hindess 1996, 75). However, these general claims must be supplemented by understanding that the ways we define autonomy reiterate specific kinds of power relationships. In the case of kids, our collective understanding of how and why kids should learn to be self-governing intersect with norms about gender, sexuality, age, and class that are often presented as natural and thus "permanent and invariable" (Phillips 2002, 336). Consequently this chapter primarily focuses on the normative dimension of autonomy, in which individuals are compelled to be self-governing in specific ways in order to be granted the privileges of maturity. The production of autonomous, mature subjects also means the proliferation of norms whereby society determines who constitutes a mature subject and through which subjects relate to themselves. These proliferating norms also create new forms of subjectivity, in this case the new category of development called the adolescent.

To demonstrate the relationship that exists between autonomy and self-limitation I examine the discourse concerning physical maturity, especially sexuality, and immature subjects. I examine both the theoretical role of kids in modern democratic theory and actual practices to show how the intense interest in kids is central to modern conceptions of the autonomous subject. I begin with an exploration of three theorists who wrote extensively about the role of child-rearing in democracy—Locke, Rousseau, and Kant—and how their focus on the child relates to the overall view of the centrality of individual self-governance to collective self-governance in democracy. All three focus on the role of self-disciplining the body, a foregrounding of micropolitical issues in the shadow of their macropolitical projects (Popiel 2008). The chapter then turns to the practical question of the disciplining of the bodies of children through two examples. I first look at the "adolescent," a classification generated in the nineteenth century. The adolescent was fundamentally defined by physical development coupled with moral underdevelopment, giving rise to the need for new physical disciplines to control their sexuality. From the general analysis of adolescence I examine the development of age of consent and statutory rape law as constructions of "girls" as incapable of autonomous consent and thus requiring the intervention of the law, medicine, and psychiatry. The purpose of the analysis of "childhood" is to demonstrate the ways in which autonomy is constructed against the border between "mature" and "immature" subjects that is necessary for determining who counts as a political agent. "Children" are considered less than full subjects who are nonetheless central to how we think about our own political subjectivity and our own autonomy. The paradoxes of autonomy manifest themselves in the ideas and practices that circulate around and on teenaged bodies and demonstrate the normative dimension of autonomy.

Educated Guesses: Political Theorists Raise the Child

While children[1] rarely speak in political theory, they often are spoken about. Many political theorists have written about them within their very adult discussions of the political sphere. The interest in children is indicative of their role, literal and figurative, in our conceptualization of political citizenship. Within modern democratic theory children represent the prepolitical subject who must be cultivated in order to become capable of participating in democratic governance. Many recent texts have analyzed citizenship or civic education, arguing for the need for children to understand the workings of their democratic system and liberal culture in order to become participants (see Dewey 1963; Gutmann 1987; Ryan 1998; Levinson 1999; Kymlicka 1995). But political education does not only or even primarily have to do with informing children about their political system. Political education must produce autonomous subjects capable of making individual and collective decisions and thus is an education in self-governance.

"Childhood"—understood as emergence from immaturity—is used by political theorists as a period for the construction of autonomous subjects who must learn how to exhibit self-governance prior to participation in governance with others. The figure of the child represents the individual who lacks full autonomy and rights because of a perceived lack of ability to responsibly use that autonomy; they must be coerced in order to develop their capacity to self-rule. As one liberal theorist puts the paradox:

> The conditions required to develop a skill or disposition such as autonomy are both logically and empirically different from the conditions required for its exercise. Adults' exercise of autonomy may be best protected by safeguarding a variety of traditional liberal freedoms. But children's development of autonomy may be best promoted by *coercing children*. (Levinson 1999, 52, emphasis added)

Within modern political thought, the child emerges as an important metaphor for political progress as well as an object of political intervention. The symbolic value of "childhood" is captured in the first few lines of Kant's infamous "What Is Enlightenment?" when he declares "Enlightenment is man's release from his self-incurred tutelage. Tutelage is man's inability to make use of his understanding without direction from another" (1996, 17). The use of immaturity here is to characterize pre-Enlightenment history as a "childish" period of tutelage in which individuals did not make full use of their reason. Enlightenment, the achievement of political and social maturity, is populated by individuals who make full use of their capacity to reason. While Kant wags his fingers at pre-Enlightenment adults' collective "childishness," he argues the remedy is autonomy: "Nothing is required but freedom" (1996, 22).

While Kant refers here to an audience of (age-wise) adults, he invokes a unique feature of modern childhood. Echoing his theory of moral autonomy, political maturity is not characterized by blind obedience to an external set of (adult) rules but through the proper exercise of freely chosen self-restrictions that demonstrate "enlightenment."

The goal of an autonomous, self-regulating subject is achieved not through negative means of restriction or punishment, but through training the immature subject in the proper uses of freedom. Once the formerly immature subject is capable of legislating for himself, others will no longer need to legislate for him.

Childhood in modernity marked a shift in the conceptualization of children from being miniature adults to being adults-in-the-making, potential subjects who needed to be cultivated. As political theory moved away from a paternalist model of thinking about political power in which subjects were considered to be subject to the paternal father of the king, so too did thinking about children shift from a purely paternalist model. Children were no longer subjects preparing to be subject to authority, trading one patriarch for another; they were subjects preparing to be active participants in their own governance (Archard 1993, 85–86).

Childhood, understood as a stage of *temporary* immaturity, presents a problem for the political theorist invested in self-governing subjects. The child must learn how to govern himself[2] in order to become a mature adult, but he is perceived as lacking those attributes that enable him to be self-governing and therefore equal to his adult counterparts. In other words, political theorists interested in the shaping of mature, self-governing subjects must find a way to force children to be free while avoiding forms of coercion that might prevent the child from learning how to govern his own behavior. The ultimate goal is not just behavior modification but to train children in modifying their own behavior. Children exist in a suspended state as potentially autonomous subjects who lack the rights, respect, and freedoms afforded to fully autonomous agents who must endure discipline in order to earn their freedom.

The idea that autonomy is an ability that must be cultivated makes children of interest to democratic theorists as potentially autonomous subjects. Early democratic theorists faced a difficulty, reflected perhaps most clearly in Rousseau's *The Social Contract*, that good government requires good people; if the government is to govern less, the people must govern themselves more. They must have the capacity of self-limitation for their own good and must possess enough reason to govern with others. The significance of educating for autonomy is highlighted by the fact that three of the most prominent political theorists of the era not only included extensive discussions of children in their other political writings but also wrote or lectured extensively on the topics of education and childrearing. Kant, Locke, and Rousseau found children important enough to include analyses of contemporary practices of education alongside their more "adult" ruminations on epistemology, metaphysics, and politics. The three authors differ significantly on questions of political authority but converge on a similar belief that political and moral maturity is learned through proper training aimed at achieving the goal of autonomy. None of these three theorists raised an actual child[3] but nonetheless felt compelled to think about the education of children. This point of convergence yields insight into how all three of them conceptualized the development of autonomous capacities within subjects, a process that is neither natural nor necessary but requires the intervention of mature adults.

The three texts I will focus on are lesser-known works of the authors but are nonetheless critical supplements to their overall projects. Kant, Locke, and Rousseau were all theorists concerned with moral and political autonomy, and their works on education—*Paedagogik*, *Some Thoughts concerning Education*, and *Emile*, respectively—reflect a concern that the child-rearing techniques of parents in their era were in fact hindering the emergence of both mature political subjects and mature political societies. I examine three overlapping themes emerging from the texts as significant for the relationship between children and autonomy. First, they agree that the capacity for reason is learned through the management of the physical experiences of the body, leading to an investment in the physical education of children. Second, the most important physical capacities subject to self-limitation are sexual urges that are particularly threatening to the capacity to self-govern. This focus on sexuality is highly gendered, leading to different educational strategies by sex and, consequently, different political roles for the sexes. Finally, the development of autonomous capacities through the body is linked with the possibility of democracy. The failure to learn appropriate self-limitation is a problem not only for the child but for society as a whole. Thus, intervention into the lives and bodies of children is necessary to encourage their autonomy.

The concern for children in democratic theory mirrors the decline of authoritarian modes of governance in the public and private spheres. Locke took mothers to task for what he perceived as coercive and restrictive behaviors, such as swaddling or corseting children, which were physically and intellectually oppressive. The goal in these views of children was not to teach them to blindly follow authorities or mechanically obey rules but to view themselves as self-governing subjects who were capable of managing their own behavior, desires, and instincts. Children needed to learn to want to follow rules rather than being forced to do so by their parents. Kant describes this paradoxical task as learning "how to compel the will while fitting it to use its liberty," seeking to cultivate the child's capacities while simultaneously urging them to channel those capacities toward the responsible actions of an autonomous subject (Kant 1992, xvi). The child must learn to obey the moral law but in such a way that the child learns that this obedience is not coerced but freely willed.

The body is a primary instrument through which children are to be trained to use their reason. Rousseau emphasizes physicality as a key component of childhood, placing great importance on the cultivation of physical strength and arguing that the goal is to "prepare the way for his control of his liberty and the use of his strength by leaving his body its natural habit, by making him capable of lasting self-control, of doing all that he wills when his will is formed" (1911, 34). The relationship between self and body, however, is not merely one of developing physical strength and control but also acknowledging that "the desired values of rationality and self-control could not be divorced from the ability to experience the world physically" (Popeil 2008, 4).

A primary technique for training the mind and body is the learning of proper responses to physical stimuli. Locke's section titles provide a hint of the role of physical education in the management of desire with headings like "hardening the body," "not too warm clothing," "diet," "against strong drinks," and "actions of the bowels." He defends his focus on the physicality of the child arguing "how necessary health is to our business and happiness; and how requisite the strong constitution, able to bear hardships and fatigue, is to one that will make any figure in the world is too obvious to need any proof" (1902, 2). Locke claims that bodily discipline can cultivate the faculty of reason through the management of physical sensations. For example, he argues that a child's feet should be kept constantly damp in order to develop a habit of physical discomfort to train the child to ignore or overcome intense physical sensations (1902, 4–5).

Rousseau quite famously employs physical discomfort to train the child to respond appropriately to sensation. He discusses at length the importance of learning from mistakes, particularly physical discomfort and pain that teaches the child not only how to avoid intense sensations but also how to manage those sensations autonomously:

> Should he fall or bump his head, or make his nose bleed, or his fingers, I shall show no alarm, nor shall I make any fuss over him; I shall take no notice. . . . If he finds I take no notice, he will soon recover himself, and will think the wound is healed when it ceases to hurt. This is the time for the first lesson in courage and by bearing slight ills without fear we gradually learn to bear greater. (1911, 48)

Kant embraces a similar model of training, though he consistently views children as developing in stages, the first being submissive training, in which the child learns to follow rules, and moral training, in which the child develops his own rules. He discusses "hardening the child" to prevent him from becoming too "effeminate" by, for example, having him sleep on a hard bed and avoiding exciting him with food that is too spicy, strong, or warm (1992, 37–39). As the language of effeminacy suggests, while Kant is interested in the political education of children, boys, as the future citizens, are his primary concern. In the second stage the child is given freedom to play games, cultivating the body and in the pursuit of self-given goals or ends; he argues that "the more a child's body is strengthened and hardened in this way, the more surely will he be saved from the ruinous consequences of over-indulgence" (1992, 64).

The concern with the body is focused primarily on the management of sensation, avoiding extremes of pleasure and pain. This delicate balance requires cultivating the body's ability while simultaneously cultivating the ability to control physical impulses. For Rousseau these are related:

> The body must be strong enough to obey the mind; a good servant must be strong. I know that intemperance stimulates the passions; in the course of time it also destroys the body; fasting and penance often

produce the same results in the opposite way. The weaker the body, the more imperious its demands. The stronger it is, the better it obeys. All sensual passions find their home in effeminate bodies; the less satisfaction they can get the keener their sting. (1911, 24)

The physical passions that are the cause for the greatest concern are the sexual passions, receiving attention in all three texts focused on managing the development of mature heterosexuality. Significantly, Rousseau's fictional tutelege of Emile terminates with his pupil's marriage, marking his passage from childhood into mature subjectivity, becoming a citizen, husband, and father (Zerilli 1994, 39). The onset of puberty is cause of special concern to Rousseau as the period when the body has the greatest capacity and a lack of self-restraint, "everything about him enflames his imagination" (1911, 216). At this time, Rousseau introduces a lesson on the deferral of satisfaction by introducing Emile to Sophy, his wife-to-be, who can serve as an image that encourages him to be chaste until he can satisfy his desires within the institution of marriage.[4] Only when he can engage in proper reproductive sexual relations that reproduce the social order may he indulge these physical desires.

Kant also ends the educative period with marriage and fatherhood, arguing that education must continue until "the youth has reached that period of his life when nature has ordained that he shall be capable of guiding his own conduct; when the instinct of sex has developed in him, and he can become a father himself, and have to educate his own children" (1992, 26). Taking up the issue of sexual education, he says that children should not be shielded from sexuality (since they will be exposed to sexual information and stimuli) and adults should provide information when children seek it. Yet Kant is chiefly concerned that the knowledge given helps them to control rather than indulge their bodily passions. Sexuality must be directed toward socially productive channels—reproductive sex within marriage—or it can be disruptive to the self and society.

Kant's fear of masturbation exemplifies his anxiety about the disruptive nature of unmanaged sexual desires. Self-pleasuring, repeatedly called an "animal desire" is a demonstration of a failure to place limits on the self and selfishly indulging in physical desires rather than deferring pleasure for more productive opportunities. He warns:

Nothing weakens the mind as well as the body so much as the kind of lust which is directed toward themselves, and it is entirely at variance with the nature of man. But this also must not be concealed from the youth. We must place it before him in all its horribleness, telling him that in this way he will become useless for the propagation of the race, that his bodily strength will be ruined by this vice more than by anything else, that he will bring on himself premature old age, and that his intellect will be very much weakened. (1992, 117)

The extensive warning by Kant demonstrates this linkage between autonomy and self-limitation. He is chiefly concerned with providing the child with facts and skills that will guide him toward the self-governance of his desires both for his own good and for the good of society. This link ties the inculcation of autonomy to broader democratic goals. While early childhood involves following the dictums and rules of others, the child must gradually develop a capacity to think and decide for himself. However, not all decisions are considered valid, and autonomous subjects must make correct decisions to demonstrate their autonomy. Just as Kant describes the process of enlightenment as a gradual emergence of self-governance out of previous systems of rule, so too is childhood a gradual enlightenment of the subject, establishing a new relationship to himself. Kant refers to this as "voluntary obedience," learning to submit to limitations by choice that ultimately "prepares the child for the fulfillment of laws he will have to obey later, as a citizen" (1992, 86). As the passage on masturbation suggests, the stakes are quite high both for individuals and for society at large. The management of sexual desires is the ultimate test, requiring the deferral of desire and pleasure in order to achieve "higher" ends. Governing one's self is both training for and evidence of the capacity to govern with others in a democratic society while failure to properly self-regulate may be grounds for exclusion from participation in societal self-governance.

Childhood, as a state of immaturity characterized not just by chronological age but also by perceived lack of self-governance, is a source of anxiety within a self-governing society.[5] On the one hand is the belief that individuals can have a duty to be self-governing, while on the other hand is the recognition that subjects must be disciplined to learn how to engage in the necessary physical and moral behaviors deemed markers of maturity. The process of maturation requires the suppression of personal desires in order to be regarded as autonomous. Yet the line between maturity and immaturity must be continually maintained with constant vigilance to manage the desires that are never eradicated, only managed. The anxiety expressed about the emergent sexuality of children in both Rousseau and Kant is telling about the disruptive nature of the child's body and part of the reason sexuality becomes more visible in modern political thought.[6] The next section will consider how this attention to the passage from immaturity to maturity or heteronomy to autonomy through the experience of sexual maturation generates a new form of subjectivity, the adolescent, who provokes the promise and anxiety evoked by the hope of educating autonomous citizens.

The Terrible Teens

In the preceding accounts, education through the physical body culminates in entrance into the public political world. The adult body becomes a fit political participant through the most private of acts, sexual maturity. The physical and the moral are inextricably linked in the demonstration of maturity through proper engagement in heterosexuality practiced in the institution of marriage. The evidence that the subject has advanced from mere instinct to mature adulthood is the ability to channel physical desire into appropriate expressions. Sexual activity serves as a benchmark to measure autonomy through the requirement that individuals overcome desires that interfere with moral and physical discipline.

Not surprisingly, the relationship between children and sexuality has been fraught with anxiety since sex is considered an activity that requires a mature and autonomous subject. Cultural panic over child pornography, teen pregnancy, and oral sex "epidemics" all relate to a disruption in the orderly transition from animal instinct into political adult. In particular, "young adults," as almost autonomous, are a particular source of anxiety because of their potential to use their budding freedom in potentially destructive ways. Cultural preoccupation with the sexuality of adolescents demonstrates several paradoxes in our understanding of the relationship between autonomy and sexuality.[7] Teenagers are liminal subjects trapped between the more instinct-driven stages of childhood and mature personhood. They are therefore a little bit autonomous, neither fully rights-bearing subjects nor political participants, but also no longer fit for the patronizing treatment given to little kids. Adolescence as a stage of maturation subjects the individual to a range of disciplining processes that, on the one hand, seek to cultivate the autonomy of future political subjects to make free choices while, on the other hand, dictating to them which choices are appropriate for an autonomous agent.

This section examines the construction of the category of the adolescent as a sexual subject and object of intense disciplining. Characterized in discourse by physical maturation and moral immaturity, the teenager embodies several cultural tensions over autonomy and its relationship to political agency. Following an examination of the cultural construction of children's sexuality and its relationship to the construction of the category of "adolescence," I will examine the different techniques that emerged to shape the physical and moral development of adolescents.

Foucault's *History of Sexuality* is one of the most influential works on the relationship between sexuality and modern subjectivity and on the sexuality of children. Studying Victorian discourse on sexuality Foucault makes several conclusions about sexuality that are relevant. Sexuality became a central component of autonomous political subjectivity during this era in three primary ways. First, sexuality is an object of intense scrutiny and political intervention through concerns about reproduction, social hygiene, and public health. Birth rates, sexually transmitted diseases, the characteristics of the family and marriage all became matters of concern to various authorities, including the state, medical experts, and educators. Foucault writes: "Between the state and the individual, sex became an issue, and a public issue no less; a whole web of discourses, special knowledges, analyses, and injunctions settled upon it" (1978, 26). The governance of sexual practices, he states, began with the intense focus on marriage, including the legal proscription of activities seen as detrimental to marital monogamy, including prostitution, premarital sex, homosexuality, infidelity, and bestiality (1978, 38). Sexuality and the family were linked and subject to public scrutiny, regulation, and discussion, not just through the state but also through the rise in psychiatry, advice manuals, and medical professionals (see also Donzelot 1979).

Second, sexuality became relevant to personal and political identity. Sex was not merely something one did but was a part of who one was. Foucault famously declared the invention of the "homosexual" in the 1800s, a form of subjectification through a category that created a "personage, a past, a case history, and a childhood, in addition to being a type of life, a life form. . . . Nothing that went into his total composition was unaffected by his sexuality" (1978, 43). Sexuality became a form of identification and an identity, a way of relating to others as well as to oneself.

Third, Foucault argued that emergent with the centrality of sexuality to subjectivity was an intense focus on children and their sexual development. Children were viewed as innocent and asexual, mirroring centuries of understanding about children's original innocence, corrupted by adult pursuits such as sex (1978, 26–27; see also Piper 2000). The desire to shield children from sexuality led to attempts to prevent children from being exposed to or engaging in sexual activities. Techniques for disciplining children's sexuality proliferated, including physical arrangements for children's bodies and advice books for parents, doctors, and educators.

"Around the schoolboy and his sex there proliferated a whole literature of precepts, opinions, observations, medical advice, clinical cases, outlines for reform, and plans for ideal institutions" (1978, 28).[8] One of the greatest threats, however, was not sex between children but, echoing Kant, the masturbating child. The temptation to masturbate was an opportunity for the ultimate self-management of desire and caving in to that desire was indicative of personal and social failure. A primarily private act, masturbation was nonetheless a social act in that it was a form of sexuality exercised outside the institution of heterosexual marriage and a violation of proper subjectivity in giving in to personal urges. While the act itself had no harmful effects on others (in spite of supposed medical claims that it could weaken the sexual and mental performance of males), it was understood as harmful to the self as pure self-gratification, the pursuit of pleasure without a socially useful purpose. Masturbation demonstrated the link between physical self-restraint and moral development. The moral self was meant to control the physical body, and the physical body reciprocally shaped the moral self.

Critics of Foucault have noted that his history of sexuality is incomplete in its failure to consider the relationship between colonial and racial discourses and the construction of sexuality, particularly in the nineteenth century (see Stoler 1995). The perception that sexual behavior was indicative of moral capacity played a role in other forms of power relationships of the time. The masturbating child, for instance, was described as displaying "savage-like" behavior and failing to behave in a "civilized" manner. The language had both racial and class undertones in describing how the physically undisciplined activities of both the lower classes and colonized persons demonstrated their inadequacy for self-rule. Not surprisingly, the legal and social codes of colonizing agents generally involved the exportation of the sexual norms of the colonizer, including the regulation of marriage, prohibitions of nudity, and the criminalization of sodomy (Stoler 1995; Merry 1999).

The linkage between children and "savagery" had an impact not just on the perception of colonized persons; it reciprocally shaped the construction of adolescence as a specific stage of human existence. The adolescent as a particular kind of subject was understood as similar to "savages" in possessing physical capabilities that they lacked the intellectual maturity to manage. Teenagers, like colonial subjects, became subject to greater juridical control justified as being for their own good. The surveillance regulations that were applied to the bodies of adolescents were not uniform, however. As a measure of subjectivity, maturity is not defined solely by age but may also be a function of differences in race, class, gender, or sexuality (Lesko 2001, 34).

As sexuality became central to defining identity, it impacted definitions of childhood and gave rise to a new stage in childhood: adolescence. The new stage, emergent in the nineteenth century, was in part an extension of childhood made possible by shifts in production. As society moved away from the use of child labor, the health of children as well as the general population improved, contributing to longer life expectancies (Moran 2000, 15). Healthier children often entered into puberty earlier than in previous generations, but the average age of marriage and childbearing increased. Children transitioned into the world of mature, independent adulthood requiring new social strategies for coping with subjects whose physical maturity outpaced their moral development.

Adolescence became a category of popular understanding in the late nineteenth century, influenced by the 1904 publication of G. Stanley Hall's two-volume text *Adolescence: Its Psychology and Its Relations to Physiology, Anthropology, Sociology, Sex, Crime, Religion, and Education*. As the sweeping title suggests, the text depicted the adolescent as a new sort of being with a unique biological, psychological, and social existence. Combining evolutionary physiology and psychosexual development theories, the adolescent was biologically defined by puberty and the physical development of the body, which presumably signaled the development of sexual urges. Adolescence was considered a "rapid spurt of growth in body, mind, feelings and a new endowment of energy" (Hall 1904, 314). With this rapid growth came an awareness of heterosexual urges that Hall saw as confusing but necessary for the maturation of the adolescent.[9] The interpretation of these changes was profoundly marked by cultural discourses on autonomy as self-control on the one hand and racialized, gendered, and classed categories on the other. Hall drew on "recapitulation theory," or the belief that childhood development followed an evolutionary path from primitive to civilized, a belief drawing heavily on civilizational discourses that defined certain groups of persons or behaviors as belonging to primitive stages of development (Robertson 2002, 8).

The adolescent boy, defined by growing physical capabilities and sexual urges, was the source of great promise and enormous anxiety, seen as embodying "muscular masculinity" while at the same time threatening criminality and debauchery should he fail to manage his physical powers. Mirroring the stereotype of "savage man," the teenaged boy was seen as having enormous physical development without adequate moral development; he therefore was to be subject to more rigorous physical and moral training in order to become mature. The adolescent girl, on the other hand, was seen as lacking the sorts of physical impulses and desires of the boy (especially sexual desire) and needed to avoid any exertion that might deplete or diminish her future reproductive capacity (Moran 2000, 17).

Adolescence represented a period of particular anxiety for parents, society, and scholars. Against the sentimentalizing of youthful innocence, adolescence marked a phase of potential danger described as "storm and stress" (Kett 1971; Dornbusch 1989; Lesko 2001; Paris 2001). Literature in the first half of the twentieth century described the experience as a "seething period of turmoil and external strife . . . emotional instability and erratic behavior" (Zorbaugh and Payne 1935, 371). Some psychologists even went so far as to describe the teen years as a form of temporary psychosis (Zorbaugh and Payne 1935, 372). The phrase "delinquency" emerged to describe teenage behavior considered socially unacceptable, ranging from breaking the law to disobeying parents to wearing skirts considered too short.

The primary marker of adolescence was the biological event of puberty, seen not as just a physical watershed but as a moral benchmark as well. The experience of puberty defined sexual maturity, and the management of physical impulses during this period was viewed as critical for moral development. The teenage boy, in particular, was seen as a seething mass of sexual impulses that need to be restrained to guarantee moral development. As one sociologist characterized the danger of the teen: "All education rests on this principle; the continuation and the amplification of this lesson ought to lead the boy to restrain his ardent desires, to subdue his temperament, to do his duty, however disagreeable it may be" (Marro 1900, 224). Specialists in the new public health categories of "sexual hygiene," "moral hygiene," and "puberal hygiene" developed means to limit the biological force of puberty and employed means from controlling the teen's food intake and temperature as well as physical activities that were nonsexual and specifically avoided contact with the inner thighs and genital areas (Marro 1899, 1900). Precocious sexual activity could be sparked by any number of environmental stimuli, including an overly warm room, rich or spicy food, or climbing a rope.

In addition, as Rousseau warned, the boy needed vigorous physical activity of a nonsexual nature to divert his imagination away from sexual matters. The physical body was intended to be a check on the nonrational elements of the mind: "Daydreams and phantasies, thoughts that he cannot control, sudden impulses to irrational behavior occupy his attention" (Richmond 1935, 334). Not only the body but also the mind needed to be carefully regulated and monitored. Boys needed to be kept away from licentious literature and images and kept occupied with nonimaginative arts such as mathematics and (nonbiological) sciences.

The stakes involved in raising the adolescent boy were no less than the survival of democratic government, which relied on the moral development of its citizens. One sociologist and psychologist went so far as to claim that "from sexual excesses ... one notes with the deterioration of character, the loss of manly virtues. Despotic governments find in this vice the best condition for their support" (Marro 1900, 225). This passage identifies sexual activity by adolescent males as a cause of their own moral failure as adults. Sexual excess leads to "the loss of manly virtues" or an ability to act as the patriarch in the home and the good subject in politics. Sexual precocity is even seen as supporting despotism. The connection is made between the capacity to self-govern one's own body and a capacity to self-govern in the public realm through participation in democratic governance. The connection between strength of character and masculinity defines self-governance as a gendered characteristic. Yet male sexuality was not to be eradicated or conquered; it was to be channeled into socially acceptable forms of expression. Masturbation and same-sex desires were to be suppressed, while some avenues of heterosexual expression were permitted.

The connection between personal and public self-governance was gendered by characterizing the management of desire as a masculine virtue. Women joined other populations viewed as incapable of overcoming their physicality to be politically autonomous subjects. Just as women's physicality was a marker of their immaturity, the sexual practices of other cultures were used as a means of demarcating entire cultures as immature and lacking the ability and thus the right of self-governance. Treatises on the differences between civilized and savage societies highlighted the extension of the period between sexual maturity (puberty) and procreation within marriage as a mark of civilization, demonstrating the ability of its members to exercise collective self-control.[10] Early marriage or sexual behavior, especially among girls, was often used to demonstrate the backward nature of colonized societies and the lower classes (see Towns 2010, 95–96; Stoler 1995, 100–118 and 137–50; Lesko 2001). Chastity in the teen years was a means of differentiating bourgeois, civilized individuals from savages, children, and the otherwise unfit for self-rule. The upper classes had the leisure of a transitional period between childhood and adulthood because they did not have the economic imperatives of leaving the family home and working to alleviate the financial burden on the family. Consequently, sexual purity was a means of determining the potential for autonomy of specific individuals, specific cultures, and specific classes of persons.

The teen years were marked by two (at times competing at times colluding) ways of understanding the adolescent body. On the one hand was the emphasis on biology and instinct and anxiety assumed to lead to the growing desire in the adolescent body for physical pleasure. On the other hand was the discourse that adolescence required rigorous surveillance and moral direction, not only for the moral development of the individual subject but also for the very good, and indeed survival, of civilized society. Not surprisingly, a new set of disciplinary technologies proliferated, again demonstrating the entanglement of physical fitness and moral maturity. The teenage years were seen as a stage characterized by *becoming* in which the self is shaped by constant activity that transforms leisure into work on the self (Rose 1999; Foucault 1986). Adolescent girls were segregated from boys in physical activity but often engaged in physical fitness programs considered appropriate for the sex and future reproductive capabilities. Women's physical education worked not on training or competition for sport but on lifelong health practices and health maintenance (Verbrugge 1997, 293).

For boys, more rigorous physical activity was planned through schools, the rise of organized sports, and new organizations aimed at their simultaneous moral and physical development. Organizations such as the Young Men's Christian Association (YMCA) and the Boy Scouts combined rigorous physical activity and the development of a masculine body and attitude with moral and often religious training. Boys' physical activity was more likely to emphasize competition, strength, and physical domination. While sex was rarely explicitly mentioned, preventing it was a motivating factor and a constant concern. Physical activity was meant to redirect sexual urges and to give a channel to what were seen as men's natural, but controllable, physical desires.

As with adults, the idea of the subject in the process of becoming through rigorous surveillance, by self and others, was not just about the individual subject but was linked to social and political well-being. Into the twentieth century, the physical development of the boy intensified as an important location for the development of national strength. For instance, in 1960 President Kennedy wrote "The Soft American" for *Sports Illustrated*, in which he linked a decline in physical fitness to America's "falling behind" the Soviet Union in the Cold War. He claimed that physical weakness was as much to blame as scientific shortcomings for the Soviet Union winning the space race. He wrote, "The harsh fact of the matter is that there is also an increasingly large number of young Americans who are neglecting their bodies— whose physical fitness is not what it should be—who are getting soft. And such softness on the part of individual citizens can help to strip and destroy the vitality of a nation" (1960, 16). He links social well-being to the physical health of its individuals, establishing a personal responsibility for the body as a political duty. Kennedy characterizes a feminized body, a "soft" body, as a threat to democracy in its demonstration of a failure to self-regulate the body. These failed subjects may also lead to a failed democracy since self-governance on a personal level is also linked to the self-governance of the body politic.

Political agency is inscribed as a permanent duty of self-maintenance and restraint made necessary by the freedom to shape ourselves. Our own autonomy makes us responsible for rigorously improving ourselves but also responsible for the vitality of the entire body politic. Kennedy continues:

> No matter how vigorous the leadership of government, we can fully restore the physical soundness of our nation only if every American is willing to assume responsibility for his own fitness and the fitness of his children. We do not live in a regimented society where men are forced to live their lives in the interest of the state. We are, all of us, as free to direct the activities of our bodies as we are to pursue the objects of our thought. But if we are to retain this freedom . . . then we must also be willing to work for the physical toughness on which the courage and intelligence and skill of man so largely depend. (1960, 19)

The publication of "The Soft American" provided the justification for the establishment of the President's Council on Fitness, which monitored the physical activities of Americans and suggested guidelines and activities for attaining physical fitness. The council's main activity, though, was to continually gauge the health of American youth through the President's Physical Fitness Test and to establish and maintain guidelines for physical education in schools. Continual monitoring and measuring of our children was to be accompanied by individual vigilance to ensure that children (and adults) met our physical and moral standards.

The emphasis on the development of the self through the body led to another transformation in social relations: the adolescent also became a consumer. The maintenance of the physical body, including practices of hygiene, appearance, and fitness, created new forms of consumption. The teenage body created a market for managing the teenage body from training bras to acne remedies to teen magazines and age-appropriate clothing. The capacity for leisure time and play was linked with class relationships. Children were distanced from public spheres of work, while adolescents were associated primarily with public places of consumption, such as cinemas or malls (Sanchez-Eppeler 2000, 819–23). The adolescent body confronted a very adult capitalist conundrum: the impetus to consume was confronted by the necessity of exercising self-restraint in order to remain a productive member of society. Increasingly, adolescence has become a form of lifestyle consumption in which identity is expressed through consumer choices (Matt 2002; Lowe 1995, 134–35). This tension has a sexual charge for teenagers as well. Their consumption, generally aimed at physical attractiveness and social acceptance, is also a process of gendering and sexualizing the body. At the crossroads of political, social, and economic forces the adolescent body has been subject to study, monitoring, surveillance, disciplining, and outright control. The danger posed by these adolescent bodies has generated a variety of policies and practices entailing nearly permanent intervention into the lives and bodies of adolescents.

Adolescents appear trapped in a double bind. Nonengagement in sexual activity characterizes their existence as immature political subjects, justifying the denial of full autonomy. Engagement in sexual activity, however, is also interpreted as immaturity or the inability to make proper choices, further justifying their subjection. Autonomy is understood as a relationship to the body where the primary threats are the body's own desires. Suspended on the bridge between instinctual nature and adulthood, the teenager is in need of external guidance to achieve the necessary self-control to advance to maturity. The teenage body exemplifies Foucault's paradox of governmentality, that autonomy is fostered by external intervention by parents, the schools, the culture, and the law. The apparent biological basis of the category of adolescence lends itself to the appearance of being a "natural" stage of development. More careful analysis, however, reveals the ways that the category of adolescence is the product of an array of power relationships that present themselves as natural. The ways in which self-government can be related to relationships of domination will be illustrated in the final section, which turns to concerns about the sexuality of teenage girls. If the autonomy of boys has been dependent on the cultivation of their capacity to manage their sexuality, sexuality has been used as a means of denying girls autonomy. The final section shows how the normative dimension of autonomy can reinforce forms of social power such as gender.

The Difficult Subject of Girls

Adolescence as a category and a politicized subject emerged within a discourse about the achievement of political subjectivity through management of the body as a demonstration of the capacity for autonomous action. The emergent teen subject reiterates the linkage between maturity and autonomy and between physical and moral discipline. The primary focus on the moral education of boys was linked to their political education and their capacity to become autonomous subjects. Girls would become women, who were ruled in the private sphere of the family, while boys were to go on to become political subjects, engaging in the governance of themselves and others. Teenagers of both sexes were seen as insufficiently self-governing, leading to the establishment of various institutions of physical and moral training intended to create individuals capable of exercising their liberty in socially beneficial ways. The exclusion of girls from thorough political and moral education is not merely an artifact of their actual historical condition at this time; it reflected broader views about the relationship of the physical body to autonomy. By virtue of their relationship to their bodies and sexuality, women were characterized as perpetual minors. While this gendered view of maturity is no longer explicit or preserved in the law, the discourse of sexual maturity is still highly gendered in ways that explicitly deny female autonomy. While male adolescents were considered potential subjects, they nonetheless were and remain less than full political agents until the age of majority, or after. Legally, minors are subject to greater restrictions than adults and are particularly subject to regulation of their bodies, including restrictions on working hours, sexual activity, smoking, and even drinking (until the age of twenty-one, well past the age of majority). The position of adolescents as less than capable agents in many ways reinforces feminist arguments that women, because they are considered of primarily through their bodies, are seen as less capable subjects. Women, because of a supposed inability to overcome their physicality—menses, pregnancy, etc.—are often considered as less rational and/or less capable (Bordo 1993). Postcolonial scholars have often noted that colonized and racialized subjects are also often defined by their physical characteristics and are, in turn, sexualized (Stoler 1995). In a similar manner, adolescents as a class defined by their physical bodies and understood as under siege from the physical experience of puberty can be understood as agents who must learn to manage their physicality in order to be considered full political subjects. Indeed, the legal status of women in the nineteenth century can be interpreted as that of permanent minor, always under the care of an adult male (Field 2001).

Locke, Rousseau, and Kant, however, all saw their hypothetical pupils at least in part in terms of their physical bodies, and this corporeality did not exclude them from eventual political agency. Autonomy, in their accounts, is achieved not by the triumph of moral maturity over physicality. Physical and moral maturity must be interconnected to achieve autonomy. Rousseau declares that he would not tutor a sick child because anyone whose physical state is not fully under their control cannot fully internalize his moral lessons. Autonomy requires full mastery of physical impulses and desires and channeling them into socially (re)productive activities. But this mastery is possible only with moral training through the body. All the authors saw a substantive difference between gendered bodies, highlighting the role of sex and reproduction in differentiating between men and women and, in turn, between autonomous and heteronomous subjects.

Adolescent boys under constant siege from their biological urges become moral and political agents through an apparent management of their physical bodies and insertion into the moral order through acceptable (hetero)sexuality[11]—or other means of physical self-care[12]—in adulthood. The presence of impulses themselves is not the problem; rather the inability to manage them is the marker of immaturity. The boy's body becomes a self-managing body, with a masculine, heterosexist ideal for political membership. Girls fall out of this discussion, not because they are viewed only through their bodies and not as rational beings, but because of how the self-managed body is understood, discussed, and constructed. Male sexuality is perceived as active, and the ability to manage that activity is evidence of autonomy. Female desire is either absent or disruptive, evidence of a failure of autonomy. In this section I will consider how the adolescent girl is subject to intense social control that seeks to both manage and protect her body while simultaneously defining the girl as less than autonomous. I will first consider how the body of the girl is configured as outside of political considerations and, second, how constructions of the impossibility of a teen girl's "consent" reinforces her apolitical status while politicizing her body. Autonomy becomes an exclusive category by denying the political agency of the girl; she lacks autonomy and therefore must be subject to political authority and the management of her body. The need for public intervention is then offered as evidence of her lack.

Girls themselves make very rare appearances in political theory. Two significant exceptions are Plato's *Republic* and Rousseau's *Émile*, which adopt two competing approaches to the inclusion of women and girls in the polity. However, while Plato and Rousseau differ on the inclusion of women in an ideal polity, they use surprisingly similar terms for understanding femininity. They consider the sexual nature of the female body a threat to public order because of its subversion of a political community opposed to the private, individual family.

Plato's *Republic* takes contradictory attitudes toward women. Plato sees women as lacking sufficient reason to belong in the ruling classes: "The great mass of multifarious appetites and pleasures and pains will be found to occur chiefly in children and women and slaves, and, among freemen ... in the inferior multitude" (1945, 125). Women's lack of ability to check their own impulses again lumps them into a category with children, dooming them to a permanent state of minority, a status shared with slaves and the "inferior" classes. In spite of this sweeping claim, Plato nonetheless allows women to be philosopher kings and receive an equal education. Women, on his account, were theoretically able to belong to the ruling class. He states: "The wives of our Guardians, then, must strip for exercise, since they will be clothed with virtue, and they must take their share in war and the other social duties of guardianship" (1945, 155). Plato stresses the physical elements of citizenship here—physical strength and the ability to go to war—which are usually used to differentiate sexes and exclude women. He erases differences written on the body, allowing women to enter into the public sphere.

Rousseau was critical of Plato's position, arguing that he could include women as governors only by transforming them into men, ironically a complaint shared by feminist critics of Plato. Rousseau's response, however, is hardly feminist. Instead, he argues that women's uniqueness ought to be preserved by insulating them from the political world. He does so in his own text by relegating Sophy, the girl, to the final chapters, in which her only role is as the wife-to-be of his pupil. In training to become master of the domestic domain, Sophy need not be educated in the same physical or moral sense that her male counterpart, Émile, endures. According to Rousseau, girls "must be trained to bear the yoke from the first . . . and submit themselves to the will of others" (1911, 332). Women's reproductive capabilities require that she be banished to the private realm and protected, a position making her dependent and therefore incapable of the autonomy necessary for political life. For Rousseau, maintaining the sexual division of labor is a means of assuring the maintenance of public order, which requires the gendering of social relations (see Weiss 1993; Wingrove 2000).

In spite of surface differences between these two accounts, they share a common exclusion of the girl. Either children are potential citizens and therefore receive physical and moral education, or they are potential mothers and therefore need not receive such training. Girls are privatized, and their own physicality, particularly their sexuality, becomes grounds for the exclusion. Since girls are not considered to be future citizens, they do not need to learn how to govern themselves and thus patriarchal control over their bodies and their choices is no problem for democracy. Their physical bodies, particularly their sexuality, are understood not only as invalidating their potential participation in the public sphere, but also as a threat to those who can and do participate. Presenting a distraction, the body of the girl is excluded for the good of public decision making. The exclusion of girls is related both to their perceived inability to control their bodies and the importance of guaranteeing social reproduction, which necessitates policing female bodies.

This exclusion of the girl from serious political life is mirrored in descriptions of the lives of teenagers. Girls are often considered in literature informed by psychoanalysis or psychology, the effect of which often is to individualize the experience of girls, to miss larger trends in their lives, or to perceive of them as pathological (see Driscoll 2002; Malson 1998). Even cultural studies—a field that has vigorously studied teenage subcultures—tends to marginalize the cultures of girls. Male teenage subcultures are often seen as subversive and directly confronting class and race hierarchies while girls subcultures are interpreted as materialistic—reinforcing capitalist patriarchy—or insignificant in confronting hegemony (see McRobbie 1991; Driscoll 2002). Anxiety over teenaged boys has shifted from strictly sexual concerns to issues of violence, for example, the concern over school violence after the shooting at Columbine High School. Girls, on the other hand, are still considered subject to physical threats seen as individual problems that pose social costs, ranging from eating disorders to teen pregnancy.

Teenage girls, positioned as physical objects by both the discourse of adolescence and their own femininity, are perceived as nonautnomous agents and therefore lacking in political agency. Popular and legal discourse has often reproduced the subject-position of girls through the policing of their bodies because of a perceived inability to do it themselves. Although they themselves are not seen as political agents, their actions may have dire political consequences and thus are subject to increased monitoring, discipline, and control.

To consider the construction of the body of the "girl" as nonautonomous I will consider the construction of a sexual "age of consent," a practice that brings together institutional, social, and cultural discourses about autonomy and girlhood. Rather than engaging in an exhaustive review of the age of consent and its legal corollary, statutory rape, I will consider two key moments in the construction of girlhood, first the historical emergence of an age of consent at the turn of the century and, second, the new use of statutory rape in reforms of the welfare system in the United States in the 1990s. These laws position girls as incapable of consent and use their sexual activity as evidence of that incapacity. This evidence is used to justify paternalist intervention, whether by social or religious institutions or by the law. Girls are thus understood to be improper political subjects who cannot manage their desire and who thereby pose a threat to the social order. The logic of consent—often seen as providing a limitation on paternalist intervention by the state by tying the legitimacy of the government to the consent of the governed—is in fact used as a paternalist justification for the denial of female autonomy. Consequently, the norm of self-governance is used as an exclusionary discourse that reinforces power relationships defining appropriate gender and sexuality.

Age of consent laws in the United States emerged in the nineteenth century, primarily as a means of protecting young girls from the advances of older men. The legal category of statutory rape was invented at the turn of the century to denote a new type of illegal sexual activity. Statutory rape implied that a minor was not capable of giving genuine consent to sexual activity and that sexual activity with those under the age of consent—regardless of their professed desire or role in initiating the contact—would be considered a crime. The law has been applied almost exclusively to girls engaging in heterosexual sex and boys engaging in homosexual sex. In both cases the corrupting influence of an older male is presumed to have overcome the minor's ability to properly make decisions, making the sex essentially coerced. Since most prosecutions of statutory rape are initiated by the parents of the minor rather than from a complaint by the minor herself, the law clearly depicts the female adolescent as in need of special protection provided by those who know better about her sexual maturity.[13]

The idea that girls (or homosexual boys) are unable to consent is significant in political terms since the capacity to consent defines the liberal political subject as one able to participate in the social contract and thus in her own governance. Locke, for instance, excludes children along with "lunatics and idiots" because they are unable to reason and are therefore unable to give reasoned, informed consent (1902, 34). Full recognition as a political subject requires demonstration of control over the body, often through sexual self-limitation. Sexual and political consent are linked through the discourse of maturity. Girls cannot have legitimate sexual encounters because they lack the maturity to govern themselves and, reciprocally, they may not govern themselves politically because they are incapable of properly managing themselves personally. Teenage boys engaging in male homosexual behavior become similarly positioned, denied a right to self-governance because of a perceived lack of self-governance in appropriately refusing the sexual advances of other males. Their poorly moderated desires place these boys in a category similar to that of girls, unable to control their bodies and thus in need of the law to step in and regulate for them. The justification for the legislation is protection of these feminized subjects from heteronomy or control by others (older males) or by their own improper desires. The effect is a differential relationship to the law for girls and nonheterosexual boys—particularly of certain races or classes—that defines them as permanent children.[14] Over time the arguments in favor of age of consent laws shifted from fear of exploitation by older men to the failure of girls to regulate themselves. Ironically, as the norm of sexual autonomy results in the rolling back of state-enforced sexual norms, the regulation of bodies gendered as female does not dissipate precisely because the self-regulation of bodies becomes a more important marker of maturity. Since girls are not considered to be future citizens they do not need to learn how to govern themselves and thus patriarchal control over their bodies and their choices is no problem for democracy.

A brief, though by no means exhaustive, examination of the origins and uses of consent laws enables an examination of the cultural construction of the girl body and various attempts to control and resist the disciplining of this body. The meaning of "consent" in relationship to teenage girls' sexuality demonstrates changing understandings of the meaning of autonomy in relationship not just to girls, but also to various groups in society. Age of consent laws had existed throughout much of American history, but a concerted effort to increase the age—which in most states ranged from a low of seven to a high of twelve—was launched in the late nineteenth century (Pivar 1973).[15] A coalition of female reformers and social purists waged a campaign to increase the age for a variety of reasons. Social purists campaigned against all forms of perceived immoral behavior from premarital sex to alcohol consumption. These campaigns often crossed paths with the suffrage movement or groups like the American Female Moral Reform Society, which argued, on the one hand, that male sexual privilege contributed to the oppression of women and, on the other, that women's heightened sense of morality required special dispensation.

Early reform campaigns emphasized the childlike quality of girls and the sexual innocence of childhood (see Robertson 2001, 2002). Supporters and detractors who believed any sex with unmarried women ought to be prosecuted portrayed adolescent girls (and sometimes women) as incapable of sexual desire and men as seducers (Campbell 1890). Class relations shaped interpretations of the threat of sexual relations. Lower-class girls were seen as particularly vulnerable not only because they tended to enter the public sphere at an earlier age in order to earn a living, thereby exposing themselves to men, but by virtue of the environment in which they were raised, perceived to be inadequate for teaching girls the proper moral attitude toward sexuality. As one pamphlet entitled *Danger to Our Girls* warned:

> We will accept the simple fact that to day there are dangers surrounding the girls, and they are largely growing into womanhood robbed of their power in integrity, self-reliance and reserve. We must try to learn what these dangers are, and try to overcome them, and place in their stead those wholesome influences about girlhood that shall help it rise to full tide of womanly energy. (Ballard 1900, 2)

Sexual promiscuity and criminality (prostitution) were often associated as consequences of the social conditions of poverty. Lower-class girls, often forced to work to support themselves and their families, were most vulnerable. Their position also meant that they were subject to increasing measures of social control, including legal and medical intervention into their lives ranging from mandatory physical exams to nightly curfews.

The increasing attention to women's sexual lives was not only about teaching women to say no; it also enabled some classes of women to exert new control over their sexual lives. African American women sought a remedy from patterns of sexual exploitation by white men and often supported statutory rape measures because they hoped the laws would give women new legal leverage against male sexual advances (Giddings 1984, 86). In addition to age of consent laws, women-led groups often campaigned for greater political, economic, and social power both for African Americans and women as a means of removing women from potentially exploitative situations.

The success of purity campaigns relied heavily on traditional views about gendered sexuality, positioning women as victims and men as perpetrators. Punitive measures were therefore often seen as appropriate for male offenders viewed as psychologically deficient (Ohi 2000, 198) while girls were often seen as in need of social guidance, whether from state-run institutions or from older women from the appropriate class. These campaigns were largely successful in increasing the age of consent from sixteen to eighteen. The consequence was not only a new legal category but also an expansion of the juvenile courts and the growth of a therapy industry to identify and reform delinquent girls (see Jackson 2000).

Ironically, the pursuit of statutory rape convictions resulting from an increase in the age of consent led to a new recognition of adolescent sexuality and the possibility of female desire (Robertson 2001, 782–83). As a consequence, explanations shifted from male seduction to female delinquency, particularly the lack of morals among young lower-class girls. Increasingly, sexuality was seen in private terms as a part of the interior, psychological self, and therefore individuals were seen as possessing an increasing right to sexual privacy immune from legal and social intervention.[16] Yet even as the legal regulation of sexuality focused less on punitive measures, women's sexual activity was not perceived as the manifestation of mature sexual desire. Sexual activity by girls reflected not their autonomous self but an undeveloped self, and thus girls could not be afforded privacy relative to their sexuality. As one moral crusader argued:

> Ignorance of selfhood is a constant pitfall to youth. Ignorance of self and its faculties is not virtue. Virtue is a strong power. Self-control must include knowledge of self also. The highest human faculty is that of sex in its mental and physical powers. It is the one most closely related to individual life, and to all social life. There is no faculty more subject to

the will and the mind, and none in which there is so great a need for intelligent control. (Ballard 1900)

Crusaders avoided criminalizing the sexually active teen but instead created a category of sexual delinquency as well as appropriate mechanisms for teaching girls about sexual morality and reforming those who had strayed. Boys' delinquency was characterized primarily by criminal activity whereas most girls were detained due to moral infractions defined mostly as engaging in sexual activity. The means of averting precocious sexuality included informal and formal mechanisms of social control. One of the primary mechanisms was the growth of women's organizations—usually organized by mothers—aimed at providing role models and counseling for young girls. The Working Girls' Society in New York advertised its purpose as mentoring young women specifically on matters of sexuality: "At a time when a girl's head is naturally full of romance, love, and marriage, it is most desirable that her older lady friend should encourage her to talk about the men she is seeing, and the attentions she receives from them" (Powell 1886, 5–6). In addition, groups like the Women's Christian Temperance Union (WCTU) advocated teaching girls "industry and self-reliance" by encouraging their domestic labor in the home. Girls were also to engage in a closely monitored exercise regimen to encourage "the life forces of the development of the muscular system and the enlarging of the mind." Such a regimen "represses the activity of the nervous forces, which control the emotional nature and thus prevent the premature activity of the sexual system" (Ballard 1900).

Mothers were placed at the center of the moral development of girls and were expected to direct the sexual development of their daughters, making women the instruments of social control. Sexual activity by teen girls was considered a failure of the mother in her responsibility to society, thereby justifying the intervention of outside agencies or the courts. Quite often the families into which these institutions reached were recent immigrant families or lower-class families who often reported their own children as a means of getting help in controlling their behavior. The consequence was a further characterization of these groups as lacking in parenting skills and virtue and subjection to higher levels of social control. The legal system intervened and often removed children from their homes or put them into state institutions if they were considered "delinquents."

In addition to the differences that class made in the construction of girl's sexuality, race played an important role. The women's movements that campaigned to protect adolescent girls were primarily middle- to upper-class and predominantly white. Enforcement of statutory rape and delinquency charges were highly racialized. The idea that a white girl would consent to sex with an African American was considered unthinkable, and therefore black men who had sex with white women of any age were assumed to be sexual predators and often were charged with rape.[17] The historical linkage between sexual crimes and race made some African American women skeptical of the legal system, and they did not participate in the institutional enforcement of statutory rape laws (see Odem 1995, 8). As a consequence, a mostly white population carried out statutory rape prosecutions. Few African American girls were affected by age of consent laws because their bodies were seen as less than pure or of less importance for the maintenance of social order (see Pivar 1973). However, various social organizations worked to increase measures that held men responsible for children resulting from unmarried sex.

Legislation of the age of consent helps to construct girls' bodies as defined by gender, age, and race, and differentiated from boys, women, and men in girls' unique inability to consent to sexual contact. The legislation extended the childhood of girls by configuring them as innocent and dependent, unable to make decisions and in need of the intervention of the family, state, and society to help them regulate their own bodies. The regulation of female sexuality achieves both the negative task of protecting women from external threats as well as the positive task of teaching girls to regulate their own internal desires.

If adolescent sexuality has become more culturally visible and accepted since the early twentieth century, age of consent laws and statutory rape continue to shape the discourse of girls' sexuality. In 1996, the federal government called for stricter enforcement of statutory rape laws in order to curb teen pregnancy as a part of welfare reform in the Personal Responsibility and Work Opportunity Reconciliation Act of 1996. The state of California responded by independently pursuing the prosecution of fathers of children born to minors, with or without the support of the minor or her parents. The decision reflected anxiety over teenage pregnancy and, particularly, acts to police the sexuality of adolescent girls.[18] These forms of intervention have class and racial implications in the construction of the body of a girl and of categories of nonautonomous subjects in need of legal, social, and moral protection. Welfare reform has placed sexual regulation at the center of social policy by emphasizing individual responsibility in the arenas of income generation and reproductive management. As a consequence, particular subjects are subject to greater monitoring, surveillance, and regulation. This paternalism is justified by arguing that such actions will cultivate the autonomy of its subjects and make them more socially responsible (Smith 2007, 41–44).

The targeting of teen pregnancy and sexual activity in welfare reform reflected the perceived link between teen pregnancy and illegitimacy to poverty and the receipt of public assistance (Weinstein 1998, 122). Teen pregnancy became an issue of heated public debate in the 1970s when rates of pregnancy among white teens rose rapidly, though overall rates of teen pregnancy were declining (see Luker 1997, 8–10; Weinstein 1998, 120–21). The response was not greater provisions for family planning or public assistance but a focus on restricting teenage sexual activity. The 1981 Adolescent Family Life Act called for public education programs promoting "self-discipline and chastity, and other positive, family-centered approaches to the problems of adolescent promiscuity and adolescent pregnancy" (Weinstein 1998, 121).

The decision to pursue statutory rape convictions was prompted by a study by the Guttmacher Institute in 1994 that demonstrated that the fathers of most babies born to minors were over the age of twenty, making the sexual relationship statutorily illegal in most states (Levine 2002, 79). The "predatory male" returned to public discourse in a new characterization of teen mothers as the victims of older males who took sexual advantage of them and refused to take financial responsibility for their children (Weinstein 1998, 127). The state of Delaware enacted the Sex Predator Act of 1996, doubling the penalty for adults convicted of statutory rape and stationing police in high schools to help identify students involved in sexual relationships with older men

(Donovan 1997, 32–33).[19] The characterization of teen mothers as victims and their partners as sexual predators enabled the construction of an apparent crisis by heightening public fears (Cocca 2002, 52).

Linked with the moral panic over the apparent sexual exploitation of girls was a public discourse that linked these pregnancies with the receipt of public assistance. In spite of the fact that teen mothers constitute a relatively small percentage of welfare recipients, teen pregnancy was seen as a major drain on public coffers. The exploitation of young women was perceived as causing welfare dependency among women and preventing them from becoming contributing members of society (see Cocca 2002; Smith 2007).

In the legal regime of welfare reform and in public consciousness, adolescent sexuality is tied closely to sexual deviance and is seen as inevitably leading to teen pregnancy and lifelong welfare dependency. The teen mother is depicted as incapable of achieving independence and thereby lacking autonomy, enabling intervention on the part of the state into her and her partner's lives. The consequence is a proliferation of punitive acts such as the denial of benefits and the prosecution of fathers, as well as a proliferation of moral condemnation of unwed motherhood because of its linkage both to bad parenting and to deviant sexuality (Smith 2007). The laws themselves have not resulted in a reduction in welfare dependency among young women because men serving jail sentences are unable to contribute financially to their child's well-being and because many girls are reluctant to participate in prosecutions. The act has had little effect on the sexual activity of men in part because of the rarity of prosecution and because the only tracking method is teenage girls who carry the child to term (Elo et al. 1999, 82–83).

The primary impact has been on the policing of female sexuality as a means of reinforcing the heterosexual nuclear family as a norm (Smith 2002; Smith 2007; Weinstein 1998). Welfare reform in general targeted women's sexuality by punishing women who refused to name the fathers of their children, thus forcing them to participate in pursuing child support. Further, the rhetoric regarding single-motherhood has reinforced state intervention in the family due to the perception of poor mothering. Senator Joseph Lieberman, speaking about welfare legislation, stated that part of the increase in unwed motherhood was due to single-mother households and the inability of those mothers to constrain their daughters' sexuality. He claimed, "Too often we are dealing here with girls growing up in poor families without a father in the house, and part of what that means is that there is not an older man in the house to protect his daughter from the unwanted advances of another older man" (quoted in Weinstein 1998, 143).

Unquestionably, adolescents are frequently coerced into sexual activity by adults. However, the legal construction of teenage girls as unable to consent reinforces the depiction of the girl as nonautonomous, and her sexuality as deviant and dangerous. As a consequence, she is continually denied autonomy not only because she herself is perceived as lacking mature control over her corporeality, but also because society itself must control her sexuality in order to maintain social order. Whether failing to exercise adequate control over the body because of predatory males or because of their own deviant desires, girls are legally, socially, and culturally constructed as nonautonomous and therefore subject to paternalist intervention. In the domain of girls' sexuality, circulating norms of autonomy are always already saturated with power relationships that rigidly structure the acceptable choices of girls.

Conclusion

If age has been an undertheorized category of political exclusion, political theorists themselves have long been concerned with ideas of maturity and immaturity, linked with notions of childhood and adulthood. Subjects in need of political tutelage require not just a thorough education in civics, or even in political values; rather, they must be thoroughly shaped through physical and moral education that enables them to be considered political subjects. Individuals must earn the right to self-determination and self-governance through a process of cultivating and controlling the self. The centrality of physical impulses as a threat to self-control and the physical body as a means of controlling these impulses has resulted in the construction of new forms of subjectivity defined by their physicality, including the adolescent and the sexual girl. These forms of subjectivity, while constructed as outside of political agency because of their uncontrolled physicality, are nonetheless political in the manner in which they construct ways of being and managing the self.

Adolescent sexuality has given rise to numerous institutions and practices that have sought to shape and manage the perceived threat of sexual precocity. The various practices relating to children and the cultivation of autonomy demonstrate the two sides of autonomy as self-governance. As a normative discourse, autonomy produces new practices of social control that delimit which behaviors and subjects are considered autonomous (and thus are allowed to exercise self-governance) and which subjects are non-autonomous (and thus may be subject to paternalist management). At the same time, autonomy has been creative in generating a new form of subjectivity, "the adolescent," along with attendant practices, disciplines, and norms associated with the new way of being. An adequate critical attitude toward the creation of new subjectivities must also document the ways the discourse of adolescence has also reinforced and generated power relationships and excluded other possibilities.

The "child" as a figure represents a set of power relationships that configure individuals as in need of guidance from others because of a perceived lack of ability to care for themselves or others. This category has included chronological children and "others" perceived of as morally immature. Further, the "delinquency" of children has also been used as justification for intervention in the lives of "adults" perceived as violating either the innocence of children or as failing to adequately protect and insulate that innocence. The category of "child" itself is unstable and has been constructed in different ways historically and theoretically. Those considered children have themselves challenged the category through their own responses to the legislation of their bodies. While discourses that construct adolescents or girls often depict them as prepolitical, they simultaneously make them the object of politicization by subjecting their bodies to intense scrutiny and intervention.

The category of the adolescent demonstrates the nagging concern within governmentality literature about how the norm of self-governance compels subjects to conform to social expectations or risk exclusion or subjection to external control. Autonomy is not only a given characteristic of subjects; it also must be actively cultivated by outside expertise and must be continually practiced by individuals. The centrality of autonomy to modern liberal democracy helps to explain why children as potential autonomous citizens are the focus of so much attention. However, the form that this attention has taken must be explored in context to understand how self-governance is always defined in ways that intersect with other existing power relationships. The processes by which autonomy is cultivated in subjects deemed immature illustrate why autonomy cannot be understood as simply an abstract set of capacities. Autonomy in the examples given is not an abstract set of norms generated by subjects, whether through subjective or intersubjective reasoning. Rather, self-governance is performed according to a set of complex and shifting power relationships through which the meaning of adequate self-governance is continually constructed and challenged. Reflection on these norms reveals not an underlying universal rationality but rather the operation of power relationships or processes of subjectification.

The following chapter builds on the insights about the connection between physical self-management and the body and the relationship of exclusion by exploring another figure of heteronomy, the drug addict. As with the adolescent, the drug addict demonstrates how autonomy functions as an exclusionary discourse that delineates the boundaries of political community. However, the chapter shifts the focus from the practices of cultivating autonomy to how failure to behave in a way deemed autonomous results in exclusion from the political community. If examining "adolescence" reveals the ways that subjects fit to govern can be made, the drug war is illustrative of the ways that self-governing subjects and self-governing communities are protected from threats to their autonomy.

3

Intoxicated Citizens

AMERICA'S DRUG WAR AND THE BODY POLITIC

> Say yes to life. And when it
> comes to drugs, just say no.
>
> —Nancy Reagan

> Nothing is true.
> Everything is permitted.
>
> —Friedrich Nietzsche,
> *Thus Spoke Zarathustra*

Upon arrival at Los Angeles International Airport (LAX) in 1986, Rosa Montoya de Hernandez was immediately detained by customs officials in a small room containing only a wastebasket. After forty-eight hours, during which Montoya de Hernandez refused to comply with customs officials who requested that she defecate in a waste-basket, she was taken to a hospital and given a pregnancy test, several X-rays, and, eventually, a laxative.[1] When the search was challenged, the Supreme Court found that the raid on Montoya de Hernandez's body was constitutional, a necessary act on the dangerous battlefield of the "War on Drugs." The protection of the integrity of national boundaries required penetrating the boundaries of Montoya de Hernandez's body.

Analyses of the drug war generally focus on the expansion of state power or the violation of individual rights. Critics of the drug war tend to criticize the apparent dissolution of civil liberties and expansion of governmental power in the face of the specter of drugs, leading to horrifying scenes like that at LAX. Supporters of strict drug regulation look to the social and individual costs of addiction and the criminal threat posed by drug smuggling. Underlying both discussions is an unrecognized appeal to the value of autonomy. On the one hand, the autonomy of the individual is threatened by the external intervention of the state on the actions of individuals. On the other, autonomous subjects experience loss of self-control to constant craving, leading to criminality and a breakdown of the social order. Looking at the drug war through the lens of autonomy provides a different interpretation of the practices of the drug war and the ways it constructs proper political subjects, expelling those deemed unfit. Unlike the child who is perceived as a potentially autonomous subject, addicts are failed subjects who, in surrendering to physical pleasure, place everyone at risk. Cultivating autonomy is about producing subjects capable of making good choices. Punishing choices, such as decisions to use drugs, is about further clarifying the choices that an autonomous subject may make. In both cases, the autonomy of the subject is always already implicated in the integrity of the political community. When subjects fail to make good choices, the consequences pose a threat to society, which is therefore justified in intervening in or punishing the choices of bad subjects.

While analysis of the drug war is often seen as an example of an expansion of the state's repressive apparatus, I will consider it as a form of what Foucault called biopower. In Foucault's terminology, biopower includes discourses designed as a means of "directing life," or the management of populations, in order to enhance what are seen as positive or desirable characteristics of that populace (Foucault 1978, 1991). The exercise of biopower involves not only state power over subjects but also discourses such as medicine, psychiatry, education, and self-help that are all aimed at improving life (Rose 1990, 2006; Dean 2009; Nadesan 2008). The drug war is thus not only about the role of state power in punishing lawbreakers but also about cultivating a healthy populace through a regime that includes forms of governance including state power, medical expertise, private industry, and cultural production.

In this chapter I will examine how the drug war uses, reproduces, and modifies the norm of self-governance through an examination of a web of different practices. This chapter examines some of the paradoxes of autonomy in context, highlighting the ways that autonomy as a normative discourse linked with the law produces contradictions, specifically in the manner that it compels the subject to self-govern in particular ways. The underlying justification for the drug war depends on a sharp delineation between autonomy and productivity on the one hand and addiction and pleasure-seeking on the other. The drug war differentiates between good and bad subjects by trying to maintain the border. However, in order to be viewed as an autonomous subject, certain choices must be forbidden. The subject must be, in some sense, addicted to autonomy in a continual willingness to self-govern and remain a good subject.

I will consider the relationship between the norm of autonomy and the practices of the drug war by examining an admittedly limited sample of potential examples. Since the body plays such a central role in both the construction of autonomy and the drug war, I focus specifically on practices that link the individual body with the metaphorical body politic. First, I explore the use of the idea of "foreignness" and its association with external violation in describing both drugs and drug users as a means of establishing the boundaries to the body politic. Second, I look at practices of constructing the boundaries of public and private through drug testing, extending surveillance into individual bodies. Finally, I consider the reproduction of the social body through examination of the treatment of pregnant drug users and the public discourse that desires to prosecute, punish, and reform bad mothers. This chapter focuses on the ways autonomy draws boundaries within the political community, generating a differential geography of bodily boundaries. The idea that democratic governance requires self-governing subjects positions subjects differently relative to legal and social discourses and thus opens some bodies up to surveillance, management, and control in a variety of ways.

Introducing Foreign Bodies

This first section considers the relationship between autonomy and the body as they have been linked in the drug war. The language of "foreignness" has played a significant part in interpreting drugs, drug users, and their relationship to autonomy. Foreign bodies pose a threat to autonomy on an individual and collective level. In individuals, a foreign body implies an intrusion into the natural boundaries of the body and, generally, a state of ill health. In a collective sense, a foreign body also implies the penetration of national boundaries by difference, a situation that in light of the war on drugs and terrorism takes on a sinister tone that implies a threat to the ability of the state to control its own boundaries and, by extension, its actions. As Honig argues, foreignness often plays a symbolic role "used to figure and perhaps manage enduring problems in democratic theory" by generating a perceived solidarity among "native" citizens (2001, 113). Projecting the problems within the body politic onto foreigners or foreignness enables a continued faith in the unity and sovereignty of the political community once it isolates or removes potential infiltration.

Foreignness is not only a concept relevant to the body politic as a community; it can also apply to the individual body. The introduction of a foreign body or substance into the body can be interpreted as a profound experience of alienation whether done voluntarily or forcibly by another. The boundary of the body is viewed as an integral part of selfhood so that the introduction of foreign bodies, whether in the voluntary ingestion of mind-altering substances or in involuntary body cavity searches, is a profound experience of foreignness within. The intoxicated subject is often described as "not in his right mind" or "not himself," indicating a profound loss of control. At the same time, the assertion of bodily integrity such as the right to refuse medical treatment, protection from unwanted sexual contact, or freedom from unwanted searches, is an integral part of the rights-bearing subject. Denying subjects' control over access to their own body would be tantamount to denying their selfhood.

The comparison between the body politic as a metaphor for the whole of the political community and the actual individual bodies of subjects is made clear in the discussion of biopolitics. In theories positing a single sovereign power tasked with maintaining social order, the figure of sovereignty was often represented as the "head" of the social body (Rasmussen and Brown 2005). With the dispersal of power in which individuals are expected to govern themselves so that the state can govern less, power is displaced onto individual bodies. At the same time, each of these bodies becomes responsible for the maintenance of the social order. Just as good citizens make good laws, healthy bodies make for a healthy body politic.

The role of governance—a term implying the whole social field and not just the state—is to "take charge of life ... through continuous regulatory and corrective mechanisms ... distributing the living into the domain of value and utility" (Foucault 1978, 226). The governance of individual bodies becomes the primary means of shaping the social body. The actual physical body is configured as particularly important as the means through which self-discipline may be learned and exhibited. The increasing importance of the body is evidenced by a heightened concern with public health and the growing influence of the medical community. If individuals are given the power to self-govern, governance also enters everyday life in the need to direct a productive life. The body is both an instrument and a location of governance; it must remain healthy, sober, and productive. The body links the health of the individual body to that of an imagined social body:

> Mastery and awareness of one's own body can be acquired only through the effect of an investment of power in the body: gymnastics, exercises, muscle-building, nudism, glorification of the body beautiful. All of this belongs to the pathway leading to the desire of one's own body, by way of the insistent, persistent, meticulous work of power on the bodies of children, or soldiers, the healthy bodies (Foucault 1980, 56).

If biopower is primarily directed at producing a healthy, productive populace, the flip side is the necessary identification of what constitutes "sickness," or threats to the health of the body or the populace. The drug war demonstrates the two sides of biopower, one that works to integrate individuals into the social whole, the other that seeks to exclude disruptive forms of subjectivity. The cultivation of a healthy body politic also necessitates the identification and treatment or excision of sickness. Proper subjects must be capable of and exhibit the signs of self-rule and self-mastery (Foucault 1991; Lowe 1995). The drug war is premised on the idea that responsibility for self-governance is threatened by individual drug use that serves as evidence of poor choices. Drug users are an affront to a well-ordered society because they willfully ingest a substance that causes the loss of self-control, antisocial behavior, and a loss of initiative and drive.

Derrida even goes so far as to say that the prohibition of drugs is necessary in liberal society because drugs themselves raise the specter of failed subjects:

> We believe our society, our culture, our conventions require [drug] prohibition. Let us rigorously enforce it. We have at stake here the health, security, productivity, and the orderly functioning of these very institutions. By means of this law . . . these institutions protect the very possibility of law in general, for only by prohibiting drugs we assure the integrity and responsibility of the legal subject, of the citizens, etc. (Derrida 1995b, 3)

Derrida implies that drugs indicate an important boundary between individual rights and social norms, which highlights the tensions between the individualizing and socializing tendencies of modern society. Individuals are autonomous and maintain the right to self-govern, but they may not choose to give up that right because to do so would undermine the foundation of a political society of free individuals. In the case of the drug user, the *choice* to ingest the drug leads to a breakdown in the ability of the subject to make further autonomous, rational decisions, a choice that is considered unacceptable.

The seriousness of the threat of intoxication is evident in the drug war where self-control over the body in the form of sobriety is a marker of autonomy while intoxication is an indication of a willful surrender of self-control. The role of the body in the drug war relates to a general discourse of privacy in American law and society. In the twentieth century, the right to privacy in legal terms has expanded to include not just property but the body. Debates over abortion rights, euthanasia, and contraception have emphasized the importance of bodily autonomy as a privilege of a rights-bearing subject. The use of bodily intervention as a signifier of status makes intrusions on and in the body more socially and politically significant; such intrusions signify the violation of the integrity of the self. Control over the body is the right and responsibility of individual subjects. Thus, when individuals fail to exercise self-control over their bodies, they enable the law to mark transgressors as improper legal subjects by intervening on the transgressing body. Bodily autonomy is meant to protect the body from external intervention, but any sign of a failure to control the body from within is seen as justification for just such intervention.

Drug use is especially threatening to autonomy because of its linkage with addiction, or the loss of self-control and a breakdown of the will that is both moral and physical. Intoxication and addiction threaten the capacity to act as an autonomous agent and therefore undermine the body politic as a whole. In justifying the strict enforcement of antidrug measures, Arthur Woods, a former New York City police commissioner, captures the paradox of the requirement to be free embodied in the logic of autonomy. In the following quotation he argues for necessary self-control among citizens for social reasons but goes on to imply that the drug itself erodes the subject's capacity for self-control, making her less responsible:

> In civilized society, since members of groups are highly dependent upon one another, there must be control, and the individual must be ready to accept limitations of his freedom of actions for the sake of the welfare of the body politic. . . . Narcotics produces shirkers, searchers for privilege and self-gratification. (quoted in Campbell 2000, 75)

The choice to introduce a foreign body disqualifies the subject from making further choices, not only because it demonstrates the subject's lack of self-control and further damages the very capacity for autonomy. Drugs are perceived as a potent signifier of a willful misuse because of their corporeality and connection—in both pro drug and antidrug literature—with a loss of control or escape from reality and responsibility. Drug use implies the loss of bodily boundaries, and therefore bodily control. First is the breaching of the physical boundary of the body in the physical act of introducing the drug into the body through ingesting, snorting, smoking, or injecting a foreign substance. Next comes the breach of the boundary of self-governance in the reported loss of relationship to reality and control (see Derrida 1995b). The initial introduction of drugs into the body leads to physical dependence and the compulsive seeking of further stimulation.

Significantly, the association of drugs with pleasure-seeking has often linked discourses on drug usage with discourses of corporeal excess, especially in terms of sexuality. Drug use is often associated with an erosion of the sexual boundaries of the user, enabling a willingness to engage in sexual behaviors otherwise unthinkable due to social or individual prohibitions (Lenson 1995, 184–86). The mind-altering substance leads to a lack of control over the body, which in turn leads

NO ONE THINKS THEY'LL LOSE
THEIR VIRGINITY HERE.
METH WILL CHANGE THAT.

MONTANA METH PROJECT
1-888-366-6384

METH
NOT EVEN ONCE.

NotEvenOnce.com

A Montana Meth ad links drug usage and sexual deviance.

to dangerous, taboo, or disgusting sexual acts.[2] Anti-meth ads run in the state of Montana demonstrate this connection between the loss of self-control and the loss of propriety. One ad shows a filthy restroom, implying that meth users, lacking any sense of proper bodily boundaries, will lose their virginity in the stall. This loss of self-control that follows from the violation of a legal norm is seen as a slippery slope that dooms the drug user to the violation of other legal and social norms. In a text about drug usage patterns, for example, sociologist and drug researcher James Inciardi uses language to emphasize the perverse corporeality permeating the atmosphere at a "crack house":

> A woman purchasing crack, with an infant tucked under her arm—so neglected that she had maggots crawling out of her diaper; a man 'skin-popping' his toddler with a small dose of heroin so the child would remain quietly sedated and not interrupt a crack-smoking session; people in various states of excitement and paranoia, couching in the corners of smoking rooms inhaling from the "devil's dick" (the stem of the crack pipe); . . . any manner and variety of sexual activity—by individuals and/or groups . . . people in convulsions and seizures brought on by drug use. (quoted in Jonnes 1996, 382)

Inciardi's narrative describes a catalog of the horrors associated with the loss of autonomy: inability to control the body (seizures), drugging

Renton plunges into his addiction in *Trainspotting*.

children, mental illness (paranoia), (maggot) infestation, and even the invocation that the crack smoker has sold her soul to the devil and is performing fellatio on him. The closing words remind the reader that these drugged bodies have ceased to be subjects, or even human, and are merely a set of grotesque behaviors fueled by drug abuse.

Popular representations of drug use, even by those accused of glorifying drug use, give the same impression of the body: grotesque, warped by drug use into strange and disgusting behavior. For example, in the 1996 Scottish film *Trainspotting*, Renton, the protagonist, is sick from heroin withdrawal. After receiving and inserting an opium suppository, he is suddenly struck by diarrhea and is forced to use what he describes as the "dirtiest toilet in Scotland." He squats over the disgusting toilet as his voiceover says, "Brilliant gold taps, virginal white marble, a seat carved from ebony, a cistern full of Chanel No. 5, and a flunky handing me pieces of raw silk toilet roll. But under the circumstances I'll settle for anywhere." The film devolves into a fantasy sequence in which Renton, desperate after losing his suppository in the toilet, dives into the filthy water, through the waste, and finds his suppository before crawling out in triumph. Drug usage is depicted as a total failure of self-control, manifesting itself in a sickening corporeal display. The subject dissolves into a horrific fantasy world where the loss of self is signified by contrasting the brute material physicality of Renton's world against the trappings of civilization recounted in the voiceover. Giving in to the bodily pleasure of the drug is also seen as giving up on public order and social rules that govern conduct and maintain a civilized society. One of the ultimate boundaries of civilized propriety has been breached as Renton literally dives into and thus becomes human waste.

The relationship between body and mind in theorizing subjectivity emphasizes that a loss of physical self-control is simultaneously a loss of personhood. The ability to maintain one's physical boundaries is considered central to reasonable subjectivity. Numerous theorists have drawn on Kristeva's idea of the abject to discuss the privileging of clean and proper bodies as good subjects (Kristeva 1982; Di Stefano 1996; Longhurst 2001; Hyde 1997). Abjection is a state of flow, and Kristeva often links the concept to corporeal flows in and out of the body that defy our concept of a unified, impenetrable subject. Longhurst writes:

> Abjection is the affect or feeling of anxiety, loathing and disgust that the subject has in encountering certain matter, images and fantasies . . . to which it can respond only with aversion, nausea, and distraction. . . . The abject provokes fear and disgust because it exposes the border between self and other. (2001, 28)

The abject represents a failure to maintain the integrity of boundaries between the self and the world, justifying the violation of bodily autonomy because that body provokes disgust because it is already soiled.[3] The drugged body is thus understood as abject, already violated, and therefore violable (Derrida 1995b; McClain 1995; Driscoll 2000). The self-inflicted violation of the self through the ingestion of foreign matter transforms the body from that of a member of the body politic into an outsider, presumably one in need of external controls.[4] Drug users become an Other, a figure of a repudiation of autonomy through the grotesque failure to properly manage the body. Addiction is understood as a breakdown of the will and slavery to a foreign substance. The rational, self-governing individual is defined against the abject addict-other.

The introduction of a foreign substance into the body is conceptu-alized as a violation of boundaries, of the body, of the self, and of the public and moral law. However, the metaphor of foreignness not only marks individual bodies but also defines the boundaries of the body politic, thus requiring an examination of the ways that drugs are used to define national boundaries through a similar logic of exclusion. In particular, the representation of drugs as a foreign influence has had an important role in shaping American national consciousness and in excluding particular groups. Specifically, drug users, pushers, and their foreign connections serve as others against which citizens may measure their own national identity.

The decision to declare the campaign against drugs as a "war" exem-plifies what Foucault describes as a feature of modern governance, an increasing tendency to refer to struggles between groups within the political body.[5] The so-called "democratic peace" is really a shift in focus from external threats to internal threats or various enemies within (Foucault 2003, 16). Ivison elaborates on the language of war as it is used to secure the boundaries of the political community. He argues that the language evokes a struggle for identity against internal and external populations that differ from the self-perceived identity of the political community. Duncan Ivison states: "The social and body poli-tic . . . began to be conceived of in terms of a struggle between different groups, and of society as saturated in relations of war," creating a situa-tion of permanent vigilance against foreign threats (1998, 563). The idea of the struggle within society links the marking and exclusion of indi-vidual bodies with the question of the body politic and larger issues of the boundaries of the body politic. The language of the "war on drugs" is more than merely a rhetorical ploy; it is also an important indication of the stakes involved in the discourse on drug prohibition. The significa-tion of drugs as "foreign" is a declaration of war not merely on foreign influences, but also on groups within the social body that are consid-ered unfit or un-American.

Numerous histories have been written about the shifting patterns of drug enforcement in the United States and their various racist and nationalist undertones. Major regulation of drug importation and usage did not begin until the late nineteenth century.[6] A wave of con-cern was prompted by prescription drug use, and much drug abuse was among white, middle-, and upper-class families. The first major federal intervention was the Harrison Act of 1914, which primarily policed the distribution of drugs through doctors but has been used as a model for narcotics enforcement. The Harrison Act marked an important turning point by delineating between medical and non-medical drugs and the appropriate legal status of each. Increasingly, the regulation of drugs has distinguished between drugs with a medicinal purpose and those used solely for recreation (Courtwright 2001b; Musto 1999; Jenkins 1999). Therefore, prohibition focused less on the toxicity of the drug or the degree or type of effect on the body and highlighted problems of pleasure-seeking and addiction.[7] Significantly, pharmaceuticals are considered acceptable and thus legal as a means of blocking pain but never as a source of pleasure (Lenson 1995). Medical and legal discourses on drug usage, while often understood as opposing one another, often worked together to reinforce the categories of dangerous drugs against their therapeutic counterparts.[8]

The metaphor of drug addiction as a disease became a useful political tool, characterizing drug usage as an epidemic or plague that required immediate intervention and cure (Driscoll 2000, 14, 60). The description of drug usage by Richard Hobson, who introduced the Eighteenth Amendment[9] into Congress, demonstrates the ways that the medical and political discourses worked together to perpetuate the idea of civilized society under siege by foreign, viral forces. His description of drug usage links metaphors of the body and the specter of a foreign invader through the trope of disease: "Drug addiction is more communicable and less curable than leprosy. Drug addicts are the principal carriers of vice diseases.... Upon the issue hangs the perpetuation of civilization, the destiny of the world, and the future of the human race" (quoted in Woodiwiss 1998, 21). Just as drug use threatened to consume the life of addicts, so too could it spread throughout society.

Decisions about which drugs were safe and legal and which were public threats have long relied on a nativist logic emphasizing that drugs represented an insidious foreign influence (Kinder 1991; Courtwright 2001a/2001b; Musto 1999; Woodiwiss 1998). Policies banning drugs such as opium, cocaine, or even heroin, all of which at one point had medicinal purposes, were sparked not by medical discoveries;

rather they were the consequence of social and political factors linking them with foreign forces. One of the earliest drug panics emerged over the use of opium, exported primarily from China, even though the cultivation of the opium poppy and the promotion of opium use were largely a product of British and American imperialism (Courtwright 2001a). Harry Anslinger, the first director of the Federal Bureau of Narcotics, linked both opium and heroin to Chinese influence and later considered "Red Chinese" drug trafficking as a conspiracy not just to profit from Americans but also, in an act of political subversion, to render the American population unproductive (Campbell 2000; Musto 1999; Jonnes, 1996). Accompanying the fear of communism was an invested fear of "white slavery," of American women lured into a life of (sex) slavery and doomed to the dual loss of autonomy through servitude and addiction (Keire 2001).

During the early twentieth century, alcohol was the focus of much attention, culminating with the passage of the Eighteenth Amendment and the brief period of prohibition. Alcohol was obtainable only for medicinal purposes, requiring a doctor's written prescription. The campaign for prohibition, active since the 1800s and with its own Prohibition Party formed in 1869 and still active, was successful in part because of moral appeals to the damaging social effects of alcohol. Temperance advocates combined medical science showing the degeneration of the body through alcohol usage with eugenics arguments that showed the mental and physical inferiority of the children of immigrants who began drinking at an early age. The manufacture of alcohol was linked to foreign influence, with claims that much of America's liquor supply originated in Germany (Furnas 1965, 334–35).[10]

The repeal of Prohibition was, in part, a pragmatic issue. The ban on alcohol had led to an enormous black market and an increase in organized crime. The expense of incarcerating individuals on alcohol offenses proved costly in a time of economic depression. However, an additional strike against Prohibition was that Americans considered alcohol as a relatively mainstream drug, and its widespread use made it a valuable commodity and a familiar drug.[11] While the usage of other illegal drugs was seen as anathema to American interests, the individual right to use alcohol was viewed as patriotic. After the passage of the Twentieth Amendment repealing Prohibition, Maryland's Leonard Weinberg declared, "In this day of Fascism and Sovietism and subjugation of the people to the domination of the state or of a man, this marks a rededication of the people of America to principles of Democracy" (quoted in Kyvig 2000, 181).

Even with the alcohol wars all but resolved, battles over other narcotics—and national identity—continued. During the Cold War, drugs were an important signifier of anti-Americanism at home and abroad. Conspiracy theories multiplied with stories of Communist drugging projects in which worker drones were created through the distribution of narcotics. Claims proliferated that drugs were being smuggled into the United States as a means of subverting democracy and the free market. When a heroin epidemic was reported among soldiers returning from Vietnam, the image of a foreign threat weakening American resolve intensified (Musto 1999; Jonnes 1996). Even worse, American drug users were contributing to the red scourge through their drug usage, a practice that eventually became linked with anti-Americanism, Communism, a breakdown in gender roles, uninhibited sexuality and miscegenation. Campbell describes the projection or drug use onto foreign influence:

> Mid-century articulations of drug users as "enemies within" acknowledged drug use as an ambivalent cultural practice that subverted notions of unitary identity, natural purity, and bodily integrity. . . . In the 1950s these frightening hybrids were conflated with anti-American political ideology. Scientific and popular representations of 1950s drug addicts cast them as a foreign presence, a signal that trouble from elsewhere was infiltrating American cities and psyches. (2000, 91)

The consistent linkage of drugs with foreign influence and political subversion continues today with the connection made between the war on drugs and the war on terrorism. President Bush made the linkage shortly after the invasion of Afghanistan—long a major exporter of the opium poppy—in a much disseminated quote: "It's so important for Americans to know that the traffic in drugs finances the work of terror, sustaining terrorists. . . . If you quit drugs, you join the fight against terror in America" ("The Anti-Drug"). The linkage between terrorism and drugs was even more widely disseminated during the Super Bowl when the Office of Drug Control Policy paid $3.5 million

"Last weekend, I washed my car, hung out with a few friends, and helped murder a family in Colombia." The "Murder a Family" campaign of the Office of National Drug Control Policy connects individual drug use to international terrorism.

to buy television and print ads with teenagers describing how they had helped to fund terrorism, the punchline being that they did so through their drug habits (Ahrens 2002, A02). As the ads suggest, individuals have sacrificed their autonomy not just in a bodily sense but also in the ability to control the effects of their actions. In one ad, a teenager who uses drugs describes setting into motion a chain of actions that culminates in the murder of a family on another continent. Simply through the ingestion of drugs, she loses control over her own actions and, in doing so, presumably threatens the autonomy of her own country by supporting the work of terrorists. She invited foreign influences into her own body and her own country through her own self-indulgence.

If drugs have become a symbol of foreign threats, they have equally been used to mark out "outsiders within," especially through a racialized depiction of drug users and dealers. The practice was explicit in the first half of the twentieth century when a racialized logic contributed to Prohibition. Since the late 1800s, alcohol had been linked with uncontrolled sexuality and, especially, with racial mixing (Woodiwiss 1998; Musto 1999; Courtwright 2001a). In the 1930s, marijuana usage was linked with the Hispanic population in the Southwest. The discourse later shifted to the African American population, and in the 1940s a series of marijuana studies concluded that marijuana encouraged sexual impulses in African American men because it "removes both anxiety and submission and therefore permits a feeling of adequacy . . . a sense of mastery denied to him by his color" (quoted in Campbell 2000, 63). A similar argument was made about cocaine, eventually outlawed not because of widespread usage among the white middle-class population but because of growing panic about use by African American men and its supposed linkage to violent behavior. Critics of the drug war often cite the panic of the 1980s over the use of crack as racially motivated since crack, as opposed to cocaine, because of its lower price, is primarily used by low-income and minority populations. Drug sentencing laws, only recently revised, punished those convicted of possession of crack cocaine more harshly than those convicted of possession of cocaine (from which it is derived), and crack remains the only drug for which first-time possession may trigger a federal mandatory life sentence (U.S. Sentencing Commission 1995: iii; Baum 1996; Musto 1999).

The narratives of foreign invasion—or foreigners within—establish a relationship between individual bodies and the body politic in which the health of one reflects on the health of the other. Drug usage is considered a threat because it challenges the capacity of individuals to be responsible, democratic citizens. The threat is summarized in the opening paragraph of the National Drug Control Strategy, published in February 2002, in which drugs are characterized as active agents of infection within the body politic:

> Illegal drug use threatens everything that is good about our country. It can break the bonds between parents and children. It can turn productive citizens into addicts, and it can transform schools into places of violence and chaos. Internationally, it finances the work of terrorists who use drug profits to fund their murderous work. Our fight against illegal drug use is a fight for our children's future, for struggling democracies, and against terrorism.

The description of the scourge of illegal drug usage sounds eerily like the loss of control experienced by individual drug users described by Inciardi. Drugs threaten not just the capacity of individuals to self-govern but also their very capacity for democratic self-rule; human agency is lost to drugs on both the individual and the national scales. The linkage ties together individual self-governance with the body politic through the metaphor of a body resisting outside influences crossing over their boundaries and wreaking havoc. Drugs represent an enemy within in their capacity to erode individual ability to self-govern, as well as an enemy without, as a foreign body introduced into an imagined pure body politic. The association of drugs with heteronomy makes their policing imperative to the maintenance of the body politic. Self-governing subjects must be addicted to their own autonomy, compelled to say no to the threat posed by foreign intoxicating substances.

Testing the Limits of Public/Private Boundaries

The linkage of addiction to heteronomy helps to establish the boundaries of subjectivity within the body politic. subjects considered self-governing possess the privilege of a right to privacy, or protection from the influence or invasion of others. In contemporary culture, autonomy is often associated not only with the right to participate in public governance but also with the right to withdraw to private space in order to pursue one's independent life project. Increasingly, cultural and legal discourses have turned to the body as one such protected "private" space. The boundaries between public and private spaces are often permeable and the body is one such place where public and private boundaries are drawn, challenged, and redrawn. Examining the legal construction of the body as a site of private ownership and public intervention reveals that bodies are never fully public or private.

The legal status of the body in relationship to the state varies across different spaces and circumstances. Since the Court adopted a standard that the body is a violable and public space when a "special need" can be established and has defined the drug war as such a special need, the war against drugs has created a complex geography of permeable and impermeable body-spaces. To examine this geography, I will take a look at the laws concerning the permissibility of searches of the body, including drug testing and body cavity searches. The Court determines when the state is allowed to intrude on the body, look in its cavities, or take its fluids to be tested. This is not to say that legal discourse is the most significant in defining the body nor is it the only discourse of bodily intervention. But Court doctrine plays an important role in reflecting and shaping public discourse about the body and has important material consequences in justifying police practices on bodies. Thus, the legal status of the body is another site of the construction of autonomy through bodily practices, shaping our understanding of subjectivity through the treatment of the body.

The most recent drug war, announced in the early 1970s by the Nixon administration and accelerating through the 1980s and 1990s, has produced profound changes in legal doctrine, especially in relationship to the public–private boundary. Perhaps the best publicized and most controversial element of drug war doctrine has been the growing encroachment on property rights, particularly surprising in an era of privatization and the expansion of private property rights (see O'Brien 2000; Nolan 2001). The Court has repeatedly been willing to reconsider the meaning of the Fourth Amendment's ban on unlawful search and seizure by expanding police powers to execute warrantless searches, to engage in property forfeiture, and to modify the rules of admissibility with regard to evidence illegally seized.[12]

The body, however, is a more ambiguous case with regard to legal status since it lacks a clear constitutional status. A right to privacy applied to the body is merely inferred from the Bill of Rights, and in drug cases the Court has generally used the search and seizure standard applied to property to consider the status of the body (O'Brien 2000; Dripps 1997). Defining the body as property has been one legal tactic that configures the body as the "property" of its owner, making it subject to the same warrant requirements and legal protections as physical property. So, for example, in the case of *Rodriques v. Furtado* (1991)[13] after several unsuccessful searches of Rodriques's apartment, the police obtained a search warrant for her apartment *and* vagina, where, they had a tip, she was stowing a heroin stash. Her body was transported to a hospital where a health care professional performed the search of her vagina, which did not yield any drugs.

The property equation made between the contents of Rodriques's apartment and the interior of her vagina made in this case does not neatly translate into a simple body as property equation. Legal standards are more ambiguous when it comes to considering the body as a public, marketable commodity. While the law allows the sale of certain regenerable bodily parts such as blood plasma, sperm, or eggs, and allows the rental of the body for surrogate motherhood, it does not allow the sale of blood or organs, though they may be donated and cease to be the property of their original owner (or her descendants).[14] Nor does the law permit the sale of the whole body in slavery. Debates over living wills and a right to die indicate a similar conflict over the right of individuals to alienate themselves from parts of their body for purposes of the market but denying individuals the right to fully alienate themselves. The implication is that the state retains the right to prevent individuals from sacrificing their autonomy to an Other, whether drugs or another individual. Autonomy is protected first by the subject and, failing that, by an external force, leaving the body suspended between individual rights and state control. Bodily spaces such as Rodriques's vagina exist in a liminal place that is neither a public space saturated by the law nor an inviolable private space that makes the inspection a criminal trespass or rape.

The complications of the body as a space of legal intervention are clear in the myriad laws that have applied questions of search and seizure to the body, particularly in issues of drug testing and body cavity searches. One of the earliest cases testing the limits of bodily intrusion on legal subjects was *Rochin v. California* in 1952.[15] After police forcibly entered Rochin's home with a warrant, police observed him swallowing an object. He was taken to a hospital and given an emetic that forced vomiting. Capsules of morphine were found in the vomitus but the Supreme Court suppressed the evidence, saying that the intrusion "shocked the conscience" of the Court, a phrase that became a standard for the Court in determining the legal limits of penetrating the body. Like the standard of "I know it when I see it" applied to obscenity, the Court's conscience is highly subjective and has yielded varying results in different historical contexts and according to the status of the body to be penetrated. Bodies become recoded as "public" according to their relationship to the state (and the body politic). Bodily intrusions, however, are justified according to two distinct logics that produce, in the Court's words, "a diminished expectation of privacy" (Rosenberg 1996). Some bodies, such as those of children, are penetrable because they are seen as potential subjects within the body politic and therefore in need of intervention for their own good. Other bodies are penetrable because of their exclusion from the body politic. Because they lack the status of autonomous subjects, the violation of their bodies is not an unwarranted exercise of power. The biopolitics of privacy create a distinction between autonomous bodies protected by the body politic and those that are seen as heteronomous and therefore violable.

Workplace drug testing is the clearest example of the monitoring of drug usage being utilized as a means of monitoring the bodies of political subjects. Drug testing is a specifically bodily practice that requires the subject to submit the body (or bodily fluids) to an authority. The test then yields information about the private activities of the body. Legal regulation of testing constructs the body as private but violable for purpose of the public good, whether for the maintenance of order or to reinforce the status of certain subjects as less than autonomous.

The Court relies on a scale of intrusiveness that determines that certain forms of testing are more intrusive and therefore require greater justification. So, for instance, the testing of blood is seen as most intrusive, urinalysis slightly less intrusive, and other forms (hair, sweat, saliva, and breath) as unintrusive (Tunnell 2004, 9–12). Literally crossing the boundaries of the body (with a needle for testing blood) or requiring that the body perform (for a urine test) are seen as violations of bodily autonomy that necessitate justification. Intrusions on the body, therefore, are construed as impinging on a private space and, presumably, the self, in much the same way that the body is regulated in the sale of body parts. To test is to imply the severity of the threat posed by drugs to the subject; the intrusion by the state is seen as less an act of violence toward the integrity of selfhood than is the utilization of drugs.

The line between public and private and the meaning of bodily intrusion are also determined by the legal parameters of who may test and where. Private companies are legally authorized to require drug testing of their employees without probable cause, though some states limit the situations in which employers may test.[16] The state, on the other hand, must provide a compelling interest. The Court's consideration of drug testing has continually described the practice not merely for the purposes of crime control—detecting and punishing drug usage—but also as a means of controlling behavior and encouraging abstinence from drug usage. Private companies may use drug tests even if they do not report the results to the state. The justification for such surveillance and disciplinary practices is not the criminal behavior itself but the belief that the behavior impinges on the subject's ability to be a proper employee and serve the social body and economic interests. Judging employees on the basis of a drug test rather than a performance review or other indication of impairment indicates the belief that the uncontrollability of the drug user exceeds other conditions that hinder performance such as insomnia, depression, or stupidity.[17]

The technology of drug testing itself provides an important insight into the meaning of drug testing as a technology of discipline. Current technologies of drug testing rely primarily on urinalysis, though new technologies also allow the testing of blood, hair, and sweat. The tests, however, cannot gauge levels of drugs present in the body, the time of ingestion, or the level of impairment to the subject. Drug tests, therefore, are not a test of behavior in the workplace or the state of intoxication of the body in the workplace. Tests give employers a glimpse into the private behavior of the tested subject since they will usually be testing the ingestion of substances away from the workplace. The ability to gauge intoxication is admittedly weak since it is dependent on the physiological makeup of the subject, the type of drug ingested, the speed the drug is metabolized, and other factors. Marijuana, for example, remains in the system long after the effects of the drug have worn off, so a subject who smoked marijuana over a weekend could test positive for drug usage for the next two weeks. On the other hand, because of the rate at which the body processes cocaine, a subject who snorted cocaine on the way to work would not test positive for drugs in the system (Robinson and Jones 2000, 9).

The goal of testing in the workplace, therefore, is not necessarily the identification of persons engaging in criminal acts; rather it is a means of affecting private behavior, enabling control of a subject's behavior beyond the workplace. Testing breaks down the public/private divide by making private behavior a matter of public record and thereby subjecting it to scrutiny and alteration. Simon describes the role that techniques of quantification like drug testing play in disciplining members of the body politic as follows:

> (1) methods for identifying those individuals likely to generate problems so that more intensive surveillance or control can be applied precisely; (2) condensation and standardization of information, and (3) proliferation of contact points where individuals provide new information to the system and can be targeted for control measures. (1993, 196)

The importance of the test is not only in the results of the test itself but also in the fear of the test that presumably will encourage subjects to police themselves. Drug testing allows employers to peer into the workplace behavior of their employees but also allows their reach to extend into the private lives of their employees by obtaining evidence of their activity and/or deterring specific private behaviors (Gilliom 1994). Testing provides a means of having some control over workers' bodies and leisure time beyond the workplace, just as drug testing extends the capacity for surveillance beyond the state.

Just as private testing is justified on the grounds that it contributes to a productive workplace, the state engages in drug testing on the grounds of protecting the boundaries and purity of the state. The Court has upheld the right of the state to test employees when a compelling state interest can be defined as trumping individual liberty. Writing for the majority in *Chandler v. Miller* (1997), Justice Ginsberg describes the state standard for intrusion as a contextual reconfiguring of public and private boundaries: "Particularized exceptions . . . are sometimes warranted based upon 'special needs beyond the normal need for law enforcement' . . . Courts must undertake a context-specific inquiry, examining closely the competing private and public interests." The special needs exception has been applied in a variety of contexts, often on pragmatic grounds, for example, allowing testing following workplace accidents or for employees carrying weapons. The drug war has been repeatedly described by the Court as a special circumstance that justifies additional legal measures. Drugs are such a threat to the body politic that testing is necessary in some circumstances to guarantee public order. The language of "foreignness" and purity reemerges in legal discourse in justifying the testing of Customs employees. Justice O'Connor, writing for the majority in the *Von Raab* (1989) decision states:

> It is readily apparent that the Government has a compelling interest in ensuring that front-line interdiction personnel *are physically fit, and have unimpeachable integrity and judgment.* Indeed, the Government's interest here is at least as important as its interest in searching travelers entering the country. . . . While reasonable tests . . . doubtless infringe some privacy expectations, we do not believe these expectations outweigh the Government's compelling interests in *safety and in the integrity of our borders.* [emphasis added]

O'Connor's decision evokes the warlike metaphor of "front-line interdiction" and draws the parallel between the erosion of personal boundaries of integrity and judgment indicated by drug use with foreign travelers breaching America's borders. The double usage of the "integrity of our borders" in both the case of the body politic and with regard to the individual agents charged with defending those borders evokes the metaphor of uncleanliness or contamination discussed in the previous section. O'Connor makes the linkage between the body's purity (physical fitness) and moral purity (integrity and judgment) and thereby ties the bodies of these subjects to the moral purity of the body politic.

These bodies are configured as public spaces because of their special importance to public order.

State practices of drug testing and the linkage with the purity of the body politic extend beyond direct agents of the state, however, into other subjects whose bodies are considered to always create a compelling state interest, such as school children.[18] Again, the state repeats the justification for intervention in the bodies of individuals, in this case children, on the basis of a threat to social welfare posed by drug abuse by non-autonomous subjects. In *Acton* (1994),[19] the Court allowed the testing of a specific class of individuals, student athletes, and affirmed that these individuals could be barred from participation if they failed the test or if they refused to be tested. The decision was significant in identifying a new testable population (with little linkage to public safety) and also in allowing the school to trump parental rights since a student could be barred even if the parents supported a child's refusal to be tested.[20] Justice Scalia's majority opinion argued that the state had an interest in the health and welfare of its children and in protecting them from harm. The school, he argued, ought to be a space expunged of negative influences to allow for their development into good citizens. Scalia's argument echoes Foucault's historical argument that the liberal state takes a vested interest in the development of children as proper members of the body politic (see Foucault 1978). Indeed, his description of a concern with developing a "dense, saturated, permanent, continuous physical environment which envelops, maintains, and develops the child's body" (1978, 282) sounds almost identical to Scalia's description of the ideal schooling environment for student athletes charged with becoming proper subjects. Drug testing presumably is intended to purify the space of the school from corrupting influences and to extend the capacity of the state to regulate behavior beyond the institutional boundaries of the state and into the home, even against the will of the parent.[21]

In *Acton* Scalia hints at a shifting geography of public and private in which the body's boundaries become permeable according to various justifications. The map is more complex, however, than a simple delineation between bodies occupying public and private spaces. Bodies exist in particular relationships to the state and thereby become more or less public according to that relationship. The implication is that individuals do not carry a right to privacy with them, but that right varies across different spaces, and those spaces may be reinterpreted according to the status of the individuals that occupy them. Scalia argues:

> The Fourth Amendment does not protect all subjective expectations of privacy, but only those that society recognizes as "legitimate." What expectations are legitimate varies, of course, with context, depending, for example, upon whether the individual asserting the privacy interest is at home, at work, in a car, or in a public park. In addition, *the legitimacy of certain privacy expectations vis-à-vis the State may depend upon the individual's relationship with the State.*[22] [emphasis added]

Scalia's argument that the boundaries of public and private are constantly being redefined not only by physical space but by the shifting relationship of individual to the body politic has important implications for individual bodies. Bodies are constantly reinterpreted in terms of their boundaries. Bodily autonomy may vary by the status of those subjects relative to the state. Some bodies are violable because their choices have subjected them to state power while others are considered so important to the state that they must be violated for the public good. In making the capacity for the state to intervene in the body a marker of the relationship of individuals to the body politic, the body becomes an important site for the production of autonomy. Some bodies are penetrable as a means of ensuring their—and society's—autonomy.

Perhaps the clearest example of bodily intrusion as an exercise of state power justified by individual failure to self-regulate exists in prisons, where rituals of bodily intrusion are regular. The Court has affirmed that within prisons random testing of inmates is permissible, as are regular body cavity searches, even in the absence of any suspicion. The prison is a unique space that transforms the body into public property:

> Once within the walls of a prison, jail, or other detention facility, the standards for what is a permissible search or seizure change. Neither a search warrant nor probable cause is required. . . . Federal regulations also exist that empower the Director of the Bureau of Prisons, as well as local prison officials, to promulgate procedures for the control and treatment of prisoners. (McClain 1995)

Prison searches serve as a ritual inspection, marking bodies occupying the institution as fully public and subject to inspection by the state. The pragmatic value of such searches includes real safety concerns for both prisoner and guards, but the violation of bodily integrity serves another important symbolic role. In *Bell v. Wolfish* (1978),[23] the Court justifies body cavity searches following all visits—even those supervised by prison officials—not just in terms of the institutional needs of the prison but also based on the status of the prison in relationship to the right to privacy. Once a basic right to privacy has been constructed, including the right to bodily integrity as a basic individual right, the revocation of that right for prisoners indicates the less than autonomous status of the prisoner. The prison authorities retain the right to violate the prisoner's body. As with the drug user who is described as lacking bodily boundaries and is depicted in grotesque rituals of abjection, the state enacts the abject status of prisoners by actively violating their bodily boundaries. Bodily cavities are occupied by the state as a means of depriving the individual of the status of private, even within their own bodies. As Scalia indicated, the boundaries of public and private are redrawn in terms of the physical space of the prison and also in terms of establishing a relationship between individuals and the state and individuals to themselves.

Practices of bodily searches enacted as a part of the drug war illustrate the complex map of public and private spaces and their relationship to the shifting constructions of autonomous subjects. In some cases, privacy is a privilege afforded to some according to their occupation of private spaces and revoked for those occupying public spaces, voluntarily or involuntarily, such as those in schools or prisons. On the other hand, private conduct is policed indirectly through techniques of surveillance that impose an image of "integrity and judgment" on individuals. The only guarantee of maintaining bodily boundaries and a private self are constant demonstrations of "self discipline and integrity." The practices of the drug war complicate a simple map of public and private spaces as well as any simple designation of the body as a public or private space. Rather, the complex discourse surrounding bodily intrusion in the drug war demonstrates that the various constructions of public and private are products of power relations that structure relationships between individual bodies and the body politic. In the construction of violable and inviolable subjects, a clear delineation between autonomy and heteronomy becomes impossible. Fear of a lack of internal control from within becomes justification for external control from without. Subjects are compelled to demonstrate their autonomy by allowing the body to yield information about its activities, while other bodies are violated because they are heteronomous, and violation is a means of continually reinforcing their subordinate status. The utilization of the expectation of autonomous self-control creates a specific matrix of power in which some bodies retain boundaries and others have porous and violable boundaries. The practices of drug testing create and reiterate the power relationships through which the boundaries of the community are drawn.

Reproducing the Body Politic

The previous sections have examined the metaphor of foreignness and the shifting boundaries of public and private. These analyses have touched on the ways that the body becomes an important site of the construction of political community through the norms of self-governance. In this third section I examine how specific bodies are targeted through the drug war with special emphasis on the importance of gender, race, and class. Turning to social reproduction, I examine the legal and cultural construction of crack babies and the discourse surrounding drugged, pregnant bodies. The push to prosecute and punish women who abuse drugs while pregnant demonstrates a concern with the corruption of national identity and the construction of pregnant women as less than fully autonomous, a discourse marked with racialized and classed constructions. The punishment of drug-using mothers reiterates the relationship between autonomy and law-making in a literal sense, bringing the power of the law to bear on the choices of individual women, and in a social sense, reinforcing power relationships related to gender and race.

The controversy over the use of drugs by pregnant women erupted in 1985 with the publication of a study by pediatrician Ira Chasnoff in the *New England Journal of Medicine*. Chasnoff reported early findings from a study with twenty-three cocaine-using women on the effects of crack use on cocaine-exposed babies. The report, followed by a later article that estimated that the number of so-called "crack babies" numbered 375,000, immediately sparked media interest and was followed by numerous scientific studies and popular representations of a supposed epidemic of crack babies. Congress undertook hearings, producing two texts: "Drug Addicted Babies: What Can Be Done?" and "Born Hooked," which advocated legislative action. The federal government acted with criminal statutes that added to the offense level for drug offenses involving underage or pregnant women and making it unlawful to distribute any controlled substance to a pregnant individual (18 U.S.C. Appx 2D1.2). Many states obliged by criminalizing drug usage by pregnant women, often prosecuting them under statutes that made the distribution of drugs to minors illegal[24] and with charges of child abuse.[25] While the Court has since ruled the mandatory *testing* of all pregnant women as unconstitutional,[26] the Court has upheld the *prosecution* of women who use drugs during pregnancy. Consequently, the decision to test is left primarily to medical authorities who must justify their suspicions, often relying on profiles about the types of women who use drugs.

Since the height of the crack baby scare, the scientific and medical community has reconsidered the long-term impacts of crack usage on children and has subsequently concluded that early studies were flawed and overestimated the impact of cocaine usage on fetuses.[27] Sensationalized journalistic reports that showed images of underweight babies and described depraved and indifferent mothers continue but have been tempered after an embarrassing case in which *Washington Post* reporter Janet Cooke lost her Pulitzer Prize after admitting she had fabricated a story about "Jimmy," an eight-year-old heroin addict being raised in a crack house (Reinarman and Duskin 1992).

The hysteria over expectant mothers using drugs, especially crack cocaine, demonstrates the role of autonomy in the process of subject formation and the position of subjects to the body politic. The pregnant addict is subjectified not just by drug usage; she is also gendered, racialized, and classed. The "special treatment," in the form of extra surveillance and discipline, given to mothers is symptomatic of the threat drug usage is seen as posing to the body politic and the reproduction of social order. The statute making the distribution of drugs to pregnant women or underaged minors a special crime indicates a special responsibility for protecting these presumably vulnerable classes. The linkage of pregnant women and children represents the gendered interpretation of drug users and is part of a long tradition of viewing women as less capable autonomous subjects and as more culpable drug users, a narrative that includes racialized elements discussed below. The singling out of pregnant women indicates the role that women (and children) play in the reproduction of the body politic. Women's special place as reproducers becomes justification for the regulation of and intervention into women's bodies, a narrative that again implicates race and class. I will address both of these points about the significance of drug using mothers in relationship to the body politic to examine the gendered nature of public and private binaries and the gendering of the national body politic.

Women have always been of special concern for drug warriors, and antidrug policies have often relied on images of women ensnared by drug abuse. Narratives about female drug abuse have often been both racialized and sexualized, depicting female drug users as oversexed and violating social boundaries regarding sexual practices. In the early twentieth century, cautionary tales emerged about women who had become "white slaves" or "opium vampires" to Chinese opium dealers. In the South in particular, stories of women driven to interracial sex during drug frenzies were used as cautionary tales for women and as justification for the regulation of narcotics. The most common description of female drug use involved the young, white, middle-class girl who was introduced by a questionable boyfriend to alcohol and gradually declined into sexual depravity and dependence on illegal drugs and nonwhite men, raising the specter of the penetration of her body by foreign substances and foreign men (Campbell 2000, chapter 4; Musto 1999; Jonnes 1996).

If this description of female drug abuse sounds quaint, it retains a degree of cultural currency. In the 2001 film *Traffic*, advertised as having an anti–drug-war message, the daughter of the national drug czar is seen as introduced to freebasing by her boyfriend and begins a decline that ends with her exchanging sex for a bed and crack with her African American dealer. In the scene that demonstrates the depth of her depravity, she digs through a bag for needles while her dealer, naked, goes to the door to confront her irate father, clad in an expensive suit. The drug users are purely physical and sexualized, particularly the nonwhite male. If intended to break with racial and class-based stereotypes of drug users by focusing on the story of a socioeconomically advantaged girl, the story repeats a similar relationship between gender and drug usage. The girl, with an insufficient sense of self and lacking willpower, gives in to peer pressure to use drugs, is unable to fight addiction, and begins a downward spiral of rejecting her family, her class, her race, and finally, her own body.

The supposed susceptibility of women to drugs and especially addiction is a reflection of gender norms that define women as less autonomous and thereby vulnerable to addiction. The reasons for women's apparent lack of autonomy are often linked to their physicality and supposed enslavement to their bodies (see Di Stefano 1996; Longhurst 2001). The description of women as lacking autonomy and as failed political subjects mirrors the representations of drug users as others. Women are often described as brute physicality, controlled by pregnancy, periods, and physical weakness that reflects their weakness of will. Historically women have often been denied access to the public sphere and participation in democratic self-governance, much in the way that drug users are considered as beyond the body politic.

Longhurst describes the ways that pregnant bodies are seen as abject and out of control in ways similar to those of the addict. Pregnant bodies are especially susceptible to leakage and sickness and often demonstrate a "need to be contained and controlled" (2001, 55) through public concern, the invasion of bodily space, and even special legal protections. Just as private drug use becomes grounds for bodily intervention by others, women's pregnant bodies become public spaces through the intensely private experience of pregnancy. The special status of reproduction in society subjects female bodies to special management that justifies external intervention into their bodies and choices.

The construction of women as less than autonomous subjects relates both to their supposed shortcomings as individuals and to broader issues of their role as reproducers of the body politic as well. Women are often deployed metaphorically as representations of the nation-state, and sexuality is of specific concern in reproducing the nation-state and its supposed purity. Notably, however, the discourse of reproducing the state does not act equally on all women's bodies; rather it varies according to their judged "fitness" as reproducers of the nation. The bodies of pregnant women are considered violable according to judgments passed on their capacity for self-governance, a judgment that often reflects assumptions about race and class that lead to the development of different strategies to deal with different kinds of women.

The family is perceived as a specific site for shaping the body politic, and parents and children are a primary target of government concern in the war on drugs. Certain families are subject to juridical power that punishes perceived deviants while others are encouraged to police themselves. While the bulk of drug war spending goes toward policing, the government spends over a billion dollars annually on programs directed toward families and antidrug education, including $180 million for the National Youth Anti-Drug Media Campaign and $5 million for the Parents Drug Corps program (NDCS 2002). Advertising strategies increasingly target parents with the implication that drug-free children are their responsibility and urge vigilant surveillance of their own children, not unlike displacing drug testing and surveillance onto private employers. The government publication *Keeping Your Kids Drug Free*, for example, gives parents advice on monitoring children's activities, questioning children about behavior, and confronting them about drug usage. More recently, The Anti-Drug, the major media wing project of the Youth Anti-Drug Media campaign, has provided pamphlets for parents that deal with talking to children about the linkage between terrorism and drugs.[28] Parental surveillance of children is now technologically enabled through the use of cell phones, pagers, and even home drug tests that enable parents to constantly monitor their children, the movement of their bodies as well as their body's "interior."

If good parenting requires constant vigilance, bad parenting is a failure with particular significance for mothers. Literature about drug usage has repeatedly emphasized the ways in which drug usage violates proper gender roles by making women hypersexual and, significantly, by encouraging them to abandon their roles as mothers

(Campbell 2000, 214–15; see also Ladd-Taylor 1998; and Boyd 1999). Testimony about drug usage by pregnant women has often cited the numerous ways the "mothering instinct" is sapped by drug usage. A Congressional witness declared, "We have never seen that, really, at this level of magnitude in the history of human experience with a substance that causes people to no longer care about being a mother, the most fundamental of drives that occurs" (Campbell 2000, 172). This sapping of the mothering instinct is described as potentially fatal for the body politic. A member of Congress summarized the threat in a Committee Report titled "Impact of Drugs on Children and Families," describing drug using mothers as tugging "not just . . . our heart strings, but also . . . our purse strings and . . . the kite strings that draw our national ambitions aloft" (quoted in Campbell 2000, 171). When mothers fail the state must step in, an indication of a failure of liberal governance as the public is forced to impinge on the private.

Some strategies have targeted parents, and mothers, as key points of intervention with potential drug users, using the family as an extension of state strategies. However, other mothers have played a substantially different material and symbolic role in the drug war. The supposed epidemic of crack mothers, discussed at the beginning of this section, highlighted the centrality of mothers in national discourse but also the fact that not all mothers are equal in relation to the body politic. The crack mother furor resulted in the criminalization of certain mothers, a move with important gendered and racialized implications for the boundaries of the body politic. Drug usage is considered grounds for declaring a parent unfit, but the patterns of detecting and punishing "bad mothers" indicate that certain populations are already deemed as insufficient. Populations whose capacity for self-governance is already in question are subject to greater surveillance and punishment.

The singling out of specific populations for state intervention reflects existing power relationships that shape how certain populations are perceived and regulated. Statistics have long demonstrated the racialized patterns of prosecution for drug usage during pregnancy. Despite studies showing that drug use during pregnancy does not vary racially, African American and Latina women account for 80 percent of women prosecuted for child abuse or delivering drugs to minors (Neuspiel 1996, 47–55; see also Paltrow 1996). The reasons for the racial disparity are numerous. Geographically, prosecutions are concentrated in areas with large minority populations, though these patterns often reflect a single aggressive legislature or prosecutor willing to pursue legal action against these women (Roberts 1997). Further, the patterns reflect racialized patterns of drug usage. Crack cocaine usage is most prevalent among minority populations, while the abuse of prescription drugs, alcohol, and marijuana is most prevalent in white populations (Roberts 1997; Koren et al. 1989; Paltrow 1996: 479). The prosecutions also reflect a class bias as well, since women who are prosecuted are usually treated in public hospitals and often by physicians they do not know personally and are more likely to report them (Roberts 1997).

The demonization of crack mothers and the punitive measures against them draw on racialized understandings of female sexuality. Crack in particular is linked with hypersexuality as the epithet "crack whore" suggests. As Roberts (1997) has noted, these images play into racial stereotypes about uncontrolled black female sexuality linked with a general unfitness for motherhood. Similar justifications were given for the disproportionate removal of black children from their homes by the state, stricter welfare laws governing single-parent families, and even the treatment of women under slavery. These practices provide insight into the perceived value of these mothers and their children. The emphasis on punitive measures (rather than drug treatment) discourages women from seeking prenatal care and implies that addicted mothers ought to have an abortion rather than become bad mothers (Roberts 1997; Paltrow 1996). The legitimacy of the choice to become a mother is already put into question among certain populations and thus their pregnancies may subject them to further disciplinary measures.

In the cases of both "good," responsible, and vigilant mothers and their others, the "bad," irresponsible, and addicted mothers, their status as less than fully autonomous justifies increased state interventions into their bodies. However, differing attitudes toward different mothers indicate a specific relationship to the state. As in the case of drug testing, different bodies are granted different levels of privacy and publicity and evoke different strategies of governance, either heightened discipline to encourage self-governance or punitive measures that reinforce exclusion from the body politic. Autonomy is used as a justification for the policing of individuals and for the reproduction and construction of differently situated forms of subjectivity.

Conclusion

The apparent antithesis between addiction and autonomy breaks down in the analysis of the drug war. The specter of addiction justifies the intervention into the lives and bodies of subjects in order to save them from the scourge of intoxication. The connection between our cultural and legal interpretation of the corporeality of addiction reveals a great deal about the relationship between the body and autonomy. Self-control of the body is central to autonomy, a concept that relies on the premise that rationality can control otherwise untamed physical impulses. Drug users' willingness to sacrifice self-control in the pursuit of pleasure justifies intervention into their body and choices. In a paradoxical turn, the idea of autonomy that challenges forms of coercive power may also justify that the use of coercive power on bad subjects. Political determinations of who counts as an autonomous subject demarcate the boundaries of political community, excluding not only drug users but also assorted "foreign bodies" associated with the deviance of drug use. The drug war illustrates that the connection between autonomy and exclusion as the failure to self-regulate can be used to identify a subject as a "foreigner" or threat to the public order. At the same time, groups already considered less than fully autonomous, such as women, may be subject to extra regulation regarding their drug usage.

The drug war further articulates the connection between autonomy and norms. In order to be seen and treated as a subject capable of self-governance, the subject must not make particular choices that are seen as showing a lack of self-control. As the history of the drug war indicates, the choices that are condemned and social interpretation of these choices are contingent, reflecting power relationships in society. Thus, for example, the "foreigner" associated with drugs shifts over time from Chinese immigrants to African American laborers to terrorist organizations overseas.

The practices of the drug war are justified by the norm of autonomy or concern with maintaining the ability of individuals to self-govern and thus to participate in democratic self-governance. These practices echo Foucault's concern that modern discourses of self-governance compel the subject to act according to norms determined externally to the subject and dictated by power relationships. Fulfilling the expectations of autonomy is to submit oneself to norms, while violating those norms is grounds for marginalization and exclusion. Autonomy does not appear as the liberating discourse that modern liberal and democratic theorists believed it could be. Instead it binds the individual to socially recognized forms of self-limitation. However, this relationship between autonomy and power may offer other political possibilities. If Foucault was worried about the ways that power couched as self-governance could conceal the operation of power relationships, he also argued that power generates resistance. The next two chapters take on the Foucauldian argument that autonomy as self-regulation can also have an ethical component that is conducive to creativity and political change.

4

Man Is a Political Animal

SELF-DISCIPLINE AND ITS BEASTLY OTHER

> I want to have my lion and eagle near me
> so that I always have hints and omens that
> help me to know how great or small my
> strength is. Must I look down upon them
> today and feel fear? And will the hour
> return when they look up to me in—fear?
>
> —Friedrich Nietzsche,
> *The Gay Science*

In 1386 an unnamed female defendant in France was charged with the mutilation and murder of a child. Following a public trial she was convicted and sentenced to death by hanging. She was dressed in the clothing of a female menial laborer and then taken to the public square, where she was disemboweled and her limbs were torn off. The king's executioner hanged her, and her carcass was left in the public square for viewing. The defendant had to be dressed prior to her public torture and execution because she was a sow.[1] In 1998, the Animal Legal Defense Fund and Marc Jurnove successfully sued the Game Farm Park and Zoo over their confinement and mistreatment of several primates living in their facility for scientific observation.[2] Decided on the grounds that the treatment of the primates interfered with the "aesthetic interest" of Jurnove, a naturalist, in seeing animals

97

in a healthy and nurturing environment, the decision set a new precedent for animals' standing in Court. The decision of the appeals Court sided with the naturalist, saying that seeing animals mistreated could be perceived as a direct harm to those with regular contact with those animals, and that persons or organizations with a vested interest in those animals could in fact have standing in the Court of law. The ruling allowed humans to file suit on behalf of animals, implying a human interest in the humane treatment of animals (see Smith 1999).

These anecdotes about animals literally before the law bear an eerie resemblance to the opening of Foucault's *Discipline and Punish* (1979). The text begins with the gruesome description of the spectacle of punishment by the crown in which revenge is taken out on the body of Damiens, the regicide who is brutally mutilated before being killed. The scene then shifts to a more mundane description of a prison timetable structuring the time of offenders. The purpose of Foucault's narrative is to set up and then undermine the apparent humanism evidenced in the less violent and spectacular modern mode of punishment. The gentler hand of punishment is simply a transformation in the hegemonic mode of power focused not on punishment after the law has been infringed but a focus on disciplining subjects to self-regulate before the violation can occur. On the surface, the comparison between human and animal treatment appears to follow the same line of argument. Indeed, popular understanding of human behavior toward animals seems to track the same story of humanization as Foucault describes. The extension of concern to the animal kingdom is evidence of reason, humanism and compassion displacing relationships of retribution, dominance, and violence. The recognition of animal rights is merely another step in the progressive move away from the violent and irrational world of premodernity.

We should, of course, be skeptical of this story. On the most obvious level, more animals are killed every day as we continue to use (and perhaps abuse) animals as food, entertainment, research subjects, property, and pets.[3] But, just as significantly, these stories are about beings described as *animals* and not *humans*.[4] Therefore, to simply impose the narrative of disciplinary power on the animal subjects of these stories is to miss an important point: the difference that animals make. If a rejection of excessive cruelty toward animals is generally accepted as a manifestation of human compassion, the changing relationships between humans and animals tells a unique story about the construction of human autonomy. Animals have been central to the definition of what it means to be human and, in particular, to be an autonomous subject. Within the scope of modernity, animals have a specific relationship to the construction of the meaning of autonomy; to be autonomous is also to be a rights-bearing subject. Thus struggles over whether animals can be rights-bearing subjects are also struggles over why (and what) humans have rights.

As in previous chapters, this chapter considers the contingent meaning of autonomous subjectivity, its relationship to specific power relations, and its role in the exclusion of certain subjects. However, this chapter shifts the focus to consider how an awareness of the entanglement of autonomy within specific power relationships might yield ethical insights, opening up space for considering different forms of political subjectivity. Can understanding the contingency of any particular configuration of rights and responsibilities also prompt us to think about how we might configure our relationships differently? If trying a pig for murder seems unthinkable today, what are the ontological underpinnings of our own conceptions of animals? What political opportunities are rendered possible or impossible within these ways of thinking, and how might we create different opportunities?

These questions are approached through an exploration of the ways the "animal" as a figure has been used to construct the meaning of autonomous subjectivity. An analysis of the ontological construction of the category of "animal" reveals the ways that ethical and political responsibility toward animals is dependent on the certainty ascribed to the categories of human and animal. Animals are often the "constitutive outside" or negative example that enables defining human subjectivity as "disembodiment and autonomy" (Wolfe 2010, xv). Any attempts to fit animals into the schema of rights without challenging the ontological assumptions that underlie the ability to differentiate between human and animal and a priori assume human as the norm will simply reiterate the power relationships embedded in the construction of these categories. As Oliver argues:

> We must reconsider our notions of autonomy and freedom in relation to animals and ourselves. Obviously the very conception of "ourselves"

and "we" comes under scrutiny when we consider animals, not just because we may decide to include animals in those designations but also because we acknowledge that animals always have been formative parts of our self-conception, an avowal that necessarily transforms it. (Oliver 2009, 22)

The chapter thus begins to bring together the two approaches toward self-governance in Foucault. As demonstrated, the expectation that individuals be autonomous has led to a heightened sense of responsibility and proliferation of rules for individual subjects as well as power relationships that have excluded certain individuals or practices. However, the will to self-govern also has creative potential when an emphasis is put on the ethical practices of the self. Foucault suggests that an embrace of the self-critical practices of subjectification in which the subject rigorously engages in critical examination can produce spaces of possibility, ways of envisioning different political relationships based on uncertainty. The recent turn toward consideration of the animal in deconstructive thought provides an opening for linking the political and ethical through a rethinking of the category of autonomy.

The chapter engages in a brief genealogy of the relationship between human and animal in modernity. I consider the role that the animal plays in political theory, where it regularly appears as a figure outside of politics that is used as a negative example for defining political subjectivity. Next is a discussion of the emergence of the animal rights movement both in practice and in theory and how its logic reinforces the ontological distinction between human and animal that makes the exclusion of animals possible. Finally, I consider other ways of looking at animals that place them at the center, rather than periphery, of our ethical imagination. Thinking about autonomy with the category of animals enables an ambitious project of rethinking all of our ethical relationships with others, and with ourselves.

Making Man the Political Animal [5]

Pinning down the relationship between humans and animals requires a definition of the categories in question, a more difficult undertaking than we might assume. My first two sections will consider the construction of a category called "animal" that is neither self-evident nor stable.[6] Indeed, I will demonstrate that the term "animal" is a shifting signifier, defined continually in relationship to "human" in ways that make both terms dependent upon one another. The deployment of the phrase "category of animal" is not meant, therefore, to refer to a set of existing creatures in the world, nor does it refer to a clearly defined set of characteristics that compose a delineated category. The "category of animal" marks out numerous imaginary spaces that share a primary purpose of defining the difference between human animal and non-human animal.

The project of boundary construction never fully succeeds precisely because a single, definitive difference cannot be located. More interesting is the normative purpose these acts of boundary construction serve in constructing political subjectivities and ways of perceiving the self and others. Historian Keith Thomas writes:

> It is an enduring tendency of human thought to project upon the natural world (particularly the animal kingdom) categories and values derived from human society and then to serve them back as a critique or reinforcement of the human order, justifying some particular social or political arrangement. . . . The diversity of animal species has been used on innumerable occasions to provide conceptual support for social differentiation among humans; and there have been few societies where "nature" has never been appealed to for legitimation and justification. (1983, 61)

While presented as an objective scientific classification, the category of animal is hardly neutral in political and ethical debates. Even at the most basic level, the categories "human" and "animal" are a sorting device that implies a fundamental difference between the two terms and a fundamental sameness within them, a distinction that has profound consequences for the treatment of individuals falling within (or between) the categories (Lawlor 2007, 3–7). Symbolic representations of animals have played an important political role, even if the discussion of animals as a political subject is a more contemporary phenomenon. Animal rights have only recently become a contentious and politicized issue in the West though animals, in various ways, have fallen under the purview of government and legal control through various forms of administration from anticruelty statutes, livestock regulation, wildlife protection, and other rules that loosely govern proper care and treatment of animals.[7] Consideration of the status of animals generally, however, has been relegated to the sphere of moral philosophy and has been of relatively little direct interest to political theorists. Animals are generally lumped into the category of, to paraphrase a number of political and moral theorists, "animals, infants, and imbeciles" or those worthy of moral consideration but never political agency or participation (Leahy 1991, 185). These marginal creatures fall under the umbrella of political authority but only as passive recipients of care and protection, though with "animals and imbeciles" this often takes the form of violent exclusion (or even elimination), confinement, or restriction.[8] The relationship with children is significant; animal-focused spectacles such as circuses and zoos are marketed to children, and much iconic imagery produced for children involves animals.[9] The implication is that animals are not to be taken seriously in the very serious world of politics.

In spite of the explicit marginalizing of animals in the sphere of politics, they are hardly absent from consideration. Indeed, it appears that many if not most political theorists have had something to say about animals, if only to justify their exclusion from the realm of the political.[10] While I cannot adequately write a thorough genealogy of the role of animals in political theory, a brief examination of the relationship between animals and politics is useful to outline the role of animals in relationship to autonomy. The exploration reveals first that animals are not a new subject of political consideration but have lurked at the edges of political theory for centuries. Second, animals are not merely a secondary consideration; they also can be seen as a vital means of understanding the modern political subject as autonomous. For the sake of sketching the general contours of the animal/autonomy relationships, I somewhat clumsily lump the deployment of animals in political theory into three broad categories. First is the hierarchical/instrumental model, in which humans and animals are clearly distinct and humans are granted degrees of dominion over them. Second is the duty model in which animals are less than full (human) moral agents but nonetheless not mere objects for human use. Third is a nostalgic model in which the difference between humans and animals is used to critique elements of human social life, often by emphasizing what humans have lost in differentiating themselves from the rest of the animal kingdom. While I will present these as conceptually distinct, they often converge or overlap, indicating the ways that animals play a figurative role in political theory, more important in defining human nature than in existing as beings in themselves.

The first deployment of animals, the hierarchical model, takes great pains to identify the boundary between humans and animals. Domination of animals is justified by their profound difference, which is then reinforced by the act of domination (Thomas 1993, 5–11). One of the earliest considerations of animals comes from Aristotle, who believed that animals, like slaves and women, were deficient in reason and therefore were appropriately subject to political rule by men. And, like slaves and women, animals were primarily physical and not mental beings and therefore were to be utilized for material purposes (Clarke and Linzey 1990, 6; Taylor 1999, 25). A similar sentiment emerged in Christian doctrine in which animals were considered creatures of God, but lower on the ladder of beings than men (and, usually, women). Aquinas, borrowing from Aristotle, argued that animals were not rational, self-directed beings and therefore had no direct relationship to God, thus making them appropriate instruments for those beings who were closer to God (Taylor 1999, 26; Leahy 1991, 80; Salisbury 1994).[11] Locke uses animals as a paradigm for property, arguing that God gave man "dominion over the lower beasts and the earth," giving humans not merely a right but a duty to make use of animals as they saw fit (Tannenbaum 1995, 542–44). All these accounts utilize animals as means for human ends.

As theological arguments were supplanted in political theory, the hierarchical relationship between man and animal was not abandoned; it was, however, justified in new ways that both shaped and reflected a new vision of human subjectivity. The most often cited (and frequently reviled) conception of animals comes from Descartes, who believed animals were mere automatons and, like machines, could be used to further human interests (Clarke and Linzey 1990, 4; Taylor 1999, 26–27). Most theorists, however, had a more complex view of animals as non-human entities but also not just objects. Their more careful thinking about animals was often a means at getting to their conception of political subjectivity. While all of these theorists agree that rationality separates (hu)man from beast and adopt a hierarchical view of their relationship, the ways that the theorists define human/animal difference is central to the emergence of the modern subject as a rights-bearer and the meaning and role of rights in human politics.

For Hobbes, another hierarchical thinker, the key to the relationship between humans and animals was the human capacity for reason and, correlatively, the ability to use language.[12] The difference was significant since reason and language gave humans the capacity to contract and thereby escape the state of nature, characterized by constant material threats (both other persons and scarcity of resources). Since animals remain in the state of nature where, without contract, there is no justice, then to use the term "justice" in reference to animals is simply incomprehensible. Further, since animals do not contract with us, we have no mutual obligation to them (nor from them) to refrain from killing one another (Taylor 1999, 30). The emphasis on the ability to reason, communicate, and give consent will be central in later conceptions of rights based on a consent model. Hobbes emphasizes that animals lie outside of the law based on human convention. If the sovereign exists above the law, because his power may not be limited, animals exist below the law because they can neither comprehend nor consent to the practices of lawgiving. Beasts thus exist in a lawless state that nonetheless is a reminder of the significance of law for human life, indicating the feral existence we would face were we to fail to consent to governance. The animal serves as the "other" to human sociality that is kept in order by the fear of natural animality and chaos and the power of the sovereign as "the manifestation of bestiality or human animality" (Derrida 2010, 26). In this hierarchical model, animals are perpetually below humans, a status used to buttress and confirm the status of humans.

While rejecting the blunt characterization of animals as existing as mere instruments of human ends, duty-based approaches to animals are similar in the emphasis on human/animal difference and the exclusion of animals from the sphere of justice. While still retaining a hierarchy, they offer a slightly different conception of the relationship between rights and justice. I use Kant as the paradigm for this approach, in part because of his highly influential notion of autonomy and the recognition of moral agency and because, unlike many theorists, he considers the status of animals at length in developing his moral theory.

From the outset Kant excludes animals on the grounds that they lack the capacity to be moral agents. As previously discussed,[13] moral agency requires the capacity for autonomy, the ability to act on reasons or a universalizable law or principle. Moral agents are able to recognize other agents as beings like themselves and worthy of moral consideration and ought therefore to treat them with respect, as an end rather than a means. Animals are "moral patients" who are worthy of consideration but not of the same sort as moral agents because they do not recognize us nor can we recognize them as moral actors.[14] This does not outright exclude animals from moral consideration but establishes a different sort of relationship; animals are not subject to rules of justice, but they do deserve consideration in terms of welfare.[15] Kant derives a degree of respect for animals not from recognition of a duty based on their intrinsic value, as is the case with humans, but from an indirect duty. For Kant, the "proper" treatment of animals—defined by avoiding mistreatment—was a means of expressing one's own moral agency or humanity. His discussion of the ethics of human–animal relationships deserves quoting at length:

> Animals are not self-conscious and they are merely a means to an end. That end is man. . . . Animal nature has analogies to human nature, and by doing our duties to animals in respect of manifestations of human nature, we indirectly do our duty towards humanity. Thus, if a dog has served his master long and faithfully, his service . . . deserves reward, and when the dog has grown too old to serve, his master ought to keep him until he dies. If then any acts of animals are analogous to human acts and spring from the same principles, we have duties toward the animals because thus we cultivate the corresponding duties towards human beings. If a man shoots his dog because the animal is no longer capable of service, he does not fail in his duty to the dog, for the dog cannot judge, but his act is inhuman and damages in himself that humanity which it is his duty to show toward humankind. (Kant 1963, 239–40)

Kant makes a strong case that animals ought not to be treated as mere instruments and that they remain the means by which we measure our own humanity, by our superiority demonstrated through extending kindness (though not justice). As often characterizes the discussion of animals, animals are creatures that may inspire sentiment and pity, but this should not be brought into the realm of politics, which ought to be governed by reason. Kant justifies the differential treatment of those assumed to be non-autonomous, a relationship that prevents them from equal consideration or participation in the political sphere.

While significantly different, the hierarchical and the duty-based approaches share a concern with politics (and morality) as a decidedly human project based on the capacity to reason and, in doing so, submitting oneself to a law (either the sovereign or the moral law). This particular conception of political agency as the activity of an autonomous subject is constructed through the figure of the animal, who is the paradigmatic case of the being that is *not* autonomous—subject to material drive, and instincts rather than reason and deliberation—and is thereby barred from participation in politics. The relationship of animals to the law is key in both accounts and indicates why rights-based advocacy of animals may present a challenge to conventional analysis of autonomy, a suggestion taken up in the final section of the chapter.

The third category of consideration, nostalgic accounts of animal life, includes critics of modern subjectivity who adopt the figure of the animal to make critical, normative political arguments. Two paradigmatic figures, Rousseau and Nietzsche, while obviously not the only possible choices, represent a different way of configuring the human via the animal. Both theorists agree that animals are different from humans but do not assume this difference implies superiority on the part of humans. They maintain the human–animal distinction but do so in order to critique, rather than elevate, human society. Significantly, animals are used as a way of demonstrating a lack of autonomy in human lives. Animals are not necessarily the appropriate model of human autonomy, but they do offer a way of unmasking human deficiency.

Rousseau reverses the role of the animal in defining autonomy and, in his *Discourse on the Origins of Inequality*, actually attempts to demonstrate that animals possess a form of autonomy that makes them more free than their slavish opposite, civilized man. The noble savage, the representative of man's original autonomy prior to corruption and alienation via society, is modeled on the orangutan.[16] Rousseau describes animals as prelinguistic and asocial but notes these attributes ensure a degree of self-sufficiency and natural peacefulness lacking in (modern) humans. Peace and order derive not from reason but from that most animal of instincts, compassion, which is our primary means of relating to others. Of course, he goes on in the *Social Contract* to construct a decidedly human political order, and the place of animals is, at best, ambiguous (he even calls those who refuse to consent "stupid animals"). The category "animal" is used differently, however, as a metaphor for better ways of conceiving the political subject. The animal is again appropriated as a means of getting at the "real" human. Animals represent a primitive form of autonomy to be appreciated but ultimately overcome in the social–human autonomy made possible through political community. Rousseau presents man as "fallen" from the heights of natural/savage man and burdened with the task of transforming the freedom of natural man into a better form of freedom in political society.

Nietzsche is similarly fascinated with animals as a means of critiquing the modern subject and modern politics, and, like Rousseau, he critiques the enthusiasm for reason in other theorists. Animal metaphors abound in Nietzsche with ambiguous consequences. He regularly compares or contrasts human behavior with that of animals, at times celebrating animal behavior, embodying the will to power in the lion, or condemning humans who engage in "herdlike" behavior. The passage that most clearly illustrates what Nietzsche finds appealing about the animal world is from *The Genealogy of Morals*, in which Nietzsche describes the behavior of birds of prey and lambs. The birds do not perceive the lambs as weak but as "tasty," while the lambs do not condemn the behavior of the birds (1967, 44–45). By embracing this amoral trait of animals, Nietzsche assumes animals live without complex modes of morality or justice. Their reliance on their drives preempts animals from developing elaborate codes of morality that would prevent natural predators from consuming their natural prey. In short, animals lack the kind of self-limiting tendencies in humans that Nietzsche sees as causing weakness.

Animals thus represent a vision of freedom distinct from the moral law, the opposite of Kantian depictions of autonomy. Like Rousseau, Nietzsche is concerned with the "enfeeblement" of man that comes from the subordination of forms of life that embrace strength, physicality, and power. In the place of reasoning man, he embraces an *embodied* form of subjectivity. Nietzsche is critical of human attitudes of superiority since, as Nietzsche notes, "with the evolving of consciousness there is always combined a great, radical perversion, falsification, superficialization, and generalization" (1974, 297) Nietzsche is particularly critical of the insistence of theorists (particularly Kant) that humans are unique in possessing morality because of their ability to formulate and obey a law independent of nature. The development of moral laws becomes, as Nietzsche puts it, the "cruelty of the categorical imperative" whereby humans relieve themselves of the difficulty of decision making through the development of "universal laws," which they may then apply to specific situations, reaffirming their own morality through their faith in the morality of the law rather than in consideration of the particular situation itself. In blind obedience to laws (institutional but also self-legislated), we are less autonomous than the animal, whose instinct allows for the capacity to change and decide in the moment. Therefore, unlike Rousseau, who mourns the loss of our original, natural form of freedom located in the past, Nietzsche also sees a human future in the figure of the animal as an ideal toward which man might strive. Nietzsche arrives at the paradoxical conclusion, therefore, that to become *Übermensche* (overmen) and transcend the limitations of humanity we must be more like animals. To take this position he presumes, like other theorists, that animals exist outside the law, a position he takes to be preferable and not indicative of animal inferiority.

While appearing rarely and often as footnotes, literally, to the human world of politics, animals have clearly played an important role in political theorizing by being the figure in opposition to political subjectivity, whether used as a negative or positive example. The conceptualization of animals as without law is a primary means of placing them outside the bounds of politics, especially as agents who might participate in governance. The differing accounts of how we ought to understand animals indicate that the category itself is not as fixed as their apparent biological roots might indicate. The contingent construction of the subject through the animal's negation demonstrates that the category of "animal" might become grounds for political contestation. Reconceptualizing the relative categories of "human" and "animal" is not merely of academic interest. It also has a profound impact on our treatment of both animals and humans since our understandings of human capacities, goals, and possibilities are tied up with an idea of its constitutive other, the animal. If animals are situated negatively against our understanding of autonomy, then suggesting that animals might fit into the concept of autonomy has potentially disruptive results for our self-understanding as the autonomous animal. Oliver describes in the stakes in vivid terms:

> The divide between human and animal is also political and sets up the very possibility of politics. Who is included in political society and who is not is a consequence of the politics of "humanity" who creates the polis itself. In this regard, politics itself is a product of the anthropological machine which is inherently lethal to some forms of "human" life. (2009, 229)

The next section considers the empirical traces of this theoretical discussion by examining how, in concrete terms, the divide between human and animal has played out in the emergence of political movements that have sought to extend legal, political, or moral consideration to animals. This history demonstrates Oliver's point that the determination of what or who falls on which side of the human–animal divide has concrete consequences for those subjects.

Sordid Tails: A Brief History with Animals

The theoretical life of animals is primarily metaphorical. Animals are useful not merely for our material lives but also for constructing our own senses of selfhood, agency, and morality. Animals appear to play a taken-for-granted role in everyday life as food, companions, or entertainment, but this apparently natural role of animals elides a long history of changing relationships between humans and animals, a complex story that also demonstrates the construction of "human" around the term "animal" and shows the contingency of our relationships to animals. The material lives of animals reflect on and modify our metaphorical constructions of the meaning of the category. Unfortunately, relatively little is known about animals historically since, generally they are not the subjects of history.[17] Nonetheless, a brief history of animals, focusing primarily on human–animal relationships within modernity, is necessary to understand their present place in politics, particularly their relationship to our understanding of the status of different human groups.

If early views of animals tended to view them solely as instruments for human ends, their uses often corresponded to this view. Feudal agriculture often brought humans and animals together, but this closeness often led to a desire to distance humans from animals conceptually in order to overcome the suggestion that physical proximity might mean moral or spiritual similarity (Salisbury 1994; Ritvo 1989; Tester 1991; Franklin 1999). Dominance over animals was considered necessary as a way to demonstrate and be reassured of human superiority. This dominance was often displayed in outward forms, ranging from the public slaughter of animals to more subtle means, such as the symbolic value of bringing the whole cooked animal carcass to the table to be publicly carved and eaten. Significantly, meat eating was generally a sign of affluence and authority since primarily wealthy landowners owned meat-producing animals as property or hunted regularly for sport. Yet if animals could symbolize human dominance, they were also perceived as a threat since wild animals were, quite literally, a physical threat and, most insidiously, infectious disease was often spread through animals. Consequently, animals often emerge symbolically as monsters or beasts and are often used as metaphors for a fear of the unknown, fate, and nature (Salisbury 1994).

Changes in social relationships via the industrial revolution and urbanization were as profound for animals as they were for humans. A multiplicity of relationships between humans and animals emerged that stratified the animal kingdom according to geography, species, and use. In both Europe and America, the shift toward capitalism, and especially mass production, had multiple effects for animals (Tester 1991; Philo 1998; Philo and Wilbert 2000; Wolch and Emel 1998). Capitalist production democratized the practice of eating meat since meat was now more readily mass-produced on commercial farms and was significantly cheaper. While meat retained its class prestige, it also became a status symbol for a rising middle class. Moreover, the increasing availability of disposable income encouraged the consumption of animals as pets, entertainment, and edutainment.[18] Zoos, circuses, and naturalist clubs increasingly turned to animals as a pastime or form of leisure. Further, as scientific understanding of animals grew, they became less mysterious and thereby less of a source of fear. Scientific knowledge pulled humans in different directions, both recognizing the incredible similarities between human and animal anatomy and demonstrating human difference. One of most significant uniquely human abilities was the capacity to generate, catalog, and transmit knowledge about animals (Foucault 1970). Humans entered into a set of dramatically different relationships that, as in the past, were an inconsistent combination of repulsion and attraction, fear and fondness, science and sentiment, kindness and cruelty.

The animal welfare movement grew during the mid- and late nineteenth century, primarily in the middle and upper classes in urbanized areas (Tester 1991; Wolch and Emel 1998). Notably, at this time social organizations such as the RSPCA (Royal Society for the Prevention of Cruelty to Animals) and its American counterpart, the ASPCA, emerged in Britain and the United States with the express goal of reducing animal suffering, especially among city-dwelling animals, such as pets or "fighting animals" (Tester 1991; Franklin 1999). Their primary objectives were to secure humane living conditions for domesticated animals by caring for homeless animals of domesticated species and improving the treatment of those already in human care. While shifting to a more duty-based approach to human interactions with animals, the animal welfare movement did not challenge the hierarchy between human and animal but remade it with humans in the role of benefactors. The impact on animals was significant, but so too was the way that the rethinking of the human—animal boundary reshaped relationships among "humans." The treatment of animals became a way to differentiate between and judge varying human groups, with cruelty toward animals interpreted as a sign of barbarity.

The role of animals in differentiating between who counts as a political agent is not unique but in fact parallels the use of various human "others" who also are excluded from political consideration because of a failure to be seen as fully human. McClure describes how a range of struggles became linked through their common ground of exclusion, a failure to achieve the status of rational, autonomous actor:

> This historical figuration of the "subject of rights" as an autonomous "individual" provided a successful historical counter to absolutist denials of participatory channels; it none the less excluded from the public

realm all sectors of the population conventionally coded as "dependent" or "other" by the dominant cultural frame: women, children, labourers, aliens, the mad, and criminals, etc. (1992, 111)

Animals are lumped under the "etc.," a broad category describing those marginal to rights discourse. The reason for the inclusion of "animals" among the excluded subjects is not because of their dependence upon humans for their survival, a description that fits only a narrow range of animal life. Rather, animals are considered nonautonomous because of their relationship to themselves.

Animals are incapable of controlling their natural instincts; they are enslaved by their bodily impulses. In this way animals were linked with others excluded from rights-assertion because of their corporeality and irrationality, a burden often imposed on a range of "others," perceived of as lacking the rationality to govern themselves. Women, for example, were viewed to be closer to animals due to the corporeality (rather than rationality) of reproductive processes in their body: "Women and maternity are closely related to animal and animality, women's bodies have been imagined as subject to, and determined by, natural processes that make them closer to animals than to men" (Oliver 2009, 17). The determination that these subjects lack autonomy because they are unable to control their physicality is grounds for denying them a role in the governance of society more generally. Women and animals were thus determined to be *not* political animals.

The tendency of society to lump together animals and other marginalized subjects led to new forms of resistance. Animal welfare movements were frequently associated with or outgrowths of suffrage and antislavery movements.[19] Suffrage organizations often called for a right to vote on the basis of women's unique role in caring, particularly for children and animals. Antislavery groups noted that slaves were often denigrated by comparing them with animals whether in visual depictions of slaves as literal animals or in the language of "brutes" or "beasts." White abolitionists made a connection between dehumanizing slaves and the abuse of animals, arguing that civilization ought not to tolerate either. Associating these human causes with animals was risky business, since their lack of autonomy had often been demonstrated through the comparison with "animal nature." Women, slaves, and animals shared a common fate in being defined by their biology[20] or by the shared perception that they lacked the capacity to be fully human. The linkage often made these social movements political allies but as often led to mutual suspicion and concerns about being identified with other marginalized groups.

If the animal welfare movement saw a connection among groups in the shared vulnerability between them, the dangers inherent in connecting an already marginalized group with animals led them to adopt a different strategy. Animal welfare groups promoted the idea that beneficence toward animals was not a sign of human weakness but of civilization, an argument that further differentiated groups of humans according to their treatment of animals. The connection between the "humane treatment of animals" and "civilized behavior" made animal welfare a popular movement for the upper classes and impacted the behaviors targeted by activism. Pet ownership was most predominant among the upper classes, who could afford the economic luxury of a companion animal. Welfare organizations focused their attention on the use of animals in sports, especially sports enjoyed by the lower class, such as cock fighting or bull baiting. These were targeted as inhumane and further evidence of the lack of civility of lower-class persons (see Tester 1991; Franklin 1999). The animal welfare movement adopted a self-perception as a humanizing force whereby, as Kant suggested, animals could be a means through which we express our humanity and superiority through our benevolence. The demonstration of humanity has, like animals, become a product of mass consumption through marketing strategies that promote proanimal products. Proanimal groups in the twentieth century have maintained a strong commercial component, often most successful in consumer strategies that promote a lifestyle of care for animals including vegetarianism, "non-cruel" cosmetics, and elaborate pet care provisions (Garner 1993; Silverstein 1996).

Throughout this history of the gradual politicization of the animal, the meanings of the terms "animal" and "human" are contingent, according to changing relationships within society. They do not represent objective, unified categories of sameness and difference. Clearly, different animals are located differently in relationship to human society according to their status as pets, property, capital, food, entertainment, or wildlife, leading to contingent ways of relating to animals and valuing them. Second, to identify a single category of "human" in relationship to animal is also clearly mistaken since relationships to animals are geographically and historically variant and, importantly, have been used as a means to separate out categories of "humans" by race, class, gender, and nationality. In a similar way, some subjects such as slaves fall in between the two categories, while others, such as women, utilize their relationship with animals to leverage political agency. Animals, as a simultaneously material and metaphorical category, have thus been used to define the autonomy of humans as well as to determine which humans are treated as autonomous subjects. If rethinking human–animal relationships can have such a profound impact on societal relationships, the question remains whether the animal rights movement that posits that animals are not outside the law has transformative potential, especially in challenging the conceptualization of autonomy that allowed the exclusion of animals in the first place.

Animal Rights and Human Rites

The category of animal has been important in defining the category of autonomy and, correlatively, the category of human subject. Consequently, animals play a role in the cultural and political history that depicts a gradual expansion of one of the most important markers of autonomy, membership in the category of the rights-bearing subject. The capacity to claim and assert rights is an important marker of autonomy since it implies a protected self that others do not have the right to impinge upon. Legal recognition of rights acknowledges the individual's status and thereby enables a demand to be treated as an autonomous being. One strategy adopted by excluded groups considered less than fully autonomous has been to claim rights and thereby demand a promotion in status. Expanding the category of the rights-bearing subject plays a dual role in enabling the claims of certain groups to be heard while reducing the power the category has when rights are claimed by particular groups at a cost to others. In a sweeping endorsement of rights, Patricia Williams writes that "the task is to expand private property rights into a conception of civil rights, into the right to expect civility from others.... Society must give rights away ... to slaves ... to trees ... to cows ... to history ... to rivers and rocks" (1991, 164–65).

Williams argues that rights-claiming is a necessary strategy for antiracist movements because the mere achievement of the status as a rights-bearing subject makes a difference by changing the conception of that social group and its relationship to other social groups as modifying the meaning of rights discourse. While Williams's argument attempts to radicalize rights themselves by extending the right to make rights claims to previously excluded groups, the use of rights by the proanimal movement may not be as radical as they first appear. At present, arguments in favor of animal rights in fact reinforce the very binaries that enable the exclusion of animals (and various others) in the first place, particularly the distinction between autonomous and heteronomous subjects. This section examines the construction of animal rights discourse by exploring the ways it apes current rights discourse rather than modifies it and, in doing so, fails to acknowledge the more politically interesting possibilities animals may offer in thinking about autonomy, rights, and ethics.

The meaning of rights can be distilled into two separate accounts: one based on rights as an expression of interest, the other emphasizing rights as a relationship of duty. In defining rights as interest, some accounts emphasize that rights are merely an expression of interest legitimated through the power of the language of rights (Meyer 2000). Others see rights as a more fundamental need, securing the basic conditions for the pursuit of interests. This view is evocative of Hobbes's conception of the social contract in which securing the basic right to life is a precondition for pursuing interests within social and political life. Not surprisingly, this view often conforms to contractual views of political rights. Rights are mutually agreed upon rules that mediate relationships or conflicts between contracting parties. The second account of rights more closely tracks Kant's understanding of the human subject, seeing rights primarily as duties, as reciprocal obligations entailed in the recognition of the other as another subject like oneself. Rights are similar to the principles we can deduce from universalizing from our own position; how would I wish to be treated in this situation? These two conceptions of rights are significant for the animal rights debate, which often approaches the question of animal rights through asking whether animals can have interests or if they qualify as moral agents.

An important commonality between these accounts is their emphasis on the necessary relational quality of rights and the role of *recognition*. Recognition-based accounts require that we identify an Other as a rights-bearing subject (or not) and act accordingly. Therefore, all rights claims are invoking a background of assumptions about who the category of rights is applicable to and what this means. As Tully argues, "Even a negotiated struggle over distribution which begins within established rules of intersubjective recognition of the actors involved often and unpredictably spills over into a struggle over the background rules" (Tully 2000, 471; see also Duttmann 2000). Significantly, the "background rules" evoked here are an understanding of rights-bearing subjects as autonomous beings capable of formulating and pursuing interests as moral agents. This emphasis on the outward expressions of rights, the expressed interest or justification for a moral action, precludes consideration of deeper concerns about the background conditions that privilege these forms of subjective agency and the ways these categories are constructed.

Wolfe calls the obfuscation of category construction "ontologizing difference" or establishing categories prior to and no longer subject to ethical, moral, and political questioning (see Wolfe 2003a, 2003b). In Kant's account, for example, before morally autonomous subjects reflect on the moral law and acts, they must first recognize the Other as another morally autonomous subject. The importance of the clarity of the category of autonomy is clear; the discourse of rights depends on the a priori distinction of autonomous or heteronomous. Presumably we know an autonomous subject when we see it, and thus we know whether to treat it as a fellow rights-bearing subject or as an other. In *The Racial Contract*, Mills (1999) describes how this moment of category construction is central to Kant's thinking and helps to explain how he is the father of both modern political philosophy and the modern conception of race. The act of moral reasoning begins not with the apprehension of the moral law but in looking at and judging the other as autonomous, and therefore similar to one's self, or heteronomous, and therefore different. Kant's anthropology divides humans into four categories of descending autonomy, from white Europeans to Native

Americans. Only Europeans qualify as fully autonomous and worthy of moral consideration (Mills 1999, 75–77). Animals, of course, were far beyond the pale of moral recognition. The identification of the Other as similar or different enables moral reasoning, but the initial ontological judgment is not itself put into question. In the act of (re) cognizing the Other, the subject inscribes the identity of the Other as difference (in this case, as heteronomous) while reaffirming the status of the subject as morally autonomous because of its ability to categorize otherness. As the previous chapters have demonstrated, the processes by which we determine whether another subject is autonomous or not is contingent on political relationships rather than determinate objective factors.

This power-laden process of recognition is particularly important when transformed into the language of rights and the law where the ontologizing of difference has definite material effects. The processes of law establish explicit rules mediating social relationships and thereby codify certain categories or metaphorical constructions of the world.[21] These constructions wield power not just by setting the terms on which recognition by others is possible, but also in establishing a relationship to the self. Coombe writes:

> Legal processes ... do more than merely reflect and reproduce dominant cultural conceptions of self, personhood, and identity in Western societies. They are ... constitutive of subjectivities. By defining and legitimating particular representations of how those in different subject positions or social groups experience their selfhood, adjudicative and legislative processes serve to maintain, reproduce and sometimes transform relations of power. (1991, 5)

The theoretical and practical relationship between rights and personhood means that to grant rights to animals would present a profound challenge to our understanding of subjectivity and the categories through which it is constructed. Animal rights would entail a dramatic shift not just in material relationships with animals but also in how we understand ourselves as rights-bearing subjects. Considering animals as subjects with rights, like us, is a fundamental challenge to the human–animal boundary and our present practices with animals. To use the phrase "animal rights," therefore, is to propose a possible shift in legal and social understandings of animals and also a revision of the general concept of rights. The claim of rights for animals either requires us to change our concepts to allow animals to fall under the category of "personhood" and may require the rethinking of the equation between personhood and the rights-bearing subject. As more social groups have made the leap from property status to personhood, the strategy of rights-claiming for animals is an important and perhaps unsurprising move for those concerned about the treatment of animals (and humans). Yet if the animal rights movement claims to radicalize our understanding of rights, its arguments tend to reinforce the depoliticization of the process of category formation.

Somewhat uniquely among social movements, the animal rights movement was largely begun by and continues to be dependent on an academic and philosophical perspective (see Silverstein 1996). Understanding how rights discourse serves as a strategy for proanimal groups requires, therefore, an understanding of the terms on which rights are claimed and whether they do, in fact, make a difference for animals. Two key figures in inaugurating the discussion of animal rights are Peter Singer and Tom Regan. Singer's *Animal Liberation*, originally published in 1970, posited that animals deserve consideration because they share with humans the one factor relevant to moral decision making: the capacity for pleasure and pain. To call Singer an advocate of animal rights is a bit misleading since Singer, a utilitarian, endorsed rights only as a rhetorical tool: "The language of rights is a convenient political shorthand. It is even more valuable in the era of thirty-second TV clips than it was in Bentham's day; but in the argument for a radical change in our attitudes towards animals, it is in no way necessary" (27). The solution for Singer is to recognize animals as worthy of moral consideration when making ethical decisions, and, he concludes, the only way to ensure we minimize the suffering of animals is to minimize our contact with them, ending our captivity of animals and our economic use of them.

Tom Regan's *The Case for Animal Rights*, explicitly endorses a strategy of rights-claiming because he believes rights discourse is a powerful means of securing a higher status for animals in moral and political decision making. His faith in rights stems from a view of rights that is closer to a Kantian approach, describing rights as the recognition of a mutual understanding between moral agents. Regan differs from

Kant, however, in his categorization or recognition of animals as moral subjects. By arguing that animals are "subjects of a life," that is, sentient beings with lives separate from ours, they deserve recognition and respect (see Regan 1983; Silverstein 1996). Thus while both see the pain experienced by an animal as cause for moral concern, Singer would define the problem as a societal commitment to reducing suffering while Regan would focus attention on the rights of the individual to be free from pain independently of other social conditions. Thus, following Singer's example, considering the morality of animal testing would require an overall accounting of the suffering inflicted if testing is continued compared with suffering inflicted if testing is ended, while for Regan the infliction of pain in the process of testing is always already a violation of the rights of the animal. In extending recognition of individual rights to animals, Regan is somewhat less clear on the practical outcome than is Singer, though his supporters generally argue that the consequence is a formal legal equality with humans, and they often use the Courts or occasionally extralegal methods (such as liberating animals from scientific laboratories) as a means of rectifying present injustice.

Translating these abstract reconstructions of the boundaries of the rights-bearing subject into actual political practices is difficult. Attempts to imagine a world of equal animal rights demonstrates many of the problems that are linked with simply defining animals as similar enough to humans to grant them rights. One example of the animal rights imaginary emerges from the Great Ape Project, an attempt to conceptualize and achieve the equal treatment of apes (as the animals most similar to humans), initiated by a consortium of scientists, philosophers, and activists (including Singer). The spirit of the project is translated into practical political terms by the three political theorists who drafted the Declaration of the Rights of Apes, a project of so-called simian sovereignty that imagines what political parity for the great apes would look like (Goodin et al. 1997). The declaration begins with a justification of the rights of animals in terms of the expansion of the traditional category of rights-bearing subject and arguing that apes exist along a spectrum of moral agency, using language that mimics the Declaration of Independence. Their solution is a "homeland for great apes" in equatorial Africa which would operate as a sovereign state, governed by trustees who "need not know anything in particular about the interests and preferences, worldviews and projects of the great apes to know that they have an interest in survival and autonomous development, without further interference from humans" (Goodin et al. 1997, 839). As the title of the declaration suggests, the struggle for simian sovereignty is considered parallel to the American Revolution, an argument that apes require territorial sovereignty and a right to self-determination as if apes and humans have not only identical rights but similar desires, aspirations, and needs.

The response to the Declaration of the Rights of Apes by Seery highlights what he calls the "tortured ambivalence" of the proponents of simian sovereignty, poking fun at the absurd consequences that can occur when the authors take apes, and themselves, too seriously. He jokingly suggests "a modified Rawlsian approach": "Let's bring those apes to the bargaining table! I would like thus to see how the difference principle plays out with primates" (1997, 854). Seery's refusal to take the proposal seriously is not a dismissal of the idea that our relationships with animals might need more consideration. Instead, he highlights the impossibility of including animals in a category of rights-bearers, as if animals could simply be integrated into our existing system of rights-claiming and rights-protecting without any modification of the political, ethical, or legal framework within which those rights are constructed.

The Great Ape project works animals (and particularly, those that look most like us) into existing categories that define the rights-bearing subject by looking for similarities or ways to claim that animals are like us. Rather than basing their accounts of how the animal alters or reconfigures the rights-bearing subject as a political act, Singer, Regan, and others again depoliticize animals by believing they can resolve the status of animals philosophically, leading to rather absurd outcomes when translated into practice. The sense of resoluteness about animals merely recapitulates the humanist confidence that characterizes the accounts excluding animals; animals can still be accommodated within the parameters of human knowledge. Settling the question of animal rights assumes we can definitively know, first, what characteristics are appropriately indicative of a rights-bearing subject and, second, if animals in fact qualify.

This philosophical move, which resolves the question of animals by continually returning to general rules based on universalizing assumptions, is captured in one of the more sophisticated contemporary accounts of animal rights. Nussbaum's *Frontiers of Justice* attempts to bring animals—along with other marginalized subjects—into the purview of justice without assuming that the subjects be "free, equal and independent" (2006, 87). Instead, she utilizes a capabilities approach that defines justice as a chance for a "flourishing life" through respecting the dignity relevant to the specific being (or species). To provide a moral foundation for the inclusion of animals, Nussbaum turns to literature, which, she argues, can provide a means of creatively identifying with our animal others and thus extending them just treatment. She argues that literature contributes to justice by "stirring in us identifications, empathetic responses, and projections that may be readily formalized in analytical propositions" (2006, 411). The underlying conceit is a human ability to know animals—whether through science or literature—and to develop a set of rules that guarantees proper moral consideration of animals. Lurking in the background is, once again, the autonomous, rule-making subject who generates the law.

These accounts do not challenge the background assumptions about the rights-bearing subject but rather simply assume that animals have been misidentified and therefore can be recategorized under the umbrella of the rights-bearing subject. They repeat the conceit that our categories, like "human," "animal," or "rights," are clear, and that we may alter them simply by arriving at the proper definitions of these terms. Declaring animals to be rights-bearing subjects because they are like us and thereby feeling justified in being their appropriate representatives is merely a repetition of power relationships and the violence of erasing animals' particularity in the generation of universal laws (see Minow 1994).

What a vigorous rethinking of the position of animals must accomplish, therefore, is to disrupt the appeal to the clarity of categories prior to thinking about ethics and politics by constantly keeping open the categories we use to identify others. Disrupting the boundary of human–animal is intended precisely to challenge our commonsense ideas about animals as different and inferior. But more fundamentally, placing animals at the center of the question of rights encourages ethical reasoning that does not rely on the ability to know the other, and to make analogies based on similarity to the known or commonality of situations. Diamond makes a similar challenge to philosophers who insist on knowing animals in our terms before we can define our ethical responsibility to them:

> It is their arguments I have been attacking . . . and not their perceptions, not the sense that comes through in their writings of the awful and unshakeable callousness and unrelentingness with which we most often confront the non-human world. The mistake is to think that the callousness cannot be condemned without reasons which are reasons for anyone, no matter how devoid of all human imagination or sympathy. Hence, their emphasis on rights, on capacities, on interests, on the biologically given; hence the distortion of their perceptions by their arguments. (1991, 334)

Diamond argues that a concern for animals is a valid project but that current arguments in favor of animal rights simply repeat the errors of an arrogant overconfidence in the capacity to develop a single, reasonable, and justifiable response to the problem of our coexistence with animals. The challenge is to think differently about the problems in ways that do not once again appropriate animals as a means of securing our identities as autonomous, rights-bearing subjects. The moment of recognition of the Other is an ethical and political opportunity that is lost when theorists continually return to preconceived identities and the formulation of generalizable rules. The goal is to imagine a different sort of politics that utilizes the instability of the autonomy/heteronomy distinction, rather than seeking to fix the categories of our political engagement. In the next section I consider a displacement of morality by ethics and examine posthumanist arguments for utilizing animals not as a marginal or difficult case for ethical reasoning but as an examplar.

From Dogmatism to Dogs

Relating his experience in a Nazi concentration camp, Levinas describes feeling treated like an animal by his human captors and consequently beginning to believe in his own inhumanity. The situation is changed, he says, by the arrival of a dog who is allowed to live among the prisoners of the camp. They befriend him, naming him Bobby, and Levinas claims that through the dog's enthusiastic recognition of the prisoners as worthy humans, they regain their humanity. He writes: "He would appear at morning assembly and was waiting for us as we returned, jumping up and down and barking in delight. For him, there was no doubt that we were men. . . . This dog was the last Kantian in Nazi Germany" (1990, 153).

After this statement, Levinas quickly retreats from his attribution of personality and specifically human qualities to Bobby. He concludes that simply because the dog treats humans as they ought to be treated does not mean the dog recognizes this duty, nor does it necessitate a reciprocal duty on the part of his human companions. So it appears that Levinas's humanity has been restored not because Bobby has recognized him but rather because Levinas recognized his difference from Bobby. The camp members regain their sense of self through refusing a relationship of duty or mutual responsibility to a dog. Levinas seems particularly haunted by the conception that if our sphere of ethical duties is extended too far it runs the risk of obliterating our humanity. He therefore feels he must reject Bobby in order to secure his own humanity. While Levinas uses Bobby to resolve his own temporary loss of human status, we may reinterpret his internal struggle about categorizing the dog as a productive, a potentially creative moment rather than a problem to be resolved. The moment of uncertainty in distinguishing between human and animal, autonomy and heteronomy is valuable in imagining other political and ethical possibilities.

In *Making All the Difference* (1990) Minow shares in the critique often made by critical legal scholars, critical race theory scholars, and feminist jurisprudence scholars that the drive for generality and universality in rights discourse often translates into a means of preserving the power of particular groups because these groups are situated differently in relationship to different rights. So, for example, the universal right to privacy, which guarantees the sanctity of individual space is predicated on a particular relationship to publicity and privacy that sees private space as the protected sphere of the individual. Women, she notes, have not been protected by this "privacy bubble" and often experience domination most intensely within the sphere of the private. Minow argues, however, that rights discourse can and ought to be thought of differently. She notes that the problem with the universalism and generality apparent in rights discourse is the process of reasoning through analogy whereby two subjects, objects, or situations are deemed similar and, therefore, a single law can be applied to both. (Or, of course, two situations are deemed different and require different laws). She suggests a form of reasoning based on difference, and our inability to formulate a general law for all particular cases is a useful way forward in developing a transformative vision of law.

Reflecting on animals as a form of difference that challenges our perception of sameness/otherness may lead to two dramatically different conclusions about the applicability of rights to the category of animal. The first is a rejection of a rights discourse in favor of a different sort of discourse. The second is to consider Minow's dilemma of difference as a challenge to rethink the category of rights. I address each of these arguments in turn before examining how, precisely, animals might be a useful means to rethink our notions of rights.

Critics of rights discourses have argued that rights cannot adequately account for our ethical responsibilities, especially in relationship to nature, because they are premised on conceptions of calculability, rules, and legality. For this reason many scholars, especially Marxists and feminists interested in the problem of animals, have argued that a different discourse is required and that the political project of human and animal emancipation ought to be carved out of a different mode of justification. Feminist scholars like Adams argue that an ethic of care ought to govern both human–human and human–animal relationships.[22] The advantage, she argues, is to foreground relationships rather than individuals and to avoid the conflicts of interest in which humans almost always win out (see Adams 1991; Adams and Donovan 1995).

In a similar vein, Marxist scholar Ted Benton draws on Marx's argument in "On the Jewish Question," believing that rights language reiterates the "duality between man and citizen" (1993, 192) and cannot account for the "embeddedness and embodiment" of social life (1993, 183).[23] He argues instead for a needs-based conception of justice—roughly equivalent to "from each according to his abilities, to each according to his needs"—that ensures that though animals, like some humans, do not participate in the same ways or to the same degree, they are still deserving of social consideration, and that society (engaging non-human and human animals) cannot flourish without all participants being granted the capacity to contribute to social development. The model, he notes, would bestow respect on animals, without whom human existence would be impossible, and would cultivate a greater appreciation for our humanity realized through engagement with nature.

Finally, while never directly addressing the question of the status of animals, Brown warns that rights may also be a discourse of entrapment that violently forces identities into being in certain forms and reifies or naturalizes them, especially for those making rights claims (Brown 1995, 2000). To name a particular group or category of persons (or animals?) as rights-claiming may lead the group to define itself as a victim (in terms of its deprivation of rights) and to prevent challenging the constructed nature of the categories that victimize them. Indeed, animal rights discourse has often operated as Brown warns it might. Philosophers and activities have often used the category of animals as if it were a fact, rather than a contingent construction and have repeated the mistake of thinking we can know animals and their correlative rights, a move that merely reiterates the human–animal binary and human certainty and superiority. Second, the discourse on animal rights has often focused on the conflictual nature of rights, continually framing animal interests as mutually opposed to those of humans, seeing the two categories as exclusive and conflictual.[24]

These accounts imply that fulfilling our responsibilities to animals requires abandoning the man-made language of rights.[25] What these arguments miss is the potential for realizing that the very definition of "human" is entangled in the discourse on rights. Using animals *differently* in conjunction with the category of rights, therefore may help us contest the meaning of humans and rights and produce new political possibilities for rights discourse. Though he rarely attaches his name to any particular project, Derrida links himself to the project of rights through precisely this angle. He argues that rights may be understood differently:

> We will reconstitute under the name of subject . . . an *illegitimately*
> delimited identity, illegitimately, but often precisely under the author-
> ity of rights!—in the name of a particular kind of rights. For it is in order
> to put a stop to a certain kind of rights, to a certain juridico-political
> calculation, that this questioning has been interrupted. Deconstruction
> therefore calls for a different kind of rights, or rather, lets itself be called
> by a more exacting articulation of rights, prescribing in a different way,
> more responsibility. (1995b, 273, emphasis in original)

Constructing a more responsible form of rights requires not merely
exposing the constructed nature of the categories of exclusion that
are necessary for the construction of rights claims, the task of the
previous sections of this chapter. The second step is to imagine how
the language of rights might be used differently, or how challenging
the assumptions that enable exclusion might fundamentally change
the nature of rights. Such a project is defended by McClure, who, like
Minow, argues that rights may have a transformative potential when
they are used to make rather than suppress difference. She suggests
that rights may become a source of change when the background condition for rights-claiming—the identity of the rights-bearing subject—
becomes contestable. She writes, "The construction of the 'subject of
rights' was, and by extension continues to be, a process consequent on
the articulation of particular and specific historical struggles" (1992,
111). With Williams she argues that the struggle for recognition as
rights-bearing subjects alters not just the subjects recognized but can
work to modify or alter material conditions more broadly (see also
Tully 2000).

The increasing number of social groups making rights claims,
McClure notes, ought to be understood not merely as claims to be
included within the category of rights-bearing subject; nor should
the claims be seen as part of the universality of rights but as rights
of "otherness" (1992, 112). Bowers refers to this phenomenon as the
queering of identities, or challenging our familiarity with our own
identity, through challenging our capacity to know and categorize the
other (see Bowers 1994). When an other makes a demand that makes it
more difficult to categorize that other, or our relationship to the other,
it can challenge and make us reformulate the background conditions
that inform our ethical and political decision making. This is not to
say that all rights claims, even by traditionally excluded subjects, can

achieve the queering of categories, but at certain times some claims do have the capacity to destabilize sedimented categories and identities. Those figures silenced by existing categories may have the most potential for changing the field of politics.

McClure draws her argument about the politicizing potential of rights from Laclau and Mouffe's discussion of radical democracy (1985, Mouffe 1996). One of the central goals articulated in the democratic project is to widen the potential spaces considered open for political contestation and, second, to realize the heightening of ethical and political responsibility entailed in continually questioning political identities and decisions. Laclau and Mouffe's project dovetails with one of the purposes of rethinking autonomy: to consider the multiple ways we can conceive of and engage in political action. Animals can fulfill a potential role in the project of democratization by politicizing a wide range of everyday practices as well as challenging the normal background conditions and assumptions of our political and ethical decisions. Animal rights claims vastly expand the range of contestable political sites to include everything from science, medicine, and agriculture to more personal practices of consumption, eating, and pet-owning. Destabilizing the category of animals achieves a second goal of democratization, keeping open our ethical background conditions and calling for a need to continually interrogate our representations of and practices toward animals. The impossibility of adequately formulating a single, responsible rule toward this other requires a sense of context-dependent ethical and political reasoning that might contribute to a more complex, flexible, and even democratic form of rights claiming that embraces the deconstruction of the category of autonomy we have been engaged in.

Otherness, Ethical Responsibility, and Political Engagement

If the conjunction between animals and rights is potentially productive, both for animals and more traditional rights-bearing subjects, I will turn now to the second half of the equation of the potential democratic role of animals in ethical consideration. This leads to the question of how considering animals as a paradigmatic rather than a marginal case for ethical and political consideration can be transformative more broadly of how we think about our ethical responsibilities to all others. I focus on the problem of representation and recognition in relationship to rights and the question of the "wholly other" to whom I am responsible as ethical questions that may suggest a revised vision of rights and autonomy.

The distinction between a generalized versus a particular (or concrete) other has been widely discussed in political theory, though rarely through the lens of animals. The general problem, as demonstrated in Minow's dilemma of difference, is that the particular interest of an individual may conflict with the general interest of a group, and vice versa. Ignoring differences within rather than just between categories of otherness can erase important considerations that are relevant for ethical actions. In the case of animals, we conceptually consider animals as a generalized others, using the category of "animal" to obscure the diversity of differences that make non-human animals as different from one another (and often more so) than they are different from their human counterparts (Derrida 2002). At the same time, humans have a remarkable tendency to individualize animals, often by anthropomorphizing them, and thereby consider, at times to excess, the needs of individual animals. Therefore, pets may receive enormous amounts of care while their owners consume meat. Or, in some cases, a single, well-known animal will be saved at enormous expense, even though the rescue may be harmful to the more general interest of the species.[26] Either approach to the non-human animal appears problematic: knowing the animal either through an overly inclusive category that erases its particularity or through a hyper-individualizing category that values only the animal's familiarity (and often use) for the individual.

A third possibility may be to embrace the strangeness of animals in the encounter. Derrida, for example, reflecting on the category of animal, takes the experience of being seen by his own cat as a starting point, imagining being seen by the other (rather than seeing and knowing the other) as the space of engagement (2002, 376–79). The individual cat is a mixture of both the mundane and familiar, the everyday experience of the family cat, and the strange and exotic, the other whom I recognize as other and who remains to some degree mysterious to me. The experience may, therefore, be a model for apprehending otherness that suspends understanding and recognition. The experience is neither general nor particular but *singular*; it presents an encounter with strangeness that cannot be reduced to familiarity or to complete disengagement. The uncertainty created through an encounter with the other in which that other cannot fit neatly into preexisting categories of knowing can challenge the sovereignty and self-identity of the subject and, in doing so, radically change the nature of ethical responsibility (Wood 2004, 131).

The second ethical problem illuminated by animals is the issue of recognition and responsibility. The (assumed) inability of animals to communicate is often seen as grounds for exclusion, especially from rights discourse, since animals are unable to make claims on us. We might consider, for example, a passage from *Alice in Wonderland* in which Alice expresses her frustration at the inability to communicate with cats because they are unable to respond in an appropriate manner:

> It is a very inconvenient habit of kittens (Alice had once made the remark) that, whatever you say to them, they always purr. "If they would only purr for 'yes,' and mew for 'no,' or any rule of that sort," she had said, "so that one could keep up with a conversation! But how can you talk with a person if they always say the same thing?" On this occasion the kitten only purred: and it was impossible to guess whether it meant "yes" or "no." (Carroll 2010, 101)

In the case of Alice, she takes the inability to respond according to the predetermined rules of her language, which she can interpret in her terms, as a failure on the part of kittens. Alice appears to be reiterating the problem Wittgenstein states as, "If a lion could talk, we could not understand," implying such a vast gulf of difference that we could not possibly play the same language game as an animal (1958, 223). Wittgenstein's conclusion leaves us with two problems. The first is the question of how to respond to the purring of a lion. If we accept our absolute difference from the world of the lion, we either must translate for the lion—again making ourselves the guardians of the animal kingdom by interpreting the purrs the animals make—or we must reduce the lion to silence, ignoring the purring as insignificant (or unsignifying?). The problem is multiplied, however, if we add that when a "human" talks, we may also fail to understand. The challenge is to move away from a model of successful recognition in which we feel we have fully recognized, or cognized and understood the other and/or the other's claims. Rather than recognition, we might consider *acknowledgment,* a more modest sense of being in the presence of an other to whom one is responsible but in uncertain and incalculable terms (Markell 2000; Derrida 1995a; Levinas 1969).

The Kantian model of recognition hinges on a simultaneous self-recognition of one's identity as a moral agent and, second, seeing, knowing, and recognizing the other as either another moral agent or something else. The recognition of self and other then allows a principle to be applied and, presumably, a principled action to follow. The animal can disrupt this circle by challenging our ability to know the other and, therefore, our ability to use the other to reflect on our own ability. Unlike previous deployments of animals as figures through which we think, emphasizing the gap in communication between human and animal does not make the human more secure in their identity (as different from the animal). Instead, the encounter with the animal is intended not merely to evoke the strangeness of the other, but also the strangeness of the self. If the category of human is an imagined identity contingent on a relationship to a category called animal, the encounter between the two is a reminder of the ways in which our own identity is dependent on these others. Yet the incapacity to ever fully know the other, and the frustration of subjects like Alice to fully translate animals into our terms, means that the boundary is always shifting and uncertain. Therefore, fitting either the self or the other neatly into categories of human and animals is always already a categorical error. To do so, however, does not eliminate the possibility of ethical action; rather it raises the bar on ethical considerations, refusing to defuse responsibility through the appropriate application of rules. Rather than either assuming a capacity to know the demands of the other or, like Wittgenstein and Alice, to declare the other incomprehensible, we might adopt a heightened responsibility for striving to recognize the claims of the other while simultaneously accepting the fundamental impossibility of doing so. The challenge is to, unlike Alice, refuse to place the burden on the kitten, to place the burden on oneself to both listen to and recognize the inadequacy of hearing the other. Derrida suggests we give up the status of the sovereign translator able to hear and act on rights claims in a rote manner.

The experience of uncertainty raises questions about how to act in conditions of uncertainty when faced with what appears to be a "wholly other" or one we have difficulty translating into our own predetermined terms "without letting formulae and maxims do the work for us" (Wolfe 2010, 96). The experience of the cat's attempts to express a demand vocally and physically may be interpreted as hunger, but this demand may be mistaken. The animal's incapacity to fully communicate its needs is not the impossibility for ethical considerations but may be a starting point. The uncertainty from attempting to engage with and be responsible toward an uncertain other is not a failure of ethics because we are unable to adopt a rule or a standard behavior that fulfills our responsibility. Derrida transforms the question of the animal into a more general form of ethical questioning that refuses a general position toward the other and, instead, argues for a recognition of totally fulfilling our obligation to the other and a simultaneous ethical imperative to do so. He writes:

> The moral question is thus not, nor has it ever been: should one eat or not eat, eat this and not that, the living or the nonliving, man or animal, but since one must eat in any case and since it is and tastes good to eat, and since there's no other definition of the good, how for goodness' sake should one eat well? (1995b, 282)

The ethical position of "eating well" is a refusal to establish a single rule that may be applied to others and that follows from the act of recognition. While Kant believes that a universal rule may be generated and applied in particular cases, Derrida urges us to continually return to the particular because it requires a deeper ethical sensibility. The animal is a useful category of difference in this instance because of its centrality outside the category of autonomy. While the animal is a unique form of difference, it shares with other groups in being seen as lacking but only because it is compared to a "carnophallogocentric"[27] model of fullness, in other words, the autonomous, free-willing subject (who is also white and male) that is placed at the center of ethical and political decisions. Confronted with the incapacity to fully recognize and fulfill our duties toward the animal, we are forced into a different mode of thinking.

What follows from this ethical project is not a concrete reconfiguration of human–animal relationships or even human–human relationships but a different vision of politics that relies on uncertainty and contingency. So Derrida is reluctant to endorse a definite path to overcome the institution of violence in the exclusion of animals, and he stops short of naming animals as rights-bearing subjects, or as he puts it "to start a support group for vegetarianism, ecologism, or for the societies for the protection of animals" (1995b, 278). Derrida is worried about any attempt to *resolve* our guilt over our relationships with animals or any dogmatic and definite claims that we can be certain we are behaving justly toward animals if we only develop the appropriate set of rules to govern our relationships.

His argument is much indebted to Nietzsche, who was profoundly troubled by the human capacity for memory, and thereby bad conscience and guilt, as a means of *alleviating* responsibility. The purpose of guilt is not to rectify a wrong but to assure oneself of one's own moral standing and, therefore, guilt is a means by which to displace responsibility (I may be doing the wrong thing but I feel bad about it, so therefore I'm still a good person).[28] Nietzsche is critical of *both* positions—that of the unapologetic carnivore and that of the dogmatic vegetarian, who share a certainty that they know the proper behavior toward animals and therefore are debt free. He notes that to declare oneself a vegetarian is to presume that you have found the appropriate ethical rule and, by following it, can assure your moral agency (1974). He refers to the certainty of moral theory as the cruelty of the categorical imperative: to apply a rule to decisions is not to take responsibility for those decisions but to feel comfortable in knowing one has applied the appropriate rule. With animals the problem is particularly acute precisely because we cannot know the appropriate action: we encounter different animals in a range of different situations all of which, he argues, ought to demand a new decision and not the application of a rule.

Derrida adopts a similar position toward the animal, arguing that its appearance as a wholly other, but one with which we can and must relate, offers an opportunity to rethink the background conditions of our ethical and political decisions. He rejects both the moral certainty of a belief in a universalizable rule of justice and toward contract models of thinking about justice as limited because it alleviates human responsibility. Any duty that can be fulfilled or debt that can be repaid is an abdication of responsibility. To be responsible, the responsibility must be infinite.[29]

The idea of an infinite responsibility that falls outside of rational consideration is meant to challenge our ability to categorize the other while at the same time reducing the sense that we can fully know ourselves as moral and political agents. The failure to ever feel fully satisfied or certain about ethical responsibility and the relationship to the other is also a sense of a loss of control, the degree of autonomy and self-control that political theorists used to delineate between the world of the human and the animal. The sense that one must eat but also the imperative that one must eat *well* is a reminder of the incapacity to fully know and understand the context and consequences of political and ethical action. The experience with the animal is an experience of a less sovereign self, able to control the context and consequences of action.

The animal-other constitutes a challenge and future for a democratic project concerned with expanding our political and ethical engagements. The shifting boundaries of the category challenge our own sense of autonomy while suggesting this may offer us new ethical and political possibilities. Thinking about autonomy relative to animals challenges our conceptions of who we are as political agents and what counts as political, keeping these questions open for contestation.

One of the more thoughtful reflections on the implications of living with animals is J. M. Coetzee's *The Lives of Animals*. Asked to give a series of lectures at Yale on the topic of animals, Coetzee instead turned to fiction, writing two short stories about a fiction writer-turned-activist who embarrasses her son by giving lectures on animal rights at his university (1999). He chooses the fictional structure to emphasize the tentative and uncertain nature of his project, considering our lives with animals. The story includes the main character's public lectures accompanied by scenes between her academic son and his philosopher wife who deeply disapprove of her actions. Animals in the story serve a metaphorical purpose, introducing strangeness into the family relationships and bringing together and introducing clashes into disciplinary units in the university as the English professor speaks to biologists, philosophers, and others. The scenes are marked by a profound sense of misunderstanding, as characters consistently misunderstand one another and their own feelings, emphasizing the very human incapacity to ever fully communicate or connect.

While academic debates are hashed out in the course of the story, Coetzee chooses to end with a moment between writer and son in which she bursts into tears, having dreamed about her carnivore son using human flesh as lampshades. Coetzee's conclusion is not to resolve the debate over animal rights, nor to inform us of our proper behavior toward animals, but to leave us with a simultaneous sense of dis-ease about our inability to resolve the debate while suggesting this discomfort may also propel us toward others. In the end the son comforts the mother, not on the premise of having arrived at an agreement or even an understanding, but in a moment of reaching out to an other. The story ends with the son's seemingly inadequate words "There, there, it will soon be over," a statement of the clear impossibility the story was meant to illustrate; the debate is far from over, and beyond either the son or the mother to control. The ending highlights the inadequacy of a form of ethical reasoning that wishes for the question of animal rights to be over, settled finally and assuring us we have fulfilled our duty. In contrast with Nussbaum's use of the literary imaginary to generate a new set of rules, Coetzee gestures toward another possibility: his fictional imagination presents an ethical possibility, continually inventing other ways of relating to our others that guarantee that contestation and ethical questioning will never be over and thus any normative order, especially that associated with autonomy, is always subject to questioning.

Conclusion

This chapter has proceeded through executed sows, talking lions, and silent cats toward the political possibility opened up by the challenge to the categories of autonomy/heteronomy, subject/object, and human/animal. The category of animal, defined by its corporeality and lack of autonomy, has demonstrated the difficulties in distinguishing between autonomy and heteronomy and the political consequences when we attempt to do so. This chapter has also gone on to examine some of the political potential of engaging in the project of questioning the categories that serve as a supposedly secure foundation for political life. The confusion of categories is not the death of the subject or an end to politics but a possibility for different ways of thinking.

The category of animal is central to our self-understanding as "humans" and to the very idea of autonomy. If autonomy as rational self-reflection is what distinguishes humans from animals, then challenging the purity of the concept goes to the heart of how we understand ourselves and how we perceive our animal-others. Animals are a part of our everyday lives, and those encounters, our interpretation of them and response to them, is an often uncritical reiteration of our own human subjectivity as different from and, usually, superior to these others. Therefore deploying a counterintuitive language of animal rights in a way that challenges the underlying assumptions that inform the ways we recognize various animals. If we suspend the placement of other beings into the categories of human/nonhuman, or autonomous/heteronmous, even for a moment, it creates new possibilities for how we might relate responsibly to that other. The political import goes beyond what we traditionally lump into the category of animals into the realm of others who may occupy a similar position beyond political or ethical consideration.

Animals have often been excluded from political consideration for a variety of reasons ranging from their lack of rationality to their inability to represent themselves in a coherent manner. If we shift the responsibility to ourselves as ethical beings, then animals present a challenge, not just an excluded class, and urge us to look for the political beyond the expected. We must look for political engagement not just in those who can represent themselves in terms we understand; we must also consider the possibility that certain subjects are always silent, or beyond our capacity to hear in familiar terms. Animals draw our attention to the silences in our political discourses. At the same time, the ideas of infinite responsibility and an irreconcilable discourse with the other imply an unpredictability and uncontrollable quality to political action. In looking at the cat, subjects do not realize their moral responsibility and, thereby, their own identity as moral autonomy. Instead, subjects are confronted with an inability to fully know or rationalize the situation or, at the same time, to fully reflect on themselves in relation to a knowable other. This form of ethical questioning creates a different sort of political subject oriented toward instability, uncertainty, and responsibility.

Ethical questions that begin with, rather than being challenged by, conditions of uncertainty and impossibility are a valuable tool in challenging the reification of power relations that masquerade as universals. However, ethical uncertainty does not exhaust the political potential of autonomy. As Wolfe, sympathetic to Derrida's position, argues, "Humans and animals may share ... a vulnerability and passivity without limit ... but what they do *not* share equally is the power to materialize their misrecognition of their situation and to reproduce that materialization in institutions of exploitation and oppression whose effects are far from symmetrical in species terms" (2010, 95). In other words, the emphasis on the uncertainty of ethics should not lead us to neglect our responsibility to interrogate the conditions of possibility of any particular exchange *and* to work to prevent the reification of power relationships that generate those conditions.

While ethical questioning can generate uncertainty and open up the space for creativity, it must (1) be attendant to the power relationships that generate the singularity of the encounter and (2) elaborate how political change takes place within these indeterminate spaces. The final chapter tackles these challenges by elaborating on the norm, associated with autonomy, of physical fitness. The purpose is to articulate the ways tensions between lawmaking and creativity within the norm of autonomy produce, in Nancy's terms, surprises. The final chapter brings together the critique of self-governance with the ethic of care in an examination of the everyday politics of the autonomous subject of advanced liberal physical culture.

5

Fit to Be Tied

EXERCISE FADS AND OUR ADDICTION
TO AUTONOMY

It is . . . the *game* of the world
that must first be thought.

—Jacques Derrida,
Of Grammatology

The death of Len Bias in 1986 from cardiac arrest following his first encounter with cocaine became one of the most successful antidrug ads. Bias, a twenty-two-year-old All-American basketball star, had just been drafted in the first round of the NBA draft by the Boston Celtics and was set to become one of the highest played professional basketball players ever. Bias's death made national headlines, not just on the sports pages, and became a national rallying cry for the war on drugs. One story that emerges from the sensational response to Bias's death is about the drug war and panic about drugs and their threat to autonomy. A second is that Bias, hardly the only young African American male to die that day of drug ingestion, was an athlete. Bias was a modified Horatio Alger who triumphed in overcoming the limitations of his body. He defied the fate of many poor young black men through the meticulous cultivation of his physical abilities. A momentary loss of self-control led to his body's betrayal. This fear of the ever-present possibility of the failure of the project of autonomy made Len Bias's story all the more haunting.

The flip side of the addict is the athlete, dedicated to the hyper-management of the body. Athletes control their body as a valuable commodity that works for them rather than against. Beyond the cultural celebration of athletes, American culture spends a great deal of time and money cultivating its own fitness. Fitness, athleticism, and other practices of controlling the body demonstrate the subject's autonomy in overcoming physical limitations. Bias's story is about a loss of control because of a moment of weakness, a step away from his athletic subjectivity. His death was described as a warning, reinforcing narratives of discipline and self-control as the defining feature of autonomous selfhood. Failure to maintain self-control at all times was at best a betrayal of the self and, at worst, a literal death of the subject. Yet a second possibility exists within the figure of the athlete, the possibility of a loss of control through the very act of controlling. If the fit body must be ever vigilant in maintaining its integrity, then it is compelled to continually work on itself. Athletes must be addicted to their own autonomy, unable to stop the continual act of striving toward physical perfection.

This chapter brings together the tensions between autonomy as law and autonomy as creativity by considering the possibility of an addiction to autonomy. This seeming contradiction captures Nancy's description of the experience of freedom being as *surprise*. Freedom is not located in the intentional liberation from power relationships but rather in the ways in which power can produce consequences that disrupt the ordinary operation of power and require us to think and act differently. In this chapter the experience of freedom is sought in the everyday practices of self-construction through discourses of health, fitness, and athleticism. The practices of constructing the self through rigorous attention to the body is reminiscent of Kant's joy in his successful self-management, but the practices of fitness can be interpreted as challenging his view of the sovereign unitary subject who practices intentional agency in the management of the body. Instead, some bodies produced by relationships of power can, in turn, challenge the very power relationships that make them possible, requiring us to reflect on our idea of autonomy and what, or who, constitutes autonomous subjectivity.

Building on the last chapter, which considered how challenging the clarity of our categories might produce new ways of relating to otherness and ourselves, this chapter will use the fitness fanatic as a way of thinking about autonomy and political agency differently. The chapter begins by examining the inextricable relationship between autonomy as law and autonomy as creativity in contemporary discourses of selfhood that emphasize self-help. I then discuss a variant of self-help culture, that is, physical fitness culture, or a cultural drive toward self-improvement evidenced by the shape of the body. The discussion then considers another seeming "other" of autonomy, the masochist who submits to the control of an other in order to find pleasure. Relating Deleuze's theory of the masochist to Foucault's care of the self as forms of political subjectivity, I then turn to ultraendurance athletes who, through the hypermanagement of their fit bodies, have become addicts, submitting their bodies to endless discipline. The fitness fanatic illustrates the two faces of autonomy, the compulsion to generate the law and the compulsion to create the self, that come together in rhetoric of self-creation through the body. On the one hand the fitness fanatic is an example of the internalization of biopolitical norms of health and wellness. On the other hand, fitness fanatics undermine the ability of these norms to stabilize into a regime of power because they enable the creation of forms of subjectivity defying normative bodily expectations.

Fitting In

Many traditional conceptions of autonomy see the body as a potential source of heteronomy and thereby as a threat to authentic, autonomous reason. As a source of physical compulsion and desire rather than rational self-reflection, the body threatens the ability to self-govern, a concern reflected in the social preoccupation with teenage sexuality discussed in chapter 2. This conventional view of the mind–body relationship sees an autonomous relationship to the self as defined by management of the body by the mind, a relationship that can be disrupted by a weak mind, as in the cases of immaturity or madness, or a weak body, defined by overly strong impulses or illness. More recent social theories, including those inspired by the biopolitical arguments of Foucault, suggest a more dynamic conception of the body in which it acts not merely as a passive medium on which power leaves its imprint but rather as a dynamic site of political engagement. Within advanced liberalism, technologies of power represent the ways that bodies, at the individual and population level, are a means of governance. Biopower includes "an explosion of numerous and diverse techniques for achieving the subjugations of bodies and the control of populations" (Foucault 1978, 140). This control, however, is not achieved by domination of the body but rather through the cultivation or channeling of specific bodily capabilities. Public health is an exemplar of biopower, developing practices aimed at the cultivation of health at the level of population, often by cultivating individual practices of bodily self-management. Programs to prevent the spread of sexually transmitted diseases, for example, seek to promulgate public rules about sexual hygiene while at the same time encouraging individuals to police their own bodies through safer sex practices (Brown 2006).

Foucault argues that while the body is saturated by power, we should not see the body as either passive or entirely subjugated by these relationships. Instead, the body is an active site of political contestation. An analysis of biopower must be aware of the ways the actions of power on the body reproduce and resist these forms of power:

> Situated in a sense between these great functionings and the body themselves with their materiality and their forces . . . one should decipher in it a network of relations, constantly in tension, in activity, rather than a privilege that one might possess . . . one should take as its model a perpetual battle rather than a contract regulating a transaction or the conquest of a territory. (1979, 26)

The fit body, as an example of biopower, provides an opportunity to consider the ways that expectations of autonomy produce technologies of power that seek to shape the body. At the same time, the norm of autonomy, as a technology of power encouraging *self*-governance, also creates forms of resistance. Self-limitation is not only the application of a norm; it can also become new ways of being.

The fit body emerges within a social and cultural milieu emphasizing the importance of physical fitness as a personal and public imperative. If the body of the demonized addict personifies uncontrolled corporeality, which must be excluded for the good of society, the athlete is the antithesis, working to manage corporeality by resisting natural urges and impulses, a pursuit deemed admirable. Addiction is characterized by a weakness of the will accompanied by the abject body that lacks boundaries, literal and figurative.[1] Fitness is described in terms that emphasize firm boundaries in language that defines the pursuit of fitness as self-discipline and that describes the fit body in terms that evoke strength, hardness, buns of steel, or six-pack abs. While practices of physical fitness are ancient, an explosion of interest in physical fitness, deemed the "fitness craze," emerged in the 1970s. The mass popularity of pursuits such as jogging and aerobics grew along with the growth of a self-help industry and a political language of self-reliance and self-control accompanying the rollback of the welfare state (Rose 1999; Cruickshank 1999). The concern with healthy minds and bodies is related to political shifts that emphasized individual choice and personal growth while demonizing institutionalized bureaucracy as imposing an impersonal set of norms from above. The justification for the receding welfare state—provided by the left as well as from the right—was the argument that social programs fostered a loss of autonomy, and welfare bureaucratization threatened the individual's sphere of self-determination, depriving selves of an opportunity to strive as well as thrive. A threat to autonomy loomed in depriving individuals of the capacity to develop their ability to govern themselves while simultaneously developing modes of surveillance that threatened to allow the state to invade the private sphere.[2]

Against this looming threat of a loss of control, a discourse of self-help emerged as a reassertion of a right to choose one's own life path. The emphasis on individual selfhood did not involve retreat into a private self; the autonomous subject of the self-help revolution was not just nostalgic for the laissez-faire liberal economic individualism of the past. Autonomy in the frame of self-help required more than just an unencumbered self with minimal intervention from external forces; real autonomy was constituted by the ability to continually create and improve on the self. The role of society was not to step aside to allow for self-discovery; it was to cultivate practices of self-improvement.

One model of this bootstrap subject is the political persona of Bill Clinton. He was famous for his "renaissance retreats," where he and fellow elite engaged in spiritual and intellectual growth. His political life was punctuated by public confessions and revelations about his private self and, especially, his personal stories of redemption and self-overcoming.[3] Self-dubbed the "boy from Hope" and the "comeback kid," he symbolized the transformation of a self-made man into a self-making man in process, warts and all. For better or worse, he shifted attention on his public office away from public action to questions of personal responsibility and private flaws.

The act of continual self-creation recasts autonomy as subject *formation*, not just the actions of a prepolitical subject who generates the law. The idea of autonomy here is close to that of Castoriadis, who locates autonomy in the creative impulse to generate something new and better. Yet if the subject creates itself, it is therefore responsible not just for its actions but for its self. The subject is put into a position of continual self-scrutiny and improvement. The subject's freedom and will are not opposed to power but rather are its necessary conditions, central to the internalization of responsibility that leads to self-policing (Foucault 1994, 292; see also Foucault 1988b). The subject of self-help captures the entwined nature of creativity and the law here, noting how the will to create the self becomes the law.

To understand the complexity of a mode of social control that works with rather than against subjective freedom, we must examine how the disciplinary society of the bureaucratic welfare state has given rise to what Deleuze called a postdisciplinary society (1997). "Postdisciplinary" describes a mode of power that goes beyond the internalization of social norms and toward the generation of a self-producing subject without any particular end. One way of understanding the difference between the two forms of power is through Fuller's distinction between the two different moralities that may inform the generation of laws (1964). One morality of legality, the morality of *duty*, establishes distinct rules for right and wrong and punishes transgressions of those rules in the interest of order. The morality of *aspiration*, on the other hand, works in the opposite direction, summoning the subject toward excellence, without definite rules for what that excellence might entail. Aspiration demands a fulfillment of one's full capacities, though without any certainty about what those capacities are; one aspires to reach a moving target, an end point that can never be achieved. Fuller borrows the metaphor of writing from Adam Smith to demonstrate the difference between the two modes of judgment. Writing may be analyzed according to the rule-bound system of grammatical correctness or in terms of aesthetic judgments that "are loose, vague, and indeterminate, and present us rather with a general idea of the perfection we ought to aim at, than afford us any certain and infallible directions of acquiring it" (quoted in Fuller 1964, 6).

While the morality of duty promises a final judgment, or a set of rules by which the subject may be evaluated on the basis of the attainment or non-attainment of the desired norm, the morality of aspiration resembles aesthetics, in which the terms of judgment may be debated. Without the possibility of attainment of a clearly defined goal, aspiration becomes the means and the end of subjectivity as it strives toward aesthetic self-production that is ongoing. Subjects not only reproduce discourses that shape their subjectivity; they also modify and multiply them as they strive toward self-creation (Cohen 1985). While disciplinary power is like the morality of duty, relying on the internalization of norms, postdisciplinary control through autonomy is closer to the morality of aspiration, engaging in the actual production and proliferation of norms through a compulsion, indeed an addiction, to cultivate autonomy.

Embedded in the advanced liberal context, the norm of autonomy often adopts an aspirational morality that emphasizes continual self-improvement and creativity but nonetheless (re)produces forms of social control. One such model of subject production has been called the "risk management" model (Rose 1999; Burchell 1996). Dealing in risk is a "proactive" form of power that seeks to anticipate threats to social order before they occur. Various discourses like public health or environmental protection work on the model of predicting future occurrences and intervening to change them. Conversely, subjects are trained to engage in the same sorts of calculations in order to manage personal risk.

Risk management is not merely about institutionalized responsibility for shaping the future of society; it is also about the responsibility of individuals to control their own futures. Risk aversion is moreover a lifestyle that works with the management of the body. Knowledge about potential risks is produced and disseminated, becoming a call to action for responsible agents to prevent various threats to the integrity of the will through threats to the body. For example, a responsibility to avoid sickness defines multiple practices of a healthful lifestyle that avoids a range of threats: pesticides, carcinogens, viruses, bacteria, high cholesterol, hypertension, genetically modified foods, and other sources of risk for the body (see Rose 1999). The duty includes strategies of knowledge production and consumption as the risk-adverse subject must take in a constant stream of information about the proliferation of risks in everyday life, ranging from crime reports to cigarette warnings to food labels. Taking in the information, the calculating subject must then make personal, life-enhancing choices as evidence of self-mastery. The failure to avoid risk—readily apparent in a subject succumbing to sickness, suffering, and pain—is a failure of autonomy, a failure to be master of one's self and to be in control of the forces of the body at all times. The cultivation of health is a project without an end-point, for the goal of a "healthy body" is not clearly defined, especially when new knowledge is constantly being produced. The cultivation of health is an ongoing project that requires constant attention to the body.

In terms of the proliferation of norms, risk society, which encourages self-limitation, captures only one component of autonomy. The aesthetic dimension of subjectivity requires not just an avoidance of threats but the active pursuit of capacity maximization. The fit body is evidence of the pursuit of self-improvement and a marker of autonomy; the subject is able to produce subjective goals and desires toward which the will aspires. Examples of the technologies that produce these responsible, calculating bodies are the entrepreneurial and therapeutic metaphors used to describe and define subjectivity (see Rose 1999). As the moniker implies, the *enterprising* subject is linked with the economy of the market, the ethic of self-maximization, and an aspiration to succeed in a competitive environment. However, the enterprise of the self extends beyond the workday to all aspects of life. Enterprise is not merely a mode of business; it is also a way of life that seeks utility maximization in all arenas:

Enterprise here designates an array of rules for the conduct of one's everyday existence: energy, initiative, ambition, calculation, and personal responsibility. The enterprising self will make a venture of its life, . . . project itself a future and seek to shape itself in order to become that which it wishes to be. (Rose 1992, 146)

In the drive to aspire, the enterprising self must also engage in the process of imagining or projecting other, better selves. Through this project of aspiration, the therapeutic subject emerges as a technology of control. Therapy is precisely the work on the self that enables the healthy, self-directing autonomous citizen to emerge. The model of therapy is an engagement in "an intense and continuous self-scrutiny, self-dissatisfaction and self-evaluation in terms of the vocabularies and explanations of expertise. In striving to live our autonomous lives, to discover who we really are, to realize our potentials and shape our lifestyles, we become tied to the project of our own identity" (Rose 1999, 93). No longer just a project of identifying and fixing pathologies, therapy is a way of relating to the self that requires continual self-scrutiny. Through various sources that draw on therapeutic language, such as popular culture, the language of therapy is disseminated as a form of subject formation.

Self-production does not have an object or goal as its end but is rather the production of the image of a potential self always just over the horizon, free from the multiple barriers to achieving autonomy, especially one's own failings and limits. As Donzelot argues, the therapeutic subject is not merely the product of self-discipline; it becomes the producer of its own inadequacies and own strategies to overcome them through the processes of self-examination. The self wills its own discipline above and beyond the demands of society: "The strength of relational technology lies precisely in the fact that it does not impose anything—neither new social norms nor old moral rules. . . . It allows them to float in relation to one another until they find their equilibrium" (Donzelot 1979, 209). The subject generates the standards to which it holds itself by imagining an ideal self against which it measures itself and continually makes adjustment both to the self and to the ideal.[4] Unmoored from universal norms to which the subject can conform, there is always room for improvement.

Through the performances of autonomy, demonstrating a will to aspire, subjects demonstrate their fitness for social life. In order to continue to be recognized as an autonomous subject, the individual must constantly act to improve the self. An individual's responsibility is to the self, but one must provide evidence of this responsibility by a will to risk avoidance and by self-cultivation. Baudrillard calls this evolution in systems of control "terrorism," implying we are held hostage both by our own anxieties about external risks while at the same time we hold ourselves hyperresponsible for having the internal control to avoid these risks (Baudrillard 1990, 35). He sees a similar mutual constitution of autonomy and control that holds the subject hostage to its own aspirations, terrified in the shadow of its own freedom:

> The problem of security . . . haunts our societies and long ago replaced the problem of liberty . . . a relatively loose, diffuse and extensive state of the system, produces liberty: a different state of the system (denser) produces security (self-regulation, control, feedback, etc.); a further state of the system, that of proliferation and saturation, produces panic and terror. (Baudrillard 1990, 37)

If a bit hyperbolic, Baudrillard's description captures the creeping expansion of the security society populated by subjects subject to their own freedom. The dense web of discipline has invented selves compelled to prove their ability to choose, and to choose properly, in constant fear of a failure to actualize themselves. Here the line between the addict and the autonomous subject becomes blurred. If addicts are subjects to physical compulsions, subject are subject to their own will to will, a compulsion to aspire and demonstrate their autonomy.

The Exercise of Power

The relationship between the control of the body and the language of self-improvement comes together in the example of the fit subject. The expectation of autonomy produces a lifestyle embodied in the ideal of a healthy body. The consumption of both literal objects and cultural discourses intersect as the individual is enabled to make lifestyle decisions that provide the evidence of an ability to make appropriate choices. The body becomes the primary site of risk aversion and self-actualization and provides material evidence of the subject's will to aspire. Autonomy and compulsion are linked in practices that define fitness. The fit self conforms to a range of ever-expanding regulative norms as a means not just of survival or health enhancement but as an ongoing project of self-creation: "In the new modes of regulating health, individuals are addressed on the assumption that they *want to be healthy*, and enjoined to freely seek out the ways of living most likely to promote their own health" (Rose 1999, 86).

The aspiration toward health, however, does not function as an attainable norm, with an endpoint evidenced by a measurable standard of healthiness. Rather, fitness is a highly individualized practice of evaluating the self, establishing personal goals, and constantly adjusting them according to new information or new goals. Glassner explains that the fit self is "not merely a well-oiled machine.... The fit body-cum-self is cognized as an information processing machine, a machine which can correct and guide itself by means of an internal expert system" (1989, 184). The failure of autonomy is marked by the clear failure to exhibit this self-control in a materially marked split between health and sickness and between fit and unfit. Failure manifests itself not just in the condition of the body but also in evidence of striving through the consumption of a proliferating range of information and fitness technologies from gym memberships to NordicTracks to Abdominators (McCormick 1999). The body is a constantly monitored site of saturated responsibility, a moral and ethical choice as well as a personal goal; fitness is a measure of social fit-ness.

The exercise of physical fitness is a technology of producing fit citizens through a variety of cultural discourses about and practices of obtaining fitness. One example of the interpretation of fitness as a means of producing autonomous free individuals is found in *Helping At-Risk Youth through Physical Fitness Programming* (Collingwood 1997). The text is a guide for service agencies to develop programs for at-risk youths. At risk youths are identified by geographic location or by behavior such as "lack of self-esteem, maladjustment, depression, stress, lack of religious beliefs" or "cognitive beliefs such as having an external locus of control (*feeling externally controlled by others rather than being self-directed*)" (Collingwood 1997, 8–9, emphasis added). The manual is informed by, and attempts to generate, a set of disciplinary practices that encourage moral training through physical training, technologies including boot camps for juvenile delinquents, midnight basketball, and survival camps for disobedient children.[5] The goal is to identify the loci of risk and harness and redirect the youths' potential through physical training that can transform them into productive, autonomous citizens. Disciplinary power utilizes physical fitness as a distraction from other disruptive physical desires, such as sexuality (see chapter 3), channeling disruptive bodily desires into more productive ones. In this instance, however, physical fitness is less about self-control than self-actualization. The at-risk youth are encouraged to craft a sense of self through processes of managing the body. Teaching youth to manage their own bodies is a larger project of training them to be productive citizens through a lifelong process of pursuing self-improvement.

The lack of fitness described as characterizing at-risk youths is perceived to stem from the absence of a self-perception as an autonomous actor. This identity is to be cultivated through practices on the body. The author identifies the chief problem as a lack of self-motivation; they are passive, lacking the control to endure pain or delay pleasure and too lazy to pursue self-improvement (Collingwood 1997, 2–6). Coming from homes with "no limits," they are described as self-centered and doomed to "valueless existence" (Collingwood 1997, 2). The goal of the fitness program, therefore, is to help adolescents "choose between health-compromising and health-enhancing lifestyles" by developing a "search for identity, a sense of autonomy, a sense of self-control, a sense of accomplishment, the concept of delayed gratification and strategies to reduce physical and psychological pain, peer pressure and stress" (Collingwood 1997, 18). The technologies used to help at-risk youth to develop their sense of identity include meticulous record keeping of their activity including workouts, eating, and sleeping habits and progress. The training program emphasizes training the body/training the self through the ability to show evidence and document those selves.

While the handbook for at-risk youths might be dismissed as a piece of pop psychology, it is merely one example of the fit body as a culturally salient model of subjectivity. The aspiration to health is no less central to the everyday practices of the at-large population, which is also constantly "at-risk" of losing their self-identity as self-willing strivers. The proliferation of information about and practices of physical fitness—from health food products, diet pills, Internet sites, home gyms, workplace gym programs, and personal trainers—is ample evidence of the power of fitness discourses. Of course, the aspiration toward health does not translate into achievement; the fit self is not necessarily manifest in actual American bodies, as constant warnings about obesity and heart disease convey. These constantly remind Americans of their failure to achieve, thus inspiring more aspiring. The proliferation of the surgeon general's reports, popularized health and medical journals, gym advertisements, and media reports serve the construction of anxiety, the proof of the failure of personal responsibility and self-fashioning and becomes an incitement to act. Individuals are compelled to consume more information about their failures and choose from the array of strategies available to overcome them.

While the construction of risk is achieved on an aggregate level in the production of a statistical blizzard of facts about unfit choices, the risk is translated into individual practices that reproduce and disseminate the ideal of aspiration. The individual body is compared to and responsible for the social body. Health is not a subjective state of well-being but a rather quantifiable and comparable statistic in which the body must speak about the fit-ness of its subject. At the individual level, measurement of fit-ness is no longer reduced to simple height and weight charts, or even blood pressure checks. Rather, it is done through complex measurements—cholesterol levels, Body Mass Index, VO_2 max, lactate threshold, bone density tests, stress tests—a set of numbers that measures their subject and provides evidence of change. To compare oneself against the proliferating norms of fit-ness, the consumer has available a range of products designed to quantify and categorize: heart rate monitors, body fat scales, calipers, thermometers, blood pressure tests. These home tests enable the charting of temporal progress as a means of proving aspiration. The purpose of knowing one's BMI is to change it; understanding one's VO_2 max enables one to develop strategies to increase exercise efficiency.

The assemblage of practices intended to monitor and control the body invokes the specter that the autonomous subject is meant to transcend, the addict enslaved to physical compulsion. The fear of a lack of self-control is highlighted in the title of the best selling nonfiction

"Running Addict": Nike pitches to the autonomy addict.

book of 1999, *The Carbohydrate Addict's Diet: The Lifelong Solution to Yo-Yo Dieting.* Found in the self-help section, the book describes lifestyle choices to "overcome cravings and help you put the individual back in charge" (from the book jacket). The carbohydrate addict is described as a slave to spikes in blood sugar levels, externally controlled by a substance rather than by the self. Companions to the book include a workbook and gram counter to enable individuals to measure their choices and chart their success as a part of a lifelong project of struggling to maintain control over the body. The implications are that within every health-seeking, autonomous individual is also the addict, unable to resist the physical impulse to eat what you want.

The threat of addiction, of losing control, is counterbalanced in the rhetoric of fitness with the promise of exercise as self-empowerment, outside of the sphere of control of substances or others. More than simply enhancing the productivity of the social body, fitness is a means of pursuing *self*-interest (Turner 1982; Featherstone 1982). The fitness industry capitalizes on the desire for autonomy through connecting it with the purchase of goods that signify healthful aspirations. The pursuit of fitness becomes one way of construction of and striving toward better selves. Fitness magazines promise a self-overcoming, conquering cravings and bodily limits in order to become the self "you never knew you could be" (Sayres 1986/1987; Duncan 1994; Estes et al. 1998). As the Nike ad suggests in demonstrating the seemingly perpetual solo ascent of the stair climber, fitness as the work on the self transcends work for others because it is production of and for the self. While you may not find fulfillment in the daily grind of work, the new self that emerges from a week of workouts is always satisfying.

While the health industry preaches the logic of self-empowerment, the body working overtime in an endless climb upward and onward seems eerily similar to Baudrillard's terror before an ever-expanding sphere of responsibility: "That health cannot be imposed, that it is contingent on the will of individuals, on their readiness toward modifying their lives and looking at them differently . . . It is the visible sign of initiative, adaptability, balance and strength of will" (Greco 1993, 370). The active production of the healthy body signifies the fit subject, the will that strives for self-improvement and thereby proves itself fit for the social body. Nike's command to be impulsive—"Just do it"—takes on a more sinister ring in relationship to the fit body.

No Pain, No Gain

The pursuit of autonomy through fitness entangles the self in an unending compulsion for self-improvement. Of course, the practices of fitness are saturated by power relationships related to consumerism, gender norms, racialized discourses, and other networks of power. The unceasing exercise of power through the body can lead to political quietism, responding to the omnipresence of power by simply accepting the inability to get outside of these power relationships. Baudrillard exemplifies this political paralysis in his use of the metaphor of obesity to describe America's obsession with self-creation. His inability to think about an alternative to either total domination by power or total liberation from power demonstrates the danger of ignoring the dynamic role of the body in power relations. He describes our insatiable appetite for free will as

> a good example of . . . this revolution in things which lies no longer in the dialectical transcendence but rather in their potentialization, in

their elevation to the second power, to the nth power—in that ascension to extremes related to the absence of rules for the game. (Baudrillard 1990, 34)

For Baudrillard, life has been completely subsumed by the operation of power that endlessly floats images that must be consumed to feed a hunger for self-affirmation and self-realization that will never be sated. The only possible response—implied by Baudrillard's title, *Fatal Strategies*—is the annihilation of the subject through a complete consumption of/consumption by the system of signs, a wallowing in the excess of cultural signifier, embracing rather than resisting power. He subordinates the body to cultural inscription and in doing so reinscribes the voluntarist subject who is able to appropriate cultural codes willingly as a strategy of resistance without concern for the material effects such strategies may have on the body, individual or social.

To escape the problems of both of these versions of fatal strategies, we may look to an alternative version of the relationship between power and performance[6] offered by Deleuze's reading of masochistic practice in "An Interpretation of Coldness and Cruelty" (1971). For Deleuze, the figure of the masochist embodies the paradoxical tension between autonomy as law and autonomy as creation. Masochistic practices highlight that power and freedom—and autonomy and addiction—are not in opposition to one another but are mutually constitutive. In bringing together these apparent opposites, the masochist is able to assume a position of subordination totally subject to both the will of an external other and the will of internal visceral desires. While the submission to external and internal desires ought to make the masochist the paradigm of failed autonomy, the masochist is active in enacting a dynamic between power and the body that transforms the powers to which it is subject, as well as the body itself. Reversing the situation of submitting to aspiration, the masochist aspires to submit.

From the position of the agent of subjection, the masochist may offer us the tools to rethink the concepts of freedom, choice, and autonomy in relationship to power, submission, and domination. While Baudrillard wallows in the submission to sign systems over which one has no control—a game without rules—the masochist offers a form of submission that is creative rather than fatal. Instead of than simply reiterating the logic of control, the masochist negotiates new, different, and dynamic power relations. The masochist's

response to the terror of social control is sublimation, a complete surrender of the self in order to pass through the position of the object of
power to reemerge as a different subject, an aspiration that produces
pleasure, rather than terror (see Cosgrove 1999).

Deleuze rescues the figure of the masochist from pathologiza-
tion in the theories of Krafft-Ebing and Freud. Their aversion to mas-
ochists closely resembles the fear of addiction that motivates the
aspiring self. Masochism, as understood in therapeutic discourse,
was a disease or pathology that represented passivity and a surrender
of one's very humanity. The masochist deliberately mocks the desire
to be free of pain, to be self-directing, and to choose one's own conditions of existence. Rejecting the overt pursuit of self-determination
"the body of the masochist became marked with all those problematic sociohistorical aspects that had been banished when the liberal subject was imagined as self-determining and free, aggressive
and self-controlled" (Noyes 1997, 6).

The masochist who seeks pleasure through submission to others,
rather than in self-possession, represents a reversal of traditional conceptions of autonomous subjectivities. As well as blurring the line
between pleasure and pain, the masochist challenges the very binaries
that sustain the idea of autonomy, including submission and freedom,
and autonomy as self-rule and addiction as self-sacrifice (see Deleuze
1971). More than just the hedonistic wallowing in pleasure in pain,
masochism is a complex strategy, the willful adoption of a mechanism
of control to pursue personal pleasure. As a strategy masochism acts
on the subject and on its object, altering both the masochist and the
law to which he submits (Noyes 1997; Foucault 1988b).

Through the strategy of submission, Deleuze believes the masochist
acts as an agent by shaping of the relationship between the masochist
and his master. First, masochistic pleasure, like the morality of aspiration, is dependent not on achievement but on the continual disavowal
or delay of pleasure. Pain becomes the possibility for imagining a form
of pleasure in the future in the absence of pain; it becomes the predi-
cate for the imagination of something outside of immediate reality.
The masochist refigures the relationship between the ideal and the
real in the continual disavowal and denial of pleasure in the moment.
The masochist enacts what Donzelot described as the "float" between
the ideal and its lack but, instead of feeling guilty for a failure to attain

the ideal, the masochist's pleasure is intensified by the future possibility of pleasure. The renunciation of pleasure therefore undermines the control function operative in the delay of gratification through the mechanism of guilt that leads to the terror of responsibility. The failure to achieve the synthesis of the ideal and the real is reinscribed as a form of pleasure.

Masochist pleasure is also a critique of the ideal of the autonomous subject as entrepreneur. The masochist defies the ability to calculate, particularly the possibility of the pursuit of self-interest modeled on a principle of exchange, whether economic, social, or sexual. The model of contract often seen as guiding exchange between autonomous subjects: that they be voluntary, that they view equivalence as the ruling principle of justice, and that they be ruled by the principle of reciprocity (Fuller 1964, 22–23). Contractual exchanges establish a relationship of obligation between subjects to repay social debts, and in these relationships, accountability is understood as a transparent relationship of debt to the other through which the self can know and realize its responsibility. The contract is a version of autonomy whereby the subject can calculate and act according to a set of predictable rules.[7] On the other hand, the relationship of reciprocity incurs a debt that ties the subject to the other:

> What the Golden Rule seeks to convey is not that society is composed of a network of explicit bargains, but that it is held together by a pervasive bond of reciprocity. Traces of this conception are to be found in every morality of duty, from those heavily tinctured by an appeal to self-interest to those that rest on the lofty demands of the Categorical Imperative. Whenever an appeal to duty seeks to justify itself, it does so always in terms of something like the principle of reciprocity ... "How would you like it if everyone acted as you propose to do?" (Fuller 1964, 200)

Contractual relationships are thus based on a sense of duty or obligation that compels the self to be accountable to others and to one's self by engaging in the fair bargain of reciprocal exchange. Individuals are forever in a position of holding themselves accountable. The demand to render accounts becomes the self-disciplining subject that seeks freedom by holding itself responsible.

The performance of the masochistic contract transforms the relationship of self-policing into one of pleasure. While obedience to the law, or a contract, is dependent on fear of punishment or the provocation of guilt, the masochist reverses this relationship and makes obedience into the pleasure that the law was intended to deny. The punishment required for the functioning of the law becomes the object of desire. The insubordination through absolute obedience is described in Reik: "The supremacy of will power apparently giving in to the will of all others. In renouncing his will he shows his insubordination ... Even if you beat me, punish me, I persevere until I attain the instinctual satisfaction" (quoted in Cosgrove 1999, 428). When the sanction becomes the object of desire, the law loses its power to punish; obedience produces the desire it was meant to suppress.[8] The parodic staging of power and control mimics the construction of power relations. The apparent submission to authority is in fact the pursuit of pleasure precisely through the mechanisms of power. Parody, however, does not always constitute a form of resistance, and pleasure is not always evidence of transgression. Rather, we must examine the ways that violence mimicked by the masochist is also an ethical project to represent very real and material experiences of pain and suffering that are the consequence of bodily practices and imagine other possible relationships to our bodies and to others.

Scarry's *The Body in Pain* (1985) is instructive in understanding the productive capacities of the experience of pain as an important feature of embodied practices. She argues that physical pain and imagination are yet another set of productive oppositions. On the one hand, the experience of pain is the unimaginative and unrepresentable; it cannot be translated into a publicly expressible form (Scarry 1985, 162). The experience of pain is therefore conceived of as passive, to be suffered, a form of objectification that renders the subject inexpressive. Like the addict, the body in pain is subject to external, coercive force. But in the process of the experience pain is transformed from a passive state to be endured into an active state by the imagination—pure will—that uses the opportunity to imagine the future (Scarry 1985, 164–65). The movement between the material experience of pain and the fictive space of the imagination is evident in Deleuze's description of the blurred boundaries between fantasy and materiality through the staged act of pain.

The ways that pain not only enables but compels the subject to re-create its material conditions, to imagine other possibilities, opens up space for change within the cybernetic circuits of control that otherwise fix the body as objects of power/pain. As masochism demonstrates, autonomy produces heteronomy in the imperative to be free, a contradiction that invents the ultimate act of freedom—to will unfreedom. The position of submission, however, is also a position of mastery, enabling the autonomous subject to fulfill its project of self-creation, to imagine itself as otherwise and act on that image. The "dominant" subject must continually invent new ways of disciplining the submissive and new forms of seeking pleasure.

The relational quality of the masochist's position implies the ethical project of engagement with self and others necessary for the autonomous will to emerge. Here masochism may be linked with the Foucauldian project of the care of the self in yet another paradoxical coupling: masochistic self-care (Foucault 1986, 299). While dependent on hierarchical relations of master and slave, Foucault notes the relationship is "at the same time regulated and open" and thereby produces indeterminate effects, the possibility for control and freedom (Foucault 1988b, 299). Foucault clearly imagines that the same discipline that has created the terror of responsibility of the self might also turn the critical impulse—the desire to self-police—into a creative force.

In the project of the care of the self, Foucault describes the work of the self as conceptualized in antiquity as a process not unlike the technologies that shape his microphysics of power. The practices of self-care demand a constant cultivation of capacity, an aspiration toward achievement through testing procedures, demonstrating the ability to exhibit self-control and self-mastery and to delay gratification. The purpose, however, was not merely to deprive or punish oneself but to avoid the loss of the self in excess (to become addicted to pleasure) and to appreciate the indulgences all the more. In other words, privation became a precondition for the intensification of pleasure (Foucault 1986; see also Foucault 1988b). The goal of the care of the self is not the passage of judgment on the subject (or an individual act). For Foucault, the critical subject becomes a speculator, examining one's self to imagine how things might have been done differently and to project a future that is different (Foucault 1986, 64).

The responsibility to aspire is transformed from a relationship of terror to an aesthetic pleasure in creation "defined as a concrete relationship enabling one to delight in oneself, as in a thing one both possesses and has before one's eyes" (Foucault 1986, 65). Here the norm of self-creation crosses from a technology of domination into a site of pleasure. The aesthetic model of judgment has the potential on the one hand to produce dissatisfaction and self-help that reiterates forms of power. On the other hand, the aesthetic self defers self-identity and relates to the self as not an achievement or discovery but as a constantly evolving aspiration: "The relationships we have with ourselves are not ones of identity; rather, they must be relationships of differentiation, of creation, of innovation" (Foucault 1985, 166). The care of the self is a constant self-othering, an operation of making oneself strange to oneself in order to aspire or imagine a self that could or might be different. The project of self-care and fit-ness share a common self-critical and creative impulse that may produce subjects that disrupt the circuits of power and lead us to think differently about autonomy and ourselves.

Athletes Anonymous

From the theoretical consideration of masochistic relationships that are able to transform power relations from within, we must turn to a consideration of actual bodies that embody the materiality of the masochist. Donzelot suggests we may seek such subversion in "the body that resists the disciplinary architectures by means of countless invisible or spectacular insurrections, the body that affirms the reality of life and denounces the unreality of that by which it would be encircled and reduced to silence" (Donzelot 1979, 234). The suggestion that bodies should not be silenced is reminiscent of Scarry's second stage of the experience of pain, the possibility to imagine other bodies. Therefore, our goal must be to locate figures that demonstrate this relationship between materiality and creativity, figures whose bodies speak to us.

One such subject may be found in a variation on the fit body. In the 1980s, the American Psychological Association named a new

"Time Sheet": Exercise constitutes work on the self.

clinical psychological disorder called the exercise addict, included in the *Diagnostic and Statistical Manual IV* (see Cole 1997, 271). The diagnosis seems implausible. The addict is understood as the failure of free will and the submission to the object. The self is rendered passive, subject to craving leading to a lack of physical and mental control (see Derrida 1995b). Like the masochist, the addict sacrifices free will and submits to the other. But what if addicts are addicted to precisely what they are supposed to seek, autonomy?

Sedgwick identifies exercise as addiction's opposite, as the desire to *control* the body, rather than being controlled by bodily needs:

> Healthy free will would belong to the person who has in mind the project of unfolding ... out of a self, a body, already understood as containing him in potentia ... in this view now a staple of medicalized discourse both lay and clinical, the ... exerciser would be the person who embodies the exact opposite of addiction. (Sedgwick, 1993, 132)

Exercise is prescribed as a strategy for resisting threats to autonomy ranging from mental illness to depression to obesity to stress to, of course, addiction itself. The fit self exercises freedom in self-actualization, in the creation of a self-produced through freely choosing healthy pursuits. However, the goal of a fit self is indeterminate, mandating that health is not an achieved object but rather a project that compels repetition for self-maintenance and improvement. The structure of behavior evokes the compulsive and repetitious action of the addict, also filling an expanding need. The will becomes limitless: "The subject is addicted to the idea of free subjectivity, addicted to the repeated act of freely choosing health—the act that is supposed to be an anti-addiction" (Cole 1997, 271).

A number of recent studies have focused on the figure of the bodybuilder as a paradigmatic example of a body that, through an excess of control, becomes a representative of the pursuit of fitness that becomes an exercise in excess.[9] The bodybuilding lifestyle takes the norms and practices of fitness to an extreme. Through rigid routines of self-denial, including extreme dieting, purposeful dehydration to reduce body fat and water retention, and supplementation—both legal and illegal—the built body exaggerates the practices of fitness and becomes a grotesque embodiment of the norm (Haber 1996, 153; Johnston 1996; Ian 1991; Klein 1993a, 1993b).

Through turning the ideal of bodily construction into an abnormal materiality, the built body can undermine other body politics dependent on the control of bodies. Notably, scholars have suggested that both male and female bodybuilders can disrupt cultural connections between the metaphorical and material elements of gender and sex. While the extreme exercise regimens and steroid usage often eliminate or de-emphasize both primary and secondary sex characteristics, male and female bodybuilders engage in the active construction of gender on bodies that appear unnatural. So, for example, female bodybuilders often wear excessive makeup and hair plugs (disguising baldness brought on by steroid usage) to feminize their bodies, which have taken on male characteristics of strength and musculature (Ian 1991; Moore 1997). The consequence is a visible remapping of gender onto inappropriate bodies, perverting the norm. Male bodybuilders can similarly subvert given understandings of masculinity. The intense scrutiny and hypermanagement of the body—including narcissistic mirror gazing and practices of dieting—lead male bodybuilders to engage in acts generally coded of feminine. The male becomes the object of the gaze because of his physicality, rather than dominating because of that strength. The muscles of the bodybuilder are cosmetic, not controlling, for display and not dominance. The virility of the male body is transformed, both literally and metaphorically into a grotesque spectacle[10] (Lingis 1994, 36–37). The physical prowess that is central to connections between masculinity and dominance becomes an aesthetic display. Like Deleuze's masochist, the male bodybuilder submits to excessive obedience to the norm, and in doing so, perverts the norm.

The bodybuilder is an easily recognizable form of bodily construction, but the overtly staged quality of the built body may be dismissed as just spectacle, an abnormality rather than a variation on the norm. If the built body is to be more than just an oddity, we must look for other bodies that manifest biopolitical strategies at the intersection between cultural norms and materiality. Lingis notes that the body is more than just a surface on which signs take form; "it puts demands on us," and therefore we must consider other bodies and what demands they put on us to rethink our relationship to our, and their, bodies. If bodybuilding is one potential masochistic strategy, can we find others?

The popularity of so-called extreme sports both embodies and transcends the bodily strategies implicated in the fit body. Fitness practices are a means to avoid ordinary bodily risks but *extreme* fitness practices become the means to invite and overcome extraordinary bodily risks. The fit self wills not only the overcoming of given risks but also the construction of new and different risks. The simultaneous practice of aspiring toward fitness and seeking practices that go beyond normal conceptions of bodily practice indicate that sports meant to stretch the limits of the body may locate a dynamic site of struggle. Ultraendurance sports, such as the Ironman Triathlon, embody the elements of masochism that emphasize the significance of corporeal practice because the body is a nexus of pain/pleasure and control/creativity. In submitting to fitness norms that seek to refine bodies to create autonomous subjects, Ironmen[11] demonstrate that autonomy can become an addiction, eroding our ability to distinguish between agency and compulsion. The bodies challenge our ability to differentiate between autonomous and nonautonomous subjects and, thereby, to make bodily norms a grounds for exclusionary practices.

According to popular mythology, the Ironman Triathlon began in 1978 in Hawaii among fifteen male Marines following an argument over whether runners or swimmers are more fit. The race—an endurance challenge of a 2.4-mile swim, 112-mile bike, and 26.2-mile run—has grown to include not only the thousand-competitor Ironman Hawaii race, but also over a dozen international competitions; it boasts over a million competitors worldwide (Maloney 1985, 60). At least a quarter of the competitors in 2000 were Iron*women*. Completing the race requires an average of eighteen to twenty-four hours of training per week as well as closely monitored sleeping and eating patterns to guarantee the body will be able to endure the intense physical stress. The triathlon, like bodybuilding, is a recreational sport that requires a level of physical ability that does not serve a practical purpose (Lingis 1994) nor do many triathletes earn a substantial amount of money in the competition.[12] The natural question that emerges is why would anyone invest such a massive amount of time and money into such a grueling endeavor, or, more broadly, under what conditions are these sorts of aspirations possible? The excessively fit bodies of Ironman competitors make sense within the cultural context that awards aspiration. We can explore the ways the Ironman perversely embodies the norm of the fit, self-creating self by examining the two elements central to the aspiring self, first, the construction of risk and, second, the narratives of self-creation that emerge out of this construction.

As we saw in our discussion of the technologies of social control, one of the primary motivators is the desire to avoid risk by engaging in preventive strategies of health management. Risk-averse practices include the production of knowledge about the self, sources of risk, and the means to avoid these risks. For the Ironman, however, a high number of hours of training plus constant management of the body's intake and output are to avoid not just average risks but also the very serious health hazards that come from endurance sports, both in the training and in the competition. The physical fitness demanded of the body in order to survive an eight-plus-hour physical ordeal makes training not just a hobby, but a life-or-death necessity. Almost one-third of all competitors in Ironman Hawaii are forced to seek medical attention during or after the event most commonly from dehydration, trauma, hyponatremia,[13] and hypothermia (Dolinar 1990, 120). Since ultraendurance sports are a relatively new phenomenon, the medical community has only recently recognized the need to develop new strategies for identifying and preventing serious medical problems in triathletes (Gastmann et al. 1998, 18). In addition to the general risks of sporting activity, including overuse injuries and general fatigue, problems specific to ultraendurance athletes have emerged. Research has found that over an extended period of years, extreme training can cause hypertrophied enlargement of the heart and valve leakage with unknown long-term consequences. (Dolinar 1990, 120). Recent studies have also demonstrated that endurance athletes suffer from damaged immune systems and are more susceptible to infectious disease (Bishop et al. 1999; Mackinnon 2000).

The response to risks has not been withdrawal from the threat, either by the athletes or by the researchers interested in their health. The solution is to *overcome* them, to produce bodies fit to endure. In the pursuit of bodily aspirations, a variety of technologies have been developed that highlight the constructed qualities of these superbodies. Technological advances in the equipment used by triathletes have shaved seconds from times, often at several thousand dollars per second. Triathletes invest in wetsuits, technologically savvy bicycles, and custom designed running shoes. All of the performance enhancing technologies involve a constant circuit of knowledge production and material practices that circulate between athletes and the scientists/ marketers who develop products. The project of building better bodies and better selves is a collective rather than an individual endeavor.

Other technologies are designed to rework the body from inside out. Many technologies have been mass-marketed to a wider spectrum of fitness enthusiasts. The technologies range from relatively inexpensive, but scientifically engineered, sports drinks, supplements, and foods, to more expensive data-producing equipment such as heart rate or body fat monitors. Other technologies are used solely to fine-tune the bodies of elite athletes. Devices ranging from oxygenated tents to lactate level testers remake the body's ability in an attempt to increase the threshold of risk, a challenge both to athletes and to scientists determined to engineer better bodies.

In the modification of bodily capacities, the bodily integrity of the Ironman is breached, and the body again becomes a site not of autonomous control but of the interface with and dependence on external forces that reshape the body and the will. If the addict is a symbol of a will sacrificed to impulses through the medium of artificial chemicals, the high-level athlete's body becomes visibly modified and dependent on externalized forces shaping the body. The addict and the athlete become dependent on technologies that are central to their self-identities and are derivative of externalized forces (Derrida 1995b).[14]

Though the risks and remedies associated with endurance sports seem extreme, these risks are a primary reason for competing. Pushing the body's limits becomes a means to the end of aspiring toward a body with new, expanding limits. The bodies that are built in the process of aspiring are superior to other bodies by virtue of their *will* to experience new and elevated sources of pain. Just as the masochist must constantly seek new ways of generating pain and pleasure, the endurance athletes represent the creative need to seek new physical risks and challenges. Indeed, the sport grew the fastest in 1983 and 1995 after ABC televised the dramatic collapses of high-profile athletes from hyperthermia and dehydration just yards from the finish line. Their crawling/walking finishes are often invoked as inspiration for fellow competitors: "I just saw somebody who wanted something so bad she was willing to do anything, crawl or whatever it took, and it just sent chills up my spine" (quoted in Carlson 2000). The experience of overcoming pain is depicted as a means of achieving a new and better self that emerges on the other side of the finish line.

In reworking the limits of the body and the will, Ironmen are also engaged in a project of reworking norms that establish natural limits in presuming biology is destiny. If the will is engaged in an ongoing process of overcoming limits, then the social norms that assign value to subjects based on embodied characteristics like gender are undermined. As the technologies of social control emphasize individual autonomy and self-creation, normalizing technologies that relate moral worth to "natural" body features—like race, gender, or able bodiedness—become less powerful.[15] In the case of bodybuilders the most obvious reconstruction of normalizing discourses on shaping of the body occurs in the instability of gendered interpretations of the meaning of bodies.

As in the case of bodybuilders, endurance athletes often subvert gendered conceptions of bodily capacity. Endurance athletes often blur primary and secondary sex characteristics, with female body fat levels dropping low enough and their musculature being developing far enough to make their body types almost indistinguishable from those of males.[16] If bodybuilding practices tend to sculpt bodies that resemble a masculinized image of the body, high levels of endurance training sculpt androgynous bodies both in appearance and performance. Significantly, the achievement of female athletes, especially in endurance sports, has begun to blur the assumption that males are physically stronger[17] (Noakes 1991, chapter 16). Just five years after the first man broke the nine-hour barrier, the first female athlete broke the same time limit. Among elites, women consistently finish in the top twenty, with the highest overall finish of a woman being in eleventh place.

As with female bodybuilders' practices of exaggerating their femininity in order to counteract the desexing of their bodies, so too have some Ironmen attempted to reinscribe their gendered character, with ambiguous effects. The most successful and famous Ironman, eight-time champion Paula Newby-Fraser, has started a company of women's fitness wear called "Iron Girl," which highlights pastel colors and floral prints. As with female bodybuilders, the consequence may be as much a shifting of gendered assumptions as a resexing of the body. The supposed fragility of femaleness—the girl—is undermined by her Iron-ic identification. Rather than recoding the athlete's body as female, it demonstrates the impossibility of imposing a naturalizing category onto a rebuilt body.

If Ironmen enact a ritual of constructing and overcoming material limits—both self- and societally imposed—they are publicly enacting the process whereby material and cultural identities emerge through practices of the body. In doing so, they evoke the masochistic care of the self through a constant redefining of limits, goals, and aspirations. However, the empowered self emerges not through a will to freedom but in a will to submit, to experience and transgress a limit. The autonomous drive is transformed into an addiction to aspire. The relationship between the bodily practices of fitness and the practices associated with addiction is not lost in clinical discourse, where an obsession with fitness has become subject to a great deal of clinical interest (Nixon 1989). Researchers have developed the seemingly contradictory category of a "positive addiction," a productive submission to practices of fashioning the self (Smith et al. 1998). The consequence is the description of a response to a supposed oversocialization that does not fall back either on the unsatisfactory choice between antisocial individualist versions of autonomy that retreat into the body and a depressing alternative of a purely docile, controlled body (Melley 1999: 202). The particular bodies that partake in the Ironman ritual allow us to see both the active quality of bodies and to simultaneously theorize how this dynamic body opens up a space for struggle.

Conclusion

These built bodies are the products of autonomous self-fashioning. Submitting themselves to the brutal law of fit-ness, they emerge as self-fashioned re-created selves. The autonomy addict presents a clear challenge to the antithesis between autonomy and heteronomy, demonstrating the ways that freedom becomes a compulsion. The blurring of conceptual clarity challenges the normative role of autonomy as a category that delineates between proper subjects and those who must be disciplined or excluded. As we saw in the previous chapter, the purpose of conceptual confusion is an extension of ethical responsibility by suspending our ability to judge the other. Without the ability to exclude the other on the assumption that the other is not autonomous, ethical action requires a more contextualized consideration of how to treat a particular other. The other productive element of this confusion is the emergence of different ways of relating to the self. The imposition of control on the site of the body is never complete, and because autonomy is about self-rule and self-creation, different forms of subjectivity emerge that challenge the way we conceive of autonomy. As Foucault describes the relationship between power and the body: "Once power produces this effect, there inevitably emerge the responding claims and affirmations of one's own body against power, of health against the economic system, of pleasure against the moral norms of sexuality ... and so the battle continues" (1980, 56). From the work on the body emerges a politics of struggle, the fashioning of selves both against and with existing forms of power.

These spectacular subjects of extreme autonomy may also be locations from which we may imagine different ways of being and different relationships to ourselves. What might these bodies enable us to imagine as possibilities for ourselves? Rose describes such a critical project in ways that echo Nancy's description of freedom as "surprise":

> One would examine the ways in which creativity arises out of the situation of human beings engaged in particular relations of force and meaning and what is made out of the possibilities of that location. These minor engagements do not have the arrogance of programmatic politics—perhaps even refuse their designation as politics at all. They are cautious, modest, pragmatic, experimental, stuttering, tentative (Rose 1999, 280).

The description of how we ought to imagine a politics of resistance within these conditions resembles Foucault's description of the body politic, which emphasizes the important linkage between power and bodies and indicates the urgency of properly approaching bodies as an important and unique site of politics. And, like the ways we think about and study bodies, our conception of politics must also be attentive to the particularities of specific projects. The dynamic between the material and the ideological is not determinate and therefore requires an approach that, as Rose suggests, is modest, careful, and attentive to the rules of the game in particular locations.

Our aspiration has been to imagine what the conditions of possibility are for the emergence of the fit body and what other possibilities are enabled by these ways of being. The creation of the aspiring subject within circuits of control also creates the possibility for new aspirations and creative projects of self-fashioning that are not outside of power but nonetheless redefine the boundaries of power. The compulsion to be autonomous is also an invitation to imagine new possibilities, new selves, new relationships, and new bodies. Through these stutterings, these self-fashioning subjects may be doing work on themselves and the world, illustrating the power and control that are the conditions for freedom and autonomy.

Conclusion

FREEDOM AND SELF-GOVERNANCE

> It is always an opening, at once in the sense of an
> unclosed system, of the opening left to the other's
> freedom, but also in the sense of an overture,
> advance, or invitation, made to someone else. . . .
> It must remain something one cannot anticipate.
>
> —Jacques Derrida,
> *Points . . . Interviews*

Within modern political thought, autonomy has played an important role in resisting various forms of power. The idea that individuals possess a capacity to reason for themselves and thus govern themselves challenged multiple forms of hierarchy and domination. The project of modern democratization is heavily invested in a vision of the subject that defines autonomy as the characteristic that enables popular sovereignty. Thus the modern political project of liberation is built on the foundation of the sovereign subject of autonomy, able to will the law and thus preserve personal freedom and social order: "The freedom offered and defended by liberal rhetoric is a freedom that is entwined with these images of a subject whose integrity is an impossible perfection, a subject who can be calculated and predicted into the future at the same time as he or she has a clarity of thought and will that directs these very promises and predictions" (Bell 1996, 82). However, the promise that the autonomous subject offered universal human emancipation has often seemed empty. Liberal proponents of the idea of autonomy argue that the failure is not in the ideal itself but lies with minor quibbles in defining precisely what constitutes autonomy or in differences over how best to defend it. Antifoundationalist critics of modernity have argued that the problem with autonomy is not an incomplete realization of the idea but in the ideal itself. The antifoundationalist critique has suggested that in ontological terms the subject is always already the product of particular conditions beyond their absolute control (Hindess 1996, 75). In normative terms, the requirement of autonomy for full recognition as a political subject leads to the exclusion of particular forms of life deemed to be inadequately autonomous. The critique of autonomy as it is conventionally understood in liberal theory is not necessarily a wholesale rejection of the political or ethical value of autonomy as a powerful political discourse. Derrida, reflecting on the ways in which subjectivity is always already the product of contextual forces, argues "this heteronomy, which is undoubtedly rebellious against the decisionist conception of sovereignty or of the exception, does not contradict; it opens autonomy on to itself; it is a figure of its heartbeat" (1997, 69).

The goal of this project has been to consider the political ideal of autonomy as self-governance, avoiding the general approach of, to borrow from Bell, "recognize, rally, and reconstruct" or, for that matter, recognize, rally, and reject (1996, 83). Instead, the purpose has been to approach the idea of autonomy not as an abstract or transcendental concept that underpins or justifies a political system but as a site of political contestation whereby the boundaries of political community are drawn by determining who or what is capable of self-governance and thereby authorizing "a whole series of exclusions, disciplinary practices, and restrictive moral and rational norms" (Newman 2003, 14). Framing the discussion is a central tension within the literature, defining autonomy, on the one hand, as the capacity to self-govern or make a law whereby subjects voluntarily limit themselves and, on the other, defining autonomy as human freedom, the capacity to act in the world and on one's self. Considering the actual effects of the ideal of autonomy, how it authorizes particular subjects and not others, opens up the concept to broader political contestation. The question is not whether particular practices are autonomy-promoting or autonomy-denying but whether particular uses of the idea of autonomy cultivate self-detachment and therefore promote political change (Foucault 1996, 303) or whether they reinforce existing power relationships. My underlying goal is similar to Honig's description of Arendt's politics: the strategy, then, is to unmask identities that aspire to contestation, to deauthorize and redescribe them as performative productions by identifying spaces that escape or resist administration, regulation, and expression. These are spaces of politics, potentially spaces of performative freedom" (Honig 1993, 226).

The examples examined in the book—adolescent sexuality, the drug war, animal rights, and endurance athletes—provide snapshots of how the norm of autonomy works in contingent, shifting ways with rather than against power. The approach deliberately avoids drawing general conclusions about autonomy, a method that reflects the strategy outlined by Honig of undermining settled assumptions in order to allow political contestation to occur and to prevent the reification of any particular regime of power. The various examples have challenged the assumption that a liberal politics of protecting or promoting autonomy is synonymous with liberty or freedom.

In broad terms, the identification of political subjectivity with autonomy or the assumption that those capable of self-governance should be permitted to engage in self-governance produces a number of effects. First is that the ideal of autonomy generates a boundary within society between those perceived of as properly autonomous and those who are not. In order to be recognized as an autonomous subject, the individual is compelled to continually produce evidence of her own autonomy through proper self-governance. This compulsion politicizes everyday life as the body is one of the most important sites whereby the self can produce evidence of self-limitation. Thus the most (apparently) private of activities such as sexuality are subject to intense scrutiny for evidence of proper self-management. Further, the ideal of autonomy then justifies intervention into the decision making and action of subjects. Intervention may take the form of punishment, as with the errant drug user, to the cultivation of autonomy, as with the willful adolescent who must be taught to tame the body.

The norm of autonomy often produces paradoxical results, as when drug users are subject to medical and juridical intervention in order to save them from their own addiction. Or, statutory rape laws protect teenaged girls from sexual coercion by denying the girls any authentic sexual agency by refusing to acknowledge their ability to consent. These products of the ideal of autonomy are highly variable, shaped by power relationships that play in a role in how we judge particular actions or subjects as autonomous or non-autonomous. The role of reflecting on autonomy, as demonstrated in chapters 3 and 4, is not to develop better ideas about autonomy but to reveal how it is constructed and deployed and thus, how it could potentially be different. In Foucault's term the goal is to "promote new forms of subjectivity through the refusal of this kind of individuality that has been imposed on us for several centuries" (Foucault 1982, 216).

Chapters 4 and 5 analyze the ways that the conventions of autonomy might be used to think and act differently, challenging the boundaries of political community (such as the human–animal divide) and undermining the certainty of political judgments (like the absolute difference between and normative value of the addict and the athlete). The ethical call of uncertainty both undermines the necessity of the present and begins the process of separating out "from the contingency that has made us who we are, the possibility of no longer being, doing, or thinking what we are, do, or think" (Foucault 1984, 574). Reflecting on the role of autonomy must reject the foundation of a political order on the assumption of the autonomous subject to be liberated and look instead to

> reveal the contingency and fragility of the self as a product of a web of contingent events and relationships, and promote cautious and piecemeal experimentation with transforming inherited vocabularies and forms of life whose maintenance and defense inflict gratuitous suffering and cruelty. (Longford 2005, 574)

The characterization of the subject as subjectification is not a surrender of the self to relationships of power but a call to be self-critical, attentive to the ways in which the self is always constructed with a given context and cognizant of the fact that these relationships could be changed. If we view autonomy not as the *end* of political life but as a *means*, we may cultivate different ways of relating to ourselves and others.

Notes

1. The Choice of Law

1. In the Second Discourse, Rousseau envisions "savage man" as an autonomous subject in his freedom from dependence on others for needs, whether physical or emotional. The subject is driven primarily by immediate needs. While this autonomous man has some interaction with others (notably in reproduction), the primary feeling is pity, which may engender some sense of responsibility to the other.

2. For a thorough discussion see O'Neill 1989, chapters 1 and 2.

3. This discussion derives primarily from *Between Facts and Norms*, Habermas's most developed theorization of the law.

4. Castoriadis's location of autonomy solely in the history of the West is a highly questionable move, one he justifies by noting that philosophy is a Western activity. Other critics have taken up this problem in Castoriadis, and I will not do so here. It is valuable to note, however, that that view reflects a tendency to see "a society" as a relatively homogenous formation with clear boundaries.

5. Many critics, most famously Habermas, have criticized Castoriadis for failing to provide criteria by which any society could evaluate its own institutions; absent these normative criteria, he gives no compelling reason why a society should choose autonomy over any other institution.

6. Subsequent chapters explore the ways that liberal theorists have always envisioned autonomy as simultaneously a given characteristic of humans and a capability that must be fostered. Locke's discussion of children, for example, which we considered in chapter 2, demonstrates that while he argued for a robust notion of "natural right" that rested heavily on a view of autonomy as natural or God-given, he nonetheless believed that autonomy needed to be cultivated from birth.

2. Mature Subjects

1. The terms "children" and "child" are not meant to be definite referents to humans of particular ages; rather, they are a category evoked in political theory whether meant literally to refer to a class of humans of a certain age or, quite often, metaphorically, to imply a state of "immaturity," which may apply to any group that fails to show the trappings of maturity. I will be challenging the boundaries of this term by examining its construction and use. "Child" has had variant historical meanings that will be discussed below.

2. While later theorists of education would certainly include girls (and sometimes women) among those being educated, the theorists discussed below do not. Since this gendered distinction is important for the argument about the relationship between physical education and political education, I will retain the gendered language.

3. Rousseau sired five children with his mistress, but he gave all of them to an orphanage for adoption.

4. Rousseau's political education is strictly gender-specific: boys are educated for citizenship while girls are relegated to the private sphere as wives and mothers.

5. The status of child was not limited to chronological children; it was also applied to colonized persons of all ages as well as women. For example, in *On Liberty*, Mill characterizes whole cultures as immature and thereby incapable of self-governance. Their immaturity justifies colonization for the purpose of helping them mature toward civilized self-rule. Mill's description of the barbarian who must learn to become self-disciplining bears numerous resemblance to actual colonial education, which often began with the reformation of the physical habits of those governed, mandating the wearing of clothing, ending traditions of bodily decoration, and, most importantly, mandating monogamy and marriage as the only appropriate (mature?) sexual relations (see Merry 1999; Stoler 1995).

6. Contemporary debates over issues like executing minors demonstrate the difficulty in clearly delineating between "adult" and "child."

7. "Adolescence" is not a category deployed by Locke, Rousseau, or Kant since, as will be discussed below, the category does not come into existence until the late nineteenth century. "Teenagers" did not exist in a modern sense. "childhood" was much shorter because children were required to work and marriage took place at a young age. Kant, for instance, designates sixteen as the appropriate age for marriage for a male student, though he does argue that tutelage may continue after this point (26).

8. Foucault here claims that the "schoolboy" was subject to the most intense scrutiny, separating him from the schoolgirl and adolescence in general. The move has some theoretical use, as it distinguishs between the forms of disciplinary power that boys were subject to and the modes of domination (differing forms of power that Foucault recognizes, while choosing to focus on disciplinary modes of power) under structures of patriarchy that girls were more likely to endure. On the other hand, this obscures the role that gender differentiation plays in the construction of the boy as subject to disciplinary power because of his potential to act as an autonomous subject as well as the ways in which our understanding of the "schoolboy" is constructed via the girl. This section considers the construction of adolescence generally in relationship to sexuality (which Foucault does not do) and the following section will examine the construction of "girl" in relationship to the entanglement of autonomy and sexuality.

9. Homosexuality was interpreted by Hall and others as a mark of immaturity in which the individual had not properly proceeded through stages of psychosexual development to make appropriate object choices (see Robertson 2001 and 2002; Ohi 2000). This view was in part influenced by Freud's characterization of homosexuality.

10. Even today the age of marriage and first sexual contact is often interpreted as a sign of "barbarity" or, in slightly more politically correct terms, "modernism." While we may express shock at the age of young men engaging in warfare, the sexual activity of young girls is still a source of horror. The existence of "child brides" in some countries can still be an indicator of how backward and inhuman a particular culture is.

11. The relationship between heterosexuality and the proper expression of the male sexual impulse can be seen in the legislation regarding sodomy in the United States. Perhaps most demonstrative is the argument that identifying as a homosexual is not a crime (or a sin) unless the individual engages in homosexual activity. The self-management of desire may be seen as mitigating the improper nature of the desire.

12. Other forms of physical culture emergent from the discourse of autonomy are discussed in chapter 5.

13. The notable exception is in cases in which the state steps in and initiates prosecution. A new California program called "vertical prosecution" pursues the fathers of children of minors, with or without the consent of her parent(s).

14. For the sake of parsimony this section will focus exclusively on the relationship of girls to age of consent laws in spite of similar, though not identical, dynamics in terms of the regulation of boys.

15. The Women's History Project at the State University of New York at Binghamton has compiled a collection of documents from the age of consent campaign on their Web site. See http://womhist.binghamton.edu/aoc/intro .htm.

16. For a thorough discussion of this shift, see Haag 1999. She attributes the shift to changing ideas about liberty moving from an emphasis on laissez-faire contract rights to more subject-centered accounts of a right to a private self uncoerced by legal or social relations.

17. Other non-white men were targeted by consent laws and prostitution statutes, though they were interpreted as commercializing sex and engaging in "white slavery." Jewish, Chinese, and French men were identified as a particular threat to female sexuality. They were viewed as "evil capitalists" more than as sexual predators; they sought financial rather than sexual gratification. See Keire 2001 for a discussion of the concept of "white slavery" and its linkage of Progressive-era discourses on the immorality of the twin evils of nonnormative sexuality and commodification.

18. Statutory rape laws continue to be applied almost exclusively to male offenders, in spite of clear evidence that of-age women do engage in sexual activity with younger partners. Charges of statutory rape against women have often involved women in positions of power (usually teachers) and are often handled as media spectacles, such as the case of Mary Jo Laturneau, the Washington teacher convicted of statutory rape after she conceived a child with her fourteen-year-old student. She was portrayed, variously, as unable to make good sexual choices because of sexual trauma in her past and/or mental illness. See Allen 2002. The Court has upheld differential treatment of boys and girls in statutory rape cases; boys and girls are seen as differently situated because of biological difference. See *Michael M. v. Superior Court* (1981).

19. The state of Idaho chose to punish both parties for the sexual activity between two consenting minors by enforcing the state's fornication statutes. Teens were identified when they applied for public assistance and were most commonly sentenced to probation, parenting classes, and counseling (see Mehta 1998, 121–22).

3. Intoxicated Citizens

1. *United States v. Montoya de Hernandez* 473 U.S. 531 (1986). Montoya de Hernandez eventually expelled several smuggled packets of cocaine. Her conviction on drug smuggling charges was upheld by the Court.

2. The discourse of sexuality is gendered and racialized. The primary fear is the erosion of the sexual boundaries of white women and their promiscuous behavior. In the case of African Americans, drugs are seen as heightening an already hypersexual identity, leading to the rape and/or corruption of white women, a discourse discussed below.

3. A similar link could be made to Court-mandated HIV tests for various populations such as prisoners and those seeking marriage licenses. The discourse surrounding HIV is significant since it distinguishes between those who contracted the virus through blood transfusions and are "innocent" (their bodies were breached by a virus through no fault of their own) and those who gave in to pleasure and made "lifestyle choices," allowing their bodies to be breached by foreign objects (needles or penises) and now by a virus (see Closen 1998).

4. This logic underlies both approaches to drug use both in the legal system and through medicalization. Either drug use is a loss of self-control for which the drug user needs to be quarantined and punished, or the drug use is an addiction for which the drug user needs treatment to regain self-control.

5. Foucault's point is not, of course, that Europe ceases to engage in wars but that the nature of wars changes, often focusing on internal rifts and struggles against social groups within the nation-state (see Foucault 2003). Notably, he does not comment on the role of colonialism in this process, though a similar process of defining an empire against its others does occur. Some theorists, such as Giorgio Agamben (1998), are critical of Foucault's omission and his focus on defining the Western, disciplined subject while neglecting the violence against the subject's others. This critique does influence the analysis that follows, especially in noting that the drug war makes precisely this distinction between the subject and its others and the distinction between subjects worthy of discipline and self-governance and those who are excluded, often violently.

6. This discussion of the history of drug regulation draws from the numerous histories of the drug war that have been written. The perspectives taken by the authors vary wildly from being explicitly anti–drug war (Baum 1996; Baggins 1998; Bertram et al. 1996; Johns 1992) to being antidrug (Jonnes 1996, Courtwright 2001a, 2001b) to attempts to write a neutral history of drug regulation (Musto 1999; Coomber 1998). While adopting different normative perspectives and purposes, the overlap among the accounts of the drug war is notable.

7. Phillip Jenkins (1999) has also noted that responses to synthetic drugs—manufactured in a lab rather than discovered—also often generate panic,

especially in media reports about "Designer drugs." Jenkins and others have noted that fears about drug usage often provoke discourses about unnatural behaviors or unnatural bodies, altered by chemistry—a strange fear in a society that warmly embraces prescription drugs for ailments.

8. The conventional wisdom about therapeutic vs. medical drugs is constantly shifting. Opium, cocaine, and heroin have all had medicinal uses at some point in history. Prescription drugs such as Vicodin, Valium, and Ritalin are often used recreationally. Therapeutic drugs often are plagued with the same problems of addictive properties and long-term health effects. This point was most clearly recognized in recent medical studies showing that the long-term brain chemistry effects of Ritalin, the drug prescribed to children with Attention Deficit Disorder, are similar to those of Ecstasy, a synthetic club drug. In addition, drugs are now ranked according to a "schedule" of legality and degree of punishment. Schedule I drugs are considered to have no medicinal purposes and are subject to the most severe restrictions. Many have pointed out that this schema appears to parallel public fears rather than medical research. So, for example, marijuana is a Schedule I drug, lumped with heroin and crack, while LSD is Schedule II.

9. The Eighteenth Amendment prohibited the manufacture and sale of alcohol.

10. Of course the connection with Germany would have been particularly salient during World War I.

11. See Courtwright 2001b. He discusses why particular drugs become widespread in their use and how this affects their regulation. Caffeine, alcohol, and nicotine are all widely used drugs, and prohibiting them would not only be difficult to enforce but costly to the economy. Thus productivity remains an important way of distinguishing between illicit and licit drugs.

12. Examples of the expansion of state powers include the repeated upholding of no-knock laws when justification could be provided. See *Richards v. Wisconsin* (1997). The most controversial provision of the drug war is forfeiture laws, whereby any property used in the commission of a drug crime may be seized and becomes the property of the state.

13. *Rodriques v. Furtado* 950F.2d 805 (1st Cir. 1991). For analysis, see Hyde 1996, chapter 1. The search of Rodriques's apartment and vagina was found to be legal.

14. See *Moore v. Regents of the University of California*, 793.P.2d 479 (Cal. 1990). See also Hyde 1997, the chapter on "Body as Property," which outlines the legal contours of proprietorship in the body. See also McClain 1995 for a

discussion of the ambiguous relationship between seeing the body as property or seeing it as sacred.

15. *Rochin v. California*, 342 U.S. 165 (1952). Curiously, the Court drew a parallel between a forced confession and the forced expulsion of the drugs, between "speaking the truth" verbally or "speaking the truth" physically. Invasion of the body is seen as particularly heinous. Writes Justice Frankfurter: "Applying these general considerations to the circumstances of the present case, we are compelled to conclude that the proceedings by which this conviction was obtained do more than offend some fastidious squeamishness or private sentimentalism about combating crime too energetically. This is conduct that shocks the conscience. Illegally breaking into the privacy of the petitioner, the struggle to open his mouth and remove what was there, the forcible extraction of his stomach's contents—this course of proceeding by agents of government to obtain evidence is bound to offend even hardened sensibilities. They are methods too close to the rack and the screw to permit of constitutional differentiation." For a consideration of the case's contemporary relevance, see Miller 1997.

16. Some states have enacted restrictions on drug testing by private companies including Maine, Vermont, Rhode Island, Connecticut, Montana, Minnesota, Iowa, Hawaii, Louisiana, Maryland, Nebraska, Oregon, and Utah. Regulations range from restricting blanket testing to applicant testing or otherwise limiting the cases in which testing may occur.

17. The skeptic might invoke the illegality of drug usage as the primary difference between these performance-hindering states. However, corporate defenders of testing policies evoke the standard of performance, not the condition of illegality, as the justification for their policies. Corporations rarely report drug users to authorities and rarely even eliminate employees automatically upon drug detection, suggesting that performance and not legality drives the practice. Many companies test for financial reasons. Insurance companies often give lower rates to companies that give drug tests on the assumption that workplace accidents will be lowered. Few executives cited this as their primary reason for the activity. For a thorough discussion of workplace testing, including interviews with those tested and those testing, see Gilliom 1994.

18. Children are often configured as in need of special care to help them cultivate their autonomy. See chapter 2.

19. *Veronia School District v. Acton*, 23 F.3d 1514 (1994) affirmed decision in *New Jersey v. T.L.O.*, 469 U.S. 325, 326 (1985).

20. Indeed, in the legal challenge by Acton, the parents were instrumental in the student's refusal to be tested and the subsequent lawsuit. The student was a seventh grader at the time of the suit.

21. In *Potawottamie School District v. Earls* the Court upheld the Acton decision and expanded the scope of testing to all students engaged in extra-curricular activities.

22. Emphasis added. Justice Scalia, opinion of the Court in *Veronia School District 47J v. Acton*, 515 U.S. 646, 115 S.Ct. 2386 (1995).

23. *Bell v. Wolfish*, 441 U.S. 520, 558 (1978).

24. This strategy was primarily used in Florida. The first woman prose-cuted for distribution of drugs to a child under eighteen was Jennifer Johnson, whose conviction was upheld by the Florida appeals Court in 1989. She was not prosecuted while the child was in utero but under the grounds that once the child had been born, drugs were delivered to the child through the umbili-cal cord in the moments before it was cut. Several other cases have since been upheld. Sentences for delivery of drugs to minors tend to be longer than for either drug use or child abuse convictions.

25. In 1996 the South Carolina Supreme Court upheld the criminal pros-ecution of a woman for child abuse through prenatal drug use in *Whitener v. State of SC*, Opinion Nr. 24468, 31 (1996).

26. *Ferguson et al. v. City of Charleston et al.*, 99 U.S. 936 (2001). The Court ruled that a state mandate given to a Charleston public hospital to develop procedures for testing women seeking prenatal care in the hospital was unconstitutional.

27. See Rosenbaum 1997. Studies now indicate that babies of cocaine and crack abusing mothers are more likely to be underweight but that many health effects are related to poverty, not the direct effects of drug usage.

28. The linkage between vigilant parenting and productive citizenship is clearly drawn in the demonization of the parents of John Walker Lindh, the so-called American Taliban found fighting with Al Qaeda forces in Afghanistan. His behavior was blamed on liberal parenting and especially a permissive mother. With new linkages made between children's drug use and terrorism, the specter haunting parents now is that they may be raising the next John Walker Lindh.

4. Man Is a Political Animal

1. The case of the hanged sow, while unusual for the attempt to human-ize the pig, is not anomalous and in fact was a part of a medieval tradition of animal trials quite common until the late seventeenth and early eighteenth

centuries. For more see Tester 1991. The executed animals were never eaten, often because they were thought to be inhabited by evil spirits.

2. *Animal Legal Defense Fund v. Glickman* 154 F. 3rd 426 (DC Cir. 1998).

3. The same, of course, could be said of the modern prisoner, who is also subject to physical torture, rape, and death within the confines of the prison.

4. Many authors on the subject of animals would protest my distinction here between human and nonhuman animals since, biologically (and for their purpose of morality), humans are animals. Since I am primarily concerned with animals as a political category I will continue to use the "human" and "animal" distinction rather than the more unwieldy "human animal" and "nonhuman animal." Since one of the goals of this chapter is to demonstrate how and why this distinction is constructed and utilized (for political ends), this linguistic move should not be seen as any sort of ontological claim (there are things called humans that are distinct from something called animals) but, as I hope to show, the distinction may serve politically useful (for humans *and* animals).

5. This phrase is borrowed from Aristotle and his definition of man in *The Politics*. The gendered quality of the statement is intentional and important. Woman is less often defined as a political animal and is often lumped with animals under the category of those who must be ruled or as lesser moral agents. The gendered nature of the rights-bearing subject is discussed at length below.

6. For a quick illustration of the ways the category of animal is understood in contingent and culturally determined ways, Foucault's preface to *The Order of Things* begins with a discussion of a Chinese system of classification of animals that includes categories like "belonging to the Emperor," "embalmed," "tame," "fabulous," and "innumerable" (1970, xv). Foucault suggests that the impenetrability of this classification scheme indicates a different way of viewing the world that understands the relationship between things quite differently, a point that suggests these classification schemes are not objective but contingent and reflect broader relationships including, most importantly for Foucault, our relationship to ourselves.

7. The term "animal rights" is usually attributed to Henry Salt, whose *The Case for the Rights of Animals* (1821) is considered the first text to seriously propose that animals ought to be afforded moral and legal rights. The term was earlier used in *A Vindication of the Rights of Beasts*, a satire mocking Mary Woolstonecraft's *The Vindication of the Rights of Woman*, which compared the absurdity of extending rights to women to extending them to "beasts."

8. The term "imbeciles" (used by Leahy 1991) is a blanket term for the developmentally disabled and, sometimes, the mentally ill. Some have

suggested that modes of behavior toward animals and the mentally ill or developmentally disabled may have some parallels, drawing yet another comparison with Foucault's *Madness and Civilization*. Foucault describes a period of time where the mentally ill were allowed to wander freely before "the Great Confinement," when they were increasingly subject to regulation and confinement in order to provide treatment and separate them from the general population (1988a). Tester (1991), for example, notes that animals were increasingly subject to confinement due to more concentrated forms of agriculture and urbanization. While even animal rights theorists (most notably Tom Regan) often use the parallel between "higher animals" and the developmentally disabled, the comparison is perhaps a bit oversimplified and misses many of the complexities of the moral status of both animals and so-called marginal humans, a point that will be elaborated later. In another curious parallel, we should note that humans who appear to have lost all consciousness are described as "vegetables," presumably even lower than animals.

9. Examples abound including popular stories, fables, and movies. Circuses and zoos are designed specifically with children in mind (see Franklin 1999). Of course, animals do take on a more adult interest in the form of hunting and fishing, agriculture, and even in modes of characterizing sexuality (see Dekkers 2000).

10. The most thorough collection that demonstrates the persistent presence is *Political Theory and Animal Rights* (Clarke and Linzey 1990), which contains excerpts from classic political theory texts on the question of animals. In his foreword, Tom Regan notes (but does not explicate) that in spite of an apparent increase in popular attention to animal rights, animals are less present in contemporary theory.

11. This glosses over many centuries of political thought but, because the primary concern is the relationship between animals and rights, I abbreviate the discussion to move on to modern political thought, where the conception of "rights" is more relevant.

12. Animals deserve mention in both Hobbes's *Leviathan* and *De Cive*. It should be noted that Hobbes named two of his most famous works, *Leviathan* and *Behemoth*, after monsters or animal figures.

13. See the discussion of Kant and moral autonomy in chapter 1.

14. Others lumped into this category by Bernard Rollins, a defender of Rawls, who adopts a similar position toward animals in *A Theory of Justice*, include children, mentally incapacitated persons, and severely mentally ill persons.

15. Kant is not the first to advocate this position. Hume, for example, thought animals deserved "gentle usage" but could not fall into the realm of

justice because they could not object to the ways we treated them. See Taylor 1999 for further discussions of the complex connections.

16. In actuality, Rousseau's description of savage man is probably a cobbled together version of accounts of orangutans and persons from colonized locations; his footnotes citing his sources often vacillate between descriptions of "orangutans," "Negroes," and "savages," but his actual description of "savage man's" behavior more closely resembles actual behavior of orangutans than any known human group.

17. This history is very geographically limited as well because most studies of animal rights focus on Britain and the United States. In addition, the role given to animals both here and in the theoretical section is obviously limited to Western discourses and is not universal. A more global history of animals would most certainly be a useful exercise in deconstructing the binary of animal–human but the scope of this chapter does not, unfortunately, allow it.

18. This is not to say that these practices were absent prior to this point, but they were commercialized in the eighteenth and nineteenth centuries, both proliferating these practices and changing their character.

19. The gendered character of animal welfare and animal rights groups persists with a vast majority of membership in organized groups being female and a number of activities associated with an animal rights perspective, most notably vegetarianism, also being gendered (see Silverstein 1996; Adams 1991). The relationship between gender and animal rights will be explicated further below.

20. Numerous examples of the associations between women and animals and between women and animals and nonwhite persons could be cited. Miles Dekkers in *Dearest Pet*, for example, explores how discourses about gender, sexuality, race, and animalism became entangled (2000). He cites, for example, the coincidental rise in Ku Klux Klan violence against African American males, usually on trumped up rape charges. He notes that at the same time in the 1930s, *King Kong* emerges as a figure in American cinema in which a beautiful white woman is kidnapped by a gigantic African gorilla who covets her. She is saved both from sexual violation by the beast and her own sentimentality (she feels sympathy for the beast) by white male hunters. See also Wolch and Emel 1995.

21. We may recall from chapter 1 Habermas's description of public law as superior to moral law because of its ability to use force to compel obedience. Here we see the force of law becoming more ominous in its ability to materialize particular identities and relationships.

22. The phrase "ethic of care" as used by feminist scholars is quite different from the ethics of care utilized by Foucault, a difference further elucidated in the next chapter.

23. While Benton uses Marx's critique of rights almost verbatim, he does not make the claim that Marx himself would have supported a proanimal position. Marx most appropriately fits into the model of hierarchical thinkers in relationship to animals. He believed they were inferior creatures because they did not have a "species being" and were not historical creatures. Whether or not Marx had an instrumental approach to nature is, of course, debatable.

24. The above mentioned argument for simian sovereignty makes just such a move when it argues that apes need territorial sovereignty because mutual noninterference is the only way to ensure ape autonomy and happiness.

25. This does not exhaust, of course, all the potential critics of rights discourse.

26. This has often happened with endangered species kept in captivity and eventually saved even though the animal ought not be allowed to breed (because of genetic or other reasons).

27. This somewhat awkward phrase is meant to incorporate the interlinkages between discourses about animals, gender, and race within "legocentrism" or the certainty of Western philosophy that has persistently convinced itself of its own purity by expunging these others that introduce uncertainty and difference.

28. Wendy Brown also draws on this argument in relationship to women in her chapter "Wounded Attachments" (1995).

29. Derrida addresses this theme multiple times in his texts but the clearest articulation of this principle comes in *The Gift of Death* (Derrida 1995a).

5. Fit to Be Tied

1. The ways in which the addict is perceived to have porous boundaries is addressed in chapter 4.

2. For two very different disciplinary approaches to the relationship between 1980s policy-making and a culture increasingly jealous of the autonomy and individuality of (some of) its citizens, see Heelas and Morris 1992, which provides a sociological perspective on social policy, and Melley 1999, which examines links between popular and literary representations of paranoia about external control.

3. President Clinton's successor, George W. Bush, also capitalized on this discourse by publicly discussing his triumph over alcoholism through religious

discovery, the implication being that his ability to face adversity and overcome it indicated a stronger character than if he had never faced adversity at all.

4. The relationship between power and the imagination described here by Donzelot is not entirely different than that described by Castoriadis (see chapter 1). However, Donzelot does not see the imagination, even images generated by the subject, as outside of power but as creating new forms of control and power.

5. Programs emphasizing physical fitness or physical training can be differentiated from other popular means of social control, including work camps and manual labor. Technologies of physical training are not just about creating productive members of society; they also entail going further to produce subjects capable of willing themselves to be productive. The product of these strategies is not the machinelike producer, but the willing subject itself.

6. The invocation of "performance" here is not to be mistaken with Butler's use of performativity, though it has some similarities. I recognize that the metaphors of performance and staging have been subject to critique (see Brown 2000) but their usage here should not be confused with a more problematic connection between performance and staging, whereby the context is rendered passive, subject to the actor. Deleuze undermines this relationship by deemphasizing the theatrical connection in masochistic behavior (which rarely occurs on an actual stage) and concerns himself with the dynamic of "atmosphere," or the ways that contexts are central to masochistic behavior.

7. Responsibility and calculability are discussed in the previous chapter, where Derrida also suggests that ethical responsibility must not be calculable and therefore requires us to think beyond models of reciprocity. These two chapters may be seen as linked in this common concern for seeking out more responsible ways for thinking about ethics.

8. In chapter 1, Habermas's defense of public law described one of the advantages of a public law over private morality is that public law carries with it the threat of coercive sanction or the force of law. The actions of the masochist foreground the force required to implement the law, uncovering the coercive center of self-governance; democratic self-governance must always be protected by the force of law. Further, in finding pleasure in coercion, the masochist seems to undermine the ability of the law to maintain order.

9. See, for example, Moore 1997, Johnston 1996, and Haber 1996. Another increasingly common genre is fieldwork studies of bodybuilders in which the researcher eventually joins the bodybuilding subculture. See, for example, Ian 1991 and Klein 1993a and 1993b.

10. In addition to the challenge to virility represented by the "feminization" of male bodybuilders through practices such as shaving the body and wearing high heels to develop calf muscles, male virility is also threatened by the literal decrease in sperm counts caused by high levels of intense physical activity and steroid usage. Male bodybuilders also frequently work as male escorts or strippers, often for male clients, another feminine position (see Klein 1993a).

11. Female competitors call themselves Ironmen. The gendered dimensions of this activity will be considered below.

12. The prize for winning the Ironman Hawaii competition, the largest winner's purse on the circuit, is $70,000, and athletes earn relatively little through sponsorship. Significantly, none of the competitors on the American triathlon team in the 2000 Olympics were full-time professional triathletes.

13. Hyponatremia is a condition in which the body's electrolytes drop to dangerously low levels.

14. The ways in which the physical manipulation of the body can challenge one's sense of self are explored by Nancy in *The Intruder*, which describes how a heart transplant transformed his relationship to his body. Posthumanist scholars have written extensively on the ways that biotechnology and the increasing use of technological means to prolong or improve life can modify our sense of the human being as a unified, sovereign entity located in a body (see Wolfe 2010).

15. Ironmen are not limited to traditional conceptions of physical fitness based on the able bodied. In 1994, the Ironman circuit added a wheelchair division to the competition.

16. A range of examples could be provided, including the female loss of menses and hormonal changes in men and women resulting from training. Other bodily *practices*, including men shaving their entire bodies to enhance performance, could be cited as examples of the blurring of gendered distinctions. The increasing number of women competing in endurance athletics may also be both a symptom and a cause of changing gender relationships as both long-distance sports (recreational or competitive) and so-called obligatory running (devoting very large portions of time to running-relating activities to the detriment of other responsibilities) are generally identified as male behaviors often identified with an idealized masculinity. Some clinicians have even classified obligatory running as a male equivalent of eating disorders in women (Nixon 1989).

17. As women have had more exposure to physical training and competition, the gap between male and female performances has narrowed. One sport where women have consistently matched or exceeded male performance is in endurance swimming.

Bibliography

Adams, Carol J. 1991. *The Sexual Politics of Meat: A Feminist–Vegetarian Critical Theory.* New York: Continuum.

Adams, Carol, and Josephine Donovan, editors. 1995. *Animals and Women: Feminist Theoretical Explorations.* Durham, N.C.: Duke University Press.

Agamben, Giorgio. 1998. *Homo Sacer: Sovereign Power and Bare Life.* Palo Alto, Calif.: Stanford University Press.

Agin, Shane. 2002. "Comment se font les enfants? Sex Education and the Preservation of Innocence in Eighteenth-Century France." *MLN* 11(7):722–36.

Ahrens, Frank. 2002. "New Pitch in Anti-drug Ads: Anti-terrorism." *Washington Post,* February 4, sec. A02.

Ahrens, Jörn. 2005. "Freedom and Sovereignty: A Fatal Relationship Outlined with Jean-Luc Nancy and Marquis de Sade." *Law and Critique* 16:302–13.

Aitken, Stuart. 2001. *Geographies of Young People: The Morally Contested Spaces of Identity.* New York: Routledge.

Allen, Tina. 2002. "Gender-Neutral Statutory Rape Laws: Legal Fictions Disguised as Remedies to Male Child Exploitation." *University of Detroit Mercy Law Review* 80:111–30.

Ames, Joy L. 1997. "*Chandler v. Miller:* Redefining 'Special Needs' for Suspicionless Drug Testing under the Fourth Amendment." *Akron Law Review* 31(2):273–96.

"The Anti-Drug." *Office of Drug Control Policy Media Campaign.* http://www.theantidrug.com.

Archard, David. 1993. *Children: Rights and Childhood.* Oxford: Oxford University Press.

Baggins, David Sadovsky. 1998. *Drug Hate and the Corruption of American Justice.* Westport, Conn.: Praeger.

Baker, Jeffrey P. 2000. "A Doctor of Their Own: The History of Adolescent Medicine." *Bulletin of the History of Medicine* 74(2):409–10.

Baker, Steven. 2000. *The Postmodern Animal*. London: Reaktion.

Baldwin, Peter C. 2002. "Nocturnal Habits and Dark Wisdom: The American Response to Children in the Streets at Night, 1880–1930." *Journal of Social History* 35(3):393–611.

Balke, Friedrich. 2005. "Derrida and Foucault on Sovereignty." *German Law Journal* 6(1):71–85.

Ballard, Judith. 1900. *A Danger to Our Girls*. Women's Temperance League. Pamphlet.

Barry, Andrew, Thomas Osborne, and Nikolas Rose. 1996. *Foucault and Political Reason: Liberalism, Neo-liberalism and Rationalities of Government*. Chicago: University of Chicago Press.

Baudrillard, Jean. 1990. *Fatal Strategies*. New York: Semiotexte.

Baum, Dan. 1996. *Smoke and Mirrors: The War on Drugs and the Politics of Failure*. New York: Back Bay Books.

Bearn, Gordon C. F. 1995. "The Possibility of Puns: A Defense of Derrida." *Philosophy and Literature* 19(2):30–35.

Bell, Vicki. 1996. "The Promise of Liberalism and the Performance of Freedom." In *Foucault and Political Reason: Liberalism, Neo-liberalism and Rationalities of Government*, edited by Andrew Barry, Thomas Osborne, and Nikolas Rose, 81–98. Chicago: University of Chicago Press.

Benhabib, Seyla. 1999. "The Liberal Imagination and the Four Dogmas of Multiculturalism." *Positions* 12(2):401–13.

Benton, Ted. 1993. *Natural Relations: Ecology, Animals and Social Justice*. New York: Verso.

Berlin, Isaiah. 2001. *Liberty: Incorporating Four Essays on Liberty*. Oxford: Oxford University Press.

Bertram, Eva, Morris Blachman, Kenneth Sharpe, and Peter Andreas. 1996. *Drug War Politics: The Price of Denial*. Berkeley and Los Angeles: University of California Press.

Bielefeldt, Heiner. 1997. "Autonomy and Republicanism: Immanuel Kant's Philosophy of Freedom." *Political Theory* 25(4):524–58.

Bishop, N., A. Blannin, N. Walsh, P. Robson, and M. Gleeson. 1999. "Nutritional Aspects of Immunosuppression in Athletes." *Sports Medicine* 28(3): 151–76.

Bordo, Susan. 1989. "The Body and the Reproduction of Femininity: A Feminist Appropriation of Foucault." In *Gender/Body/Knowledge*, edited by

Susan Bordo and Alison Jaggar, 13–33. New Brunswick, N.J.: Rutgers University Press

———. 1993. *Unbearable Weight: Feminism, Western Culture, and the Body.* Berkeley, University of California Press.

Bowers, Lisa. 1994. "Queer Acts and the Politics of Direct Address: Rethinking Law, Culture and Community." *Law & Society Review* 28 (5): 1009–34.

Boyd, Susan C. 1999. *Mothers and Illicit Drugs: Transcending the Myths.* Toronto: University of Toronto Press.

Broder, Sherri. 2002. *Tramps, Unfit Mothers, and Neglected Children: Negotiating Family in Nineteenth-Century Philadelphia.* Philadelphia: University of Pennsylvania Press.

Brown, Gillian. 2000. "Child's Play." *Differences: A Journal of Feminist Cultural Studies* 11(3):76–106.

Brown, Michael. 2000. *Closet Space: Geographies of Metaphor from the Body to the Globe.* New York: Routledge.

———. 2006. "Sexual Citizenship, Political Obligation, and Disease Ecology in Gay Seattle." *Political Geography* 25:874–98.

Brown, Wendy. 1995. *States of Injury: Power and Freedom in Late Modernity.* Princeton, N.J.: Princeton University Press.

Budd, Michael Antin. 1997. *The Sculpture Machine: Physical Culture and Body Politics in the Age of Empire.* London: Macmillan.

Burchell, Graham. 1996. "Liberal Government and Techniques of the Self." In *Foucault and Political Reason: Liberalism, Neo-Liberalism and Rationalities of Government,* edited by Andrew Barry, Thomas Osborne, and Nikolas Rose, 19–36. Chicago: University of Chicago Press.

Burchell, Graham, Colin Gordon, and Peter Miller, editors. 1991. *The Foucault Effect: Studies in Governmentality.* Chicago: University of Chicago Press.

Butler, Judith. 1990. *Gender Trouble: Feminism and the Subversion of Identity.* New York: Routledge.

———. 1993. *Bodies That Matter: On the Discursive Limits of "Sex."* New York: Routledge.

———. 2005. *Giving an Account of Oneself.* New York: Fordham University Press.

Campbell, Helen. 1890. "Poverty and Vice." *Philanthropist* 5:2–3.

Campbell, Nancy. 2000. *Using Women: Gender, Drug Policy, and Social Justice.* New York: Routledge.

Carlson, Timothy. 2000. "The Twelve Greatest Moments of the Ironman." *Outside Magazine.* http://outside.away.com/outside/events/ironman/12great.html.

Carroll, Lewis. 2010 [1865]. *The Adventures of Alice in Wonderland and Through the Looking Glass*. New York: Cosimo.

Carter, Julian B. 2001. "Birds, Bees, and Venereal Disease: Toward an Intellectual History of Sex Education." *Journal of the History of Sexuality* 10(2): 213–49.

Castoriadis, Cornelius. 1991. *Philosophy, Politics, Autonomy*. New York: Oxford University Press.

———. 1998 *The Imaginary Institution of Society*. Cambridge, Mass.: MIT Press.

Chalier, Catherine. 2002. *What Ought I Do? Morality in Kant and Levinas*. Ithaca, N.Y.: Cornell University Press.

Chasnoff, Ira J., William J. Burns, and Kayreen A. Burns. 1985. "Cocaine Use in Pregnancy." *New England Journal of Medicine*. 313:666–69.

Christman, John, editor. 1989. *The Inner Citadel: Essays on Individual Autonomy*. Oxford: Oxford University Press.

Clark, D. 1997. "On Being 'the Last Kantian in Nazi Germany': Dwelling with Animals after Levinas." In *Animal Acts: Configuring the Human in Western History*, edited by Jennifer Ham and Matthew Senior, 145–64. New York: Routledge.

Clarke, Paul, and Andrew Linzey, editors. 1990. *Political Theory and Animal Rights*. Winchester, Mass.: Pluto Press.

Closen, Michael. 1998. "The Decade of Supreme Court Avoidance of AIDS: Denial of a Certiorari in HIV-AIDS Cases and Its Adverse Effects on Human Rights." *Albany Law Review* 61(3):897–987.

Cocca, Carolyn E. 2002. "From 'Welfare Queen' to 'Exploited Teen': Welfare Dependency, Statutory Rape, and Moral Panic." *NWSA Journal* 14(2): 56–79.

Coetzee, J. M. 1999. *The Lives of Animals*. Princeton, N.J.: Princeton University Press.

Cohen, Stanley. 1985. *Visions of Social Control: Crime, Punishment and Classification*. New York: Polity Press.

Cole, Cheryl L. 1993. "Resisting the Canon: Feminist Cultural Studies, Sport and Technologies of the Body." *Journal of Sport and Social Issues* 17(2): 77–97.

———. 1997. "Addiction, Exercise and Cyborgs: Technologies of Deviant Bodies." In *Sport and Postmodern Times*, edited by Genevieve Rail, 261–76, Albany: State University of New York Press.

Collingwood, Thomas. 1997. *Helping At-Risk Youth through Physical Fitness Programming*. Champaign, Ill.: Human Kinetics.

Connolly, William E. 1991. *Political Theory and Modernity.* New York: Wiley-Blackwell.

Coombe, Rosemary. 1991. "Contesting the Self: Negotiating Subjectivities in Nineteenth-century Ontario Defamation Trials." *Studies in Law, Politics and Society* 11:3–40.

Coomber, Ross, editor. 1998. *The Control of Drugs and Drug Users: Reason or Reaction?* Amsterdam: Harwood Academic Publishers.

Cosgrove, Peter. 1999. "Edmund Burke, Gilles Deleuze, and the Subversive Masochism of the Image." *ELH* 6(2):405–37.

Cote, James. 2000. *Arrested Adulthood: The Changing Nature of Maturity and Identity.* New York: New York University Press.

Courtwright, David. 2001a. *Dark Paradise: A History of Opiate Addiction in America.* Cambridge, Mass.: Harvard University Press.

———. 2001b. *Forces of Habit: Drugs and the Making of the Modern World.* Cambridge, Mass.: Harvard University Press.

Cowan, Melissa Skidmore. 1986. "Workers, Drinks and Drugs: Can Employers Test?" *University of Cincinnati Law Review* 55 (Summer):127–51.

Critchley, Simon. 1996. "Deconstruction and Pragmatism—Is Derrida a Private Ironist or a Public Liberal?" in *Deconstruction and Pragmatism,* edited by Chantal Mouffe, 19–42, New York: Verso.

Cruickshank, Barbara. 1999. *The Will to Empowerment: Democratic Citizens and Other subjects.* Ithaca, N.Y.: Cornell University Press.

Cutrofello, Andrew. 1994. *Discipline and Critique: Kant, Poststructuralism and the Problem of Resistance.* Albany: State University of New York Press.

Dainotto, Roberto Maria. 1993. "The Excremental Sublime: The Postmodern Literature of Blockage and Release." *Postmodern Culture* 3:3. http://muse.jhu.edu/journals/postmodern_culture/v003/3.3dainotto.html.

Danesi, Marcel. 1994. *Cool: The Signs and Meanings of Adolescence.* Toronto: University of Toronto Press.

Darby, Robert. 2003. "The Masturbation Taboo and the Rise of Routine Male Circumcision: A Review of Historiography." *Journal of Social History* 36(3) 737–57.

Davis, Karen. 1995. "Thinking Like a Chicken: Farm Animals and the Feminine Connection." In *Animals and Women: Feminist Theoretical Explorations,* edited by Carol Adams and Josephine Donovan, 192–212. Durham, N.C.: Duke University Press.

Dean, Mitchell. 2009. *Governmentality: Power and Rule in Modern Societies.* New York: Sage Publications.

Dekkers, Midas. 2000. *Dearest Pet: On Beastiality*. Translated by Paul Vincent. New York: Verso.

Deleuze, Gilles. 1971. *Masochism: An Interpretation of Coldness and Cruelty.* New York: George Braziller.

———. 1995. *Difference and Repetition*. Translated by Paul Patton. New York: Columbia University Press.

———. 1997. *Negotiations: 1972–1990*. New York: Columbia University Press.

Derrida, Jacques. 1967. *Of Grammatology*. Baltimore: Johns Hopkins University Press.

———. 1980. *Writing and Difference*. Translated by Alan Bass. Chicago: University of Chicago Press.

———. 1994. *Specters of Marx: The State of Debt, the Work of Mourning, and the New International*. Translated by Peggy Kaumpf. New York: Routledge.

———. 1995a. *The Gift of Death*. Translated by David Wills. Chicago: University of Chicago Press.

———. 1995b. *Points: . . . Interviews:1974–1994*. Palo Alto, Calif.: Stanford University Press.

———. 1997. *The Politics of Friendship*. Translated by George Collins. New York: Verso.

———. 2002. "The Animal That Therefore I Am More to Follow." *Critical Inquiry* 28(1):369–418.

———. 2003. "And Say the Animal Responded?" In *Zoontologies: The Question of the Animal*, edited by Cary Wolfe. Minneapolis: University of Minnesota Press.

———. 2005. *Rogues*. Translated by Pascale-Anne Brault and Michael Naas. Palo Alto, Calif.: Stanford University Press.

———. 2008. *The Animal That Therefore I Am*. Translated by David Wills. New York: Fordham University Press.

———. 2010. *The Beast and the Sovereign*. Chicago: University of Chicago Press.

Dewey, John. 1963. *Experience and Education*. New York: Collier Books.

Diamond, Cora. 1991. *The Realistic Spirit: Wittgenstein, Philosophy and the Mind*. Cambridge, Mass.: MIT Press.

Di Stefano, Christine. 1996. "Autonomy in the Light of Difference." In *Revisioning the Political: Feminist Reconstructions of Traditional Concepts in Western Political Theory*, edited by Nancy J. Hirschmann and Christine Di Stefano, 95–116. Boulder, Colo.: Westview.

Doak, Melissa, Rebecca Park, and Eunice Lee, editors. 2000. *How Did Gender and Class Shape the Age of Consent Campaign within the Social Purity Movement, 1886–1914.* Binghamton, N.Y.: State University of New York Press.

Dodson, Kevin E. 1997. "Autonomy and Authority in Kant's Rechtslehre." *Political Theory.* 25:93–111.

Dolinar, J. 1990. "Triathlons—Not Just for Ironmen." *The Physician and Sportsmedicine.* 1810:120–25.

Donovan, Patrica. 1997. "Can Statutory Rape Laws Be Effective in Preventing Adolescent Teen Pregnancy?" *Family Planning Perspectives* 29(1). http://www.guttmacher.org/pubs/journals/2903097.html.

Donzelot, Jacques. 1979. *The Policing of Families.* Baltimore: Johns Hopkins University Press.

Dornbusch, Sanford M. 1989. "The Sociology of Adolescence." *Annual Review of Sociology* 15:233–59.

Dripps, Donald. A. 1997. "Drug Testing—Again." *Trial.* June 1.

Driscoll, Catherine. 2002. *Girls: Feminine Adolescence in Popular Culture and Cultural Theory.* New York: Columbia University Press.

Driscoll, Lawrence. 2000. *Reconsidering Drugs: Mapping Victorian and Modern Drug Discourses.* New York: Palgrave.

"Dr. Phil on Alarming Sexual Behavior among Children." 2002. On *The Oprah Winfrey Show.* Host Oprah Winfrey. Prod. Dianne Atkinson Hudson. Harpo Productions. May 7.

Duncan, Margaret C. 1994. "The Politics of Women's Body Images and Practices: Foucault, the Panopticon and *Shape* Magazine." *Journal of Sport and Social Issues* 18(1):48–65.

Duttmann, Alexander Garcia. 2000. *Between Cultures: The Struggle for Recognition.* London: Verso.

Dworkin, Gerald. 1988. *The Theory and Practice of Autonomy.* New York: Cambridge University Press.

Eburn, Jonathan P. 1997. "Trafficking in the Void: Burroughs, Kerouac, and the Consumption of Otherness." *Modern Fiction Studies* 43(1):53–92.

Elo, Irma T., Rosalind Berkowitz King, and Frank Furstenberg. 1999. "Adolescent Females: Their Sexual Partners and the Fathers of Their Children." *Journal of Marriage and the Family* 61:74–84.

Eskes, Tina, Margaret Carlisle Duncan, and Eleanor Miller. 1998. "The Discourse of Empowerment: Foucault, Marcuse and Women's Fitness Texts." *Journal of Sport and Social Issues* 22(3):317–44.

Facing Up to Fat. 1999. *About.com* URL: http://about.onhealth.com/ch1/in-depth/item/item,55528_1_1.asp.

Favre, David. 2000. "Equitable Self-Ownership for Animals." *Duke University Law Review* 50:474–502.

Featherstone, Mike. 1982. "The Body in Consumer Culture." *Theory, Culture and Society* 8:18–33.

Feinberg, Joel. 1989. "Autonomy." In *The Inner Citadel: Essays on Individual Autonomy*, edited by John Christman, 27–53. Oxford: Oxford University Press.

Field, Corinne T. 2001. "Are Women . . . all Minors?: Women's Rights and the Politics of Aging in the Antebellum United States." *Journal of Women's History* 124:113–37.

Foucault, Michel. 1970. *The Order of Things: An Archaeology of the Human Sciences*. London: Methuen.

———. 1978. *The History of Sexuality*. Vol. I. New York: Vintage Books.

———. 1979. *Discipline and Punish*. London: Methuen.

———. 1980. *Power/Knowledge*. New York: Pantheon.

———. 1982. "The subject and Power, Afterword." In *Michel Foucault: Beyond Structuralism and Hermeneutics*, edited by Herbert L. Dreyfus and Paul Rabinow. Chicago: Harvester Press.

———. 1984. "What Is Enlightenment?" In *The Foucault Reader: An Introduction to Foucault's Thought*, edited by Paul Rabinow, 32–50. New York: Penguin Books.

———. 1986. *The Care of the Self: History of Sexuality*. Vol. 3. New York: Vintage Books.

———. 1988a. *Madness and Civilization: A History of Insanity in the Age of Reason*. New York: Vintage Books.

———. 1988b. *Politics, Philosophy, Culture: Interviews and Other Writings 1977–1984*. Edited by. Lawrence Kritema. New York: Routledge.

———. 1991. "Governmentality." In *The Foucault Effect: Studies in Governmentality*, edited by Graham Burchell, Colin Gordon, and Peter Miller, 87–103. Chicago: University of Chicago Press.

———. 1994. *Ethics, subjectivity and Truth: Essential Works of Michel Foucault, 1954–1984*. Vol. 1. Edited by Paul Rabinow. New York: New Press.

———. 1996. *Foucault Live: Interviews, 1961–84*. Los Angeles: Semiotexte.

———. 2003. *Society Must Be Defended*. New York: Picador.

Francione, Gary. 1996. *Rain without Thunder: The Ideology of the Animal Rights Movement*. Philadelphia: Temple University Press.

Franklin, Adrian. 1999. *Animals and Modern Cultures: A Sociology of Human–Animal Relationships in Modernity*. London: Sage Publications.

Friedman, Marilyn. 2003. *Autonomy, Gender, Politics*. Oxford: Oxford University Press.

Frost, Liz. 2001. *Young Women and the Body: A Feminist Sociology*. New York: Palgrave.

Fuller, Lon. 1964. *The Morality of Law*. New Haven, Conn.: Yale University Press.

Fultz, Kathleen. 2000. "Griswold for Kids: Should the Privacy Right of Sexual Autonomy Extend to Minors?" *Journal of Juvenile Law* 21:40–78.

Furmola, Adam. 1999. "With Best Friends Like Us Who Needs Enemies? The Phenomenon of the Puppy Mill, the Failure of Legal Regimes to Manage It, and the Positive Prospects of Animal Rights." *Buffalo Environmental Law Journal* 6:253–89.

Furnas, J. C. 1965. *The Life and Times of the Late Demon Rum*. New York: Putnam.

Garner, Robert. 1993. *Animals, Politics and Morality*. New York: Manchester University Press.

Gastman, U., F. Dimeo, H. Huonker, J. M. Bocker, K. Steinacker, H. Peterson, J. Wieland, J. Keul, and M. Lehman. 1998. "Ultra-Triathlon-Related Blood-Chemical and Endocrinological Responses in Nine Athletes." *Journal of Sports Medicine and Physical Fitness* 381:18–23.

Geronimus, Arline. 1997. "Teenage Childbearing and Personal Responsibility: An Alternative View." *Political Science Quarterly*. 112(3):405–30.

Giddings, Paula. 1984. *When and Where I Enter*. New York: William Morrow.

Gill, Emily. 2001. *Becoming Free: Autonomy and Diversity in the Liberal Polity*. Lawrence: University of Kansas Press.

Gilliom, John. 1994. *Surveillance, Privacy and the Law*. Ann Arbor: University of Michigan Press.

Gilroy, Paul. 2000. *Against Race: Imagining Political Culture beyond the Color Line*. Cambridge, Mass.: Harvard University Press.

Glassner, Brian. 1989. "Fitness and the Postmodern Self." *Journal of Health and Social Behavior* 30:180–91.

Golder, Ben. 2008. "Foucault and the Incompletion of Law." *Leiden Journal of International Law* 21:747–63.

Goodin, Robert, Carole Pateman, and Roy Pateman. 1997. "Simian Sovereignty." *Political Theory* 25(6):821–50.

Gordon, Colin. 1986. "Question, Ethos, Event: Foucault on Kant and Enlightenment." *Economy and Society* 151:71–87.

Gordon, Linda. 1994. *Pitied but Not Entitled: Single Others and the History of Welfare, 1890–1935*. New York: Free Press.

Gostin, Lawrence. O., and David Welsher. 1990. "The AIDS Litigation Project: A National Review of the Court and Human Rights Commission Decisions, Part I: The Social Impact of AIDS." *JAMA, Journal of the American Medical Association* 263(14):1961–71.

Greco, Monica. 1993. "Psychosomatic subjects and the 'Duty to Be Well': Personal Agency within Medical Rationality." *Economy and Society* 22(3): 357–72.

Grider, Katharine. 1995. "Crackpot Ideas." *Mother Jones*. (July/August):53–56.

Grosz, Elizabeth. 1994. *Volatile Bodies*. Bloomington: Indiana University Press.

Guerrini, Anita. 1999. "A Diet for a Sensitive Soul: Vegetarianism in Eighteenth-century Britain." *Eighteenth-Century Life* 23(2):34–42.

Gutmann, Amy. 1987. *Democratic Education*. Princeton, N.J.: Princeton University Press.

Haag, Pamela. 1999. *Consent: Sexual Rights and the Transformation of American Liberalism*. Ithaca, N.Y.: Cornell University Press.

Haber, Honi Fern. 1996. "Foucault Pumped: Body Politics and the Muscled Woman." In *Feminist Interpretations of Michel Foucault*, edited by Susan Hekman. University Park: Pennsylvania State UniversityPress.

Habermas, Jürgen. 1990. *The Philosophical Discourse of Modernity*. Translated by Frederick G. Lawrence. Cambridge, Mass.: MIT Press.

———. 1996. *Between Facts and Norms: Contributions to a Discourse Theory of Law and Democracy*. Translated by William Rehg. Cambridge, Mass.: MIT Press.

Ham, Jennifer. 1997. "Taming the Beast: Animality in Wedekind and Nietzsche." In *Animal Acts: Configuring the Human in Western History*, edited by Jennifer Ham and Matthew Senior, 145–64. New York: Routledge.

Ham, Jennifer, and Matthew Senior, editors. 1997. *Animal Acts: Configuring the Human in Western History*. New York: Routledge.

Hauck, E. R., and J. A. Blumenthal. 1992. "Obsessive and Compulsive Traits in Athletes." *Sports Medicine* 14(4):215–27.

Healthy People 2000. 1991. U.S. Department of Health and Human Services Pub. No PHS 91-50213.

Heberle, Renee. 2002. "Victimization and Consent." *Hypatia* 17(3):257–64.

Heelas, Paul, and Paul Morris. 1992. *The Values of the Enterprise Culture: The Moral Debate*. New York: Routledge.

Hekman, S., editor. 1996. *Feminist Interpretations of Michel Foucault*. University Park: Pennsylvania State University Press.

Herscovici, Alan. 1985. *Second Nature: The Animal Rights Controversy*. Montreal: CBC Enterprises.

Hindess, Barry. 1996. "Liberalism, Socialism and Democracy: Variations on a Governmental Theme." In *Foucault and Political Reason: Liberalism, Neo-Liberalism and Rationalities of Government*, edited by Andrew Barry, Thomas Osborne, and Nikolas Rose, 65–80. Chicago: University of Chicago Press.

———. 1998. "Politics and Liberation." In *The Later Foucault: Politics and Philosophy*, edited by Jeremy Moss. London: SAGE Publications.

Hobbes, Thomas. 1994. *Leviathan*. Indianapolis: Hackett Publishing.

Holloway, Sarah L., and Gill Valentine, editors. 2000. *Children's Geographies: Playing, Living, Learning*. New York: Routledge.

Honig, Bonnie. 1993. *Political Theory and the Displacement of Politics*. Ithaca, N.Y.: Cornell University Press.

———. 2001. *Democracy and the Foreigner*. Princeton, N.J.: Princeton University Press.

Honneth, Axel. 1995. *The Struggle for Recognition: The Moral Grammar of Social Conflicts*. Cambridge, Mass.: Polity Press.

Hoy, David, editor. 1991. *Foucault: A Critical Reader*. New York: Blackwell.

———.1994. "Two Conflicting Conceptions of How to Naturalize Philosophy: Foucault versus Habermas." In *Michel Foucault: Critical Assessments*, edited by Barry Smart, New York: Routledge.

Hultquist, Kenneth, and Gunilla, Dahlberg, editors. 2001. *Governing the Child in the New Millennium*. New York: Routledge.

Hwang, C. Philip, Michael E. Lamb, and Irving E. Sigel, editors. 1996. *Images of Childhood*. Mahwah, N.J.: Lawrence Erlbaum Associates.

Hyde, Alan. 1997. *Bodies of Law*. Princeton, N.J.: Princeton University Press.

Ian, Marcia. 1991. "From Abject to Object: Women's Bodybuilding." *Postmodern Culture* 1(3). http://pmc.iath.virginia.edu/text-only/issue.591/pop-cult.591.

Ingold, Tim, editor. 1988. *What Is an Animal?* Boston: Unwin Hyman.

Irvine, Janice. 2002. *Talk about Sex: The Battles over Sex Education in the United States*. Berkeley: University of California Press.

Ivison, Duncan. 1998. "The Technical and the Political: Discourses of Race, Reasons of State." *Social and Legal Studies*. 7(4):561–66.

Jackson, Louise. 2000. *Child Sexual Abuse in Victorian England*. London: Routledge.

Jenkins, Philip. 1999. *Synthetic Panics: The Symbolic Politics of Designer Drugs*. New York: New York University Press.

Johns, Christine. 1992. *Power, Ideology, and the War on Drugs: Nothing Succeeds Like Failure.* New York: Praeger.

Johnston, Lynda. 1996. "Flexing Femininity: Female Body-Builders Refiguring 'the Body.'" *Gender, Place and Culture* 33:27–41.

Jones, Colin, and Roy Porter, editors. 1994. *Reassessing Foucault: Power, Medicine and the Body.* New York: Routledge.

Jonnes, Jill. 1996. *Hep Cats, Narcs, and Pipe Dreams: A History of America's Romance with Illegal Drugs.* New York: Scribner.

Kalyvas, Andreas. 1998. "Norm and Critique in Castoriadis's Theory of Autonomy." *Constellations* 5(2):161–82.

Kant, Immanuel. 1963. *Lectures on Ethics.* New York and London: Century Company.

———. 1992. *Kant on Education (Über padagogik).* Bristol: Thoemmes Press.

———. 1996. *Practical Philosophy.* New York: Cambridge University Press.

Kaplan, Louise J. 1996. "The Stepchild of Psychoanalysis, Adolescence." *American Imago* 53(3):257–68.

Keeping Your Kids Drug-Free: A How-to Guide for Parents and Caregivers. 2002. Washington, D.C.: National Youth Anti-Drug Media Campaign/ Office of National Drug Control Policy.

Keire, Mara L. 2001. "The Vice Trust: A Reinterpetation of the White Slavery Scare in the United States, 1907–1917." *Journal of Social History* 35(1):5–41.

Kennedy, John F. 1960. "The Soft American." *Sports Illustrated.* December 26.

Kerr, K. Austin, editor. 1973. *The Politics of Moral Behavior: Prohibition and Drug Abuse.* Reading, Mass.: Addison Wesley.

Kett, Joseph. 1971. "Adolescence and Youth in Nineteenth-Century America." *Journal of Interdisciplinary History* 22:283–98.

Kincaid, James. 1998. *Erotic Innocence: The Culture of Child Molesting.* Durham, N.C.: Duke University Press.

Kinder, Douglas. 1991. "Shutting Out the Evil: Nativism and Narcotics Control in the United States." In *Drug Control Policy: Essays in Historical and Comparative Perspective.* Edited by William O. Walker. University Park: Pennsylvania State University Press.

Kirby, Kathleen. 1996a. *Indifferent Boundaries: Spatial Concepts of Human Subjectivity.* New York: Guildford Press.

———. 1996b. "Re:mapping subjectivities." In *BodySpace,* edited by N. Duncan. New York: Routledge.

Kirby, Vicki. 1997. *Telling Flesh: The Substance of the Corporeal.* New York: Routledge.

Klein, Alan. 1993a. *Little Big Men: Bodybuilding Subculture and Gender Construction.* Albany: State University of New York Press .

———. 1993b. "Of Muscles and Men." *The Sciences* 33(6):2–38.

Koren, G., K. Graham, H. Shear, and T. Einarson. 1989. "Bias Against the Null Hypothesis: The Reproductive Hazards of Cocaine. " *Lancet* 8677:1440–42.

Kristeva, Julia. 1982. *Powers of Horror: An Essay on Abjection.* New York: Columbia University Press.

Kulynych, Jessica. 2001. "No Playing in the Public Sphere: Democratic Theory and the Exclusion of Children." *Social Theory and Practice* 27(2):231–64.

Kymlicka, Will. 1995. *Multicultural Citizenship.* Oxford: Oxford University Press.

Kyvig, David. 2000. *Repealing National Prohibition.* Kent, Ohio: Kent State University Press.

LaCaze, Marguerite. 2007 "Kant, Derrida, and Ethics and Politics." *PoliticalTheory* 35(6):781–805.

Laclau, Ernesto. 1996a. "Deconstruction, Pragmatism, Hegemony." In *Deconstruction and Pragmatism* edited by Chantal Mouffe, 49–70, New York: Verso.

———. 1996b. *Emancipations.* New York: Verso.

Laclau, Ernesto, and Chantal Mouffe. 1985. *Hegemony and Socialist Strategy.* London: Verso.

Ladd-Taylor, Molly, and Lauri Umansky, editors. 1998. *Bad Mothers: The Politics of Blame in America.* New York: New York University Press.

Lawlor, Leonard. 2007. *This Is Not Sufficient: An Essay on Animality and Human Nature in Derrida.* New York: Columbia University Press.

Leahy, Michael. 1991 *Against Liberation: Putting Animals in Perspective.* New York: Routledge.

Lee, Janet. 1994. "Menarche and the Heterosexualization of the Female Body." *Gender and Society* 83:43–62.

Lehmann, M. J, W. Lormes, A. Optiz-Gress, J. M. Steinacker, N. Netzer, C. Foster, and U. Castmann. 1997. "Training and Overtraining: An Overview and Experimental Results in Endurance Sports." *Journal of Sports Medicine and Physical Fitness* 37(1):7–17.

Lenson, David. 1995. *On Drugs.* Minneapolis: University of Minnesota Press.

Lesko, Nancy. 2001. *Act Your Age! A Cultural Construction of Adolescence.* New York: Routledge.

Levinas, Emmanuel. 1969. *Totality and Infinity.* Pittsburgh: Duquesne University Press.

———. 1990. "The Name of a Dog, or Natural Rights." In *Difficult Freedom: Essays on Judaism*. Translated by Sean Hand. London: Athalone Press.

Levine, Judith. 2002. *Harmful to Minors: The Perils of Protecting Children from Sex*. Minneapolis: University of Minnesota Press.

Levinson, Meira. 1999. "Liberalism, Pluralism and Political Education: Paradox or Paradigm." *Oxford Review of Education* 25(1/2):9–58.

Lindley, Richard. 1986. *Autonomy*. Atlantic Highlands, N.J.: Humanities Press International.

Lingis, Alfonso. 1994. *Foreign Bodies*. New York: Routledge.

Locke, John. 1902. *Some Thoughts Concerning Education*. London: C. J. Clay.

Longford, Graham. 2005. "Sensitive Killers, Cruel Aesthetes, and Pitiless Poets: Foucault, Rorty and the Ethics of Self-Fashioning." *Polity* 33(4):569–92.

Longhurst, Robyn. 2001. *Bodies: Exploring Fluid Boundaries*. New York: Routledge.

Lowe, Donald M. 1995. *The Body in Late-Capitalist USA*. Durham, N.C.: Duke University Press.

Luker, Kristin. 1997. *Dubious Conceptions: The Politics of Teenage Pregnancy*. Cambridge, Mass.: Harvard University Press.

MacKenzie, Catriona, and Natalie Stoljar. 2000. *Relational Autonomy: Feminist Perspectives on Autonomy, Agency, and the Social Self*. Oxford: Oxford University Press.

MacKinnon, Laurel T. 2000. "Chronic Exercise Training Effects on Immune Function." *Medicine and Science in Sports* 32(7): S369–S376.

Maloney, L. 1985. "Life Beyond Jogging—the World of the Superfit." *U.S. News and World Report* 99:60–62.

Malson, Helen. 1998. *The Thin Woman: Feminism, Poststructuralism and the Social Psychology of Anorexia Nervosa*. New York: Routledge.

Markell, Patchen. 2000. "The Recognition of Politics: A Comment on Emcke and Tully." *Constellations* 7(4):496–506.

Marro, Antonio. 1899. "Influence of the Puberal Development upon the Moral Character of Children of Both Sexes." *American Journal of Sociology* 5(2):193–219.

———. 1900. "Puberal Hygiene in Relation to Pedagogy and Sociology." *American Journal of Sociology* 6(2):224–37.

Matt, Susan J. 2002. "Children's Envy and the Emergence of the Modern Consumer Ethic, 1890–1930." *Journal of Social History* 36(2):283–302.

McClain, Linda C. 1995. "Symposium: The Sacred Body in Law and Literature: Inviolability and Privacy: the Castle, the Sanctuary, the Body." *Yale Journal of Law and the Humanities* 7(1):95–242.

McClure, Kristie. 1992. "On the subject of Rights: Pluralism, Plurality and Political Identity." In *Dimensions of Radical Democracy: Pluralism, Citizenship, Community,* edited by Chantal Mouffe, 108–27. New York: Verso.

McCormack, Derek. 1999. "Body Shopping: Reconfiguring Geographies of Fitness." *Gender, Place and Culture* 6(2):155–77.

McRobbie, Angela. 1991. *Feminism and Youth Culture: From Jackie to Just Seventeen.* Boston: Unwin Hyman.

Mehta, Juhi. 1998. "Prosecuting Teenage Parents under Fornication Statutes: A Constitutionally Suspect Legal Solution to the Social Problem of Teen Pregnancy." *Cardozo Women's Law Journal* 5:121–50.

Mehta, Uday Singh. 1999. *Liberalism and Empire.* Chicago: University of Chicago Press.

Melley, Thomas. 1999. *Empire of Conspiracy: The Culture of Paranoia in Postwar America.* Ithaca, N.Y.: Cornell University Press.

Merry, Sally Engle. 1999. *Colonizing Hawai'i: The Cultural Power of Law.* Princeton, N.J.: Princeton University Press.

Meyer, Linda Ross. 2000. "Unruly Rights." *Cardozo Law Review* 22(1):1–50.

Meyers, Diana Tietjens. 1991. *Self, Society, and Personal Choice.* New York: Columbia University Press.

Midgley, Mary. 1983. *Animals and Why They Matter.* Athens: University of Georgia Press.

Mill, John Stuart. 1859. *On Liberty.* Oxford: Oxford University Press.

Miller, Randall K. 1997. "The Limits of U.S. International Law Enforement after *Verdugo-Urquidez*: Resurrecting *Rochin.*" *University of Pittsburg Law Review* 58:884–85.

Mills, Charles. 1999. *The Racial Contract.* Ithaca, N.Y.: Cornell University Press.

Mink, Gwendolyn. 2001. "Violating Women: Rights Abuses in the Welfare Police State." *Annals of the American Academy of Political and Social Science* 79:577–98.

Minow, Martha. 1990. *Making All the Difference: Inclusion, Exclusion and American Law.* Ithaca, N.Y.: Cornell University Press.

———. 1994. "From Class Actions to 'Miss Saigon': The Concept of Representation in the Law." In *Representing Women: Law, Literature and Feminism.* Edited by Susan Sage Heinzelman and Zipporah Batshaw Wiseman. Durham, N.C.: Duke University Press.

Moore, Pamela, editor. 1997. *Building Bodies.* New Brunswick, N.J.: Rutgers University Press.

Moran, Jeffrey. 2000. *Teaching Sex: The Shaping of Adolescence in the Twentieth Century.* Cambridge, Mass.: Harvard University Press.

Moss, Jeremy, editor. 1998. *The Later Foucault: Politics and Philosophy.* London: SAGE Publications.

Mouffee, Chantal, editor. 1996. *Deconstruction and Pragmatism.* New York: Routledge.

Murji, Karim. 1998. "The Agony and the Ecstasy: Drugs, Media and Morality." In *The Control of Drugs and Drug Users: Reason or Reaction?* Edited by Ross Coomber. Amsterdam: Harwood Academic Publishers.

Musto, David. 1999. *The American Disease: Origins of Narcotics Control.* Oxford: Oxford University Press.

Nadesan, Majia Holmer. 2008. *Governmentality, Biopower and Everyday Life.* New York: Routledge Press.

Nancy, Jean-Luc. 1988. *The Experience of Freedom.* Translated by Bridget McDonald. Palo Alto, Calif.: Stanford University Press.

———. 2008. *Corpus.* New York: Fordham University Press.

National Drug Control Strategy. 2002. Washington, D.C.: Government Publications/The White House.

Neuspiel, D. 1996. "Racism and Perinatal Addiction." *Ethnicity and Disease* 6:47–55.

Newman, Saul. 2003. "Stiner and Foucault: Toward a Post-Kantian Freedom." *Postmodern Culture* 13(2). http://muse.jhu.edu/journals/postmodern_culture/v013/13.2newman.html.

Nieman, D. C., and B. K. Pedersen. "Exercise and Immune Function: Recent Developments." *Sports Medicine* 272:73–80.

Nietzsche, Friedrich. 1967 [1887]. *On the Genealogy of Morals.* Translated by Walter Kaufman. New York: Vintage Books.

———. 1974 [1882]. *The Gay Science.* Translated by Walter Kaufman. New York: Vintage Books.

———. 1995 [1883–85]. *Thus Spoke Zarathustra.* Translated by Walter Kaufman. New York: Modern Library.

———. 1999. "On Truth and Lies in a Nonmoral Sense." *The Nietzsche Pages.* February 5, 1999. http://www.usc.edu/~douglast/nietzsche.html.

Nixon, Howard L. 1989. "Reconsidering Obligatory Running and Anorexia Nervosa as Gender-Related Problems of Identity and Role-Adjustment." *Journal of Sport and Social Issues* 13(1):14–24.

Noakes, Timothy. 1991. *Lore of Running.* Champaign, Ill.: Leisure Press.

Nolan, James L. 2001. *Reinventing Justice: The American Drug Court Movement.* Princeton, N.J.: Princeton University Press.

Noske, Barbara. 1989. *Humans and Other Animals: Beyond the Boundaries of Anthropology*. London: Pluto.

Noyes, John K. 1997. *The Mastery of Submission: Inventions of Masochism*. Ithaca, N.Y.: Cornell University Press.

Nussbaum, Martha. 2006. *Frontiers of Justice: Disability, Nationality, Species*. Cambridge, Mass.: Harvard University Press.

Oberman, Michelle. 2000. "Regulating Consensual Sex with Minors: Defining a Role for Statutory Rape." *Buffalo Law Review* 48:703–892.

————. 2001. "Girls in the Master's House: Of Protection, Patriarchy and the Potential for Using the Master's Tools to Reconfigure Statutory Rape Law." *DePaul Law Review* 50:799–850.

O'Brien, David. 2000. *Constitutional Law and Politics: Civil Rights and Liberties*. New York: W. W. Norton.

Odem, Mary. 1995. *Delinquent Daughters: Protecting and Policing Adolescent Female Sexuality*. Chapel Hill: University of North Carolina Press.

Ohi, Kevin. 2000. "Molestation 101: Child Abuse, Homophobia and the Boys of St. Vincent." *GLQ* 6(2):195–248.

Oliver, Kelly. 2009. *Animal Lessons: How They Teach Us to Be Human*. New York: Columbia University Press.

O'Neill, Onora. 1989. *Constructions of Reason: Explorations of Kant's Practical Philosophy*. New York: Cambridge University Press.

Orlie, Melissa. 1997. *Living Ethically, Acting Politically*. Ithaca, N.Y.: Cornell University Press.

Osborne, Timothy. 1993. "Liberalism, Neo-Liberalism, and the 'Liberal Profession' of Medicine." *Economy and Society*. 22(3):45–56.

Palladino, Grace. 1996. *Teenagers: An American History*. New York: Basic Books.

Paltrow, Lynn. 1996. "Punishing Women for Their Behavior during Pregnancy: An Approach That Undermines the Health of Women and Children." New York: Center for Reproductive Law & Policy. http://www.crlp .org/pub_art_punwom.html 10.

Paris, Leslie. 2001. "The Adventures of Peanut and Bo: Summer Camps and Early-Twentieth Century American Girlhood." *Journal of Women's History* 12(4):47–76.

Patton, Paul. 1998. "Foucault's Subject of Power." In *The Later Foucault: Politics and Philosophy*, edited by Jeremy Moss, 64–77. London: SAGE Publications.

Phillips, Kendall. 2002. "Spaces of Invention: Dissension, Freedom, and Thought in Foucault." *Philosophy and Rhetoric* 35(4):28–45.

Philo, Chris. 1998. "Animals, Geography and the City: Notes on Inclusions and Exclusions." In *Animal Geographies*. Edited by Jennifer Wolch and Jodi Emel. New York: Routledge.

Philo, Chris, and Chris Wilbert, editors. 2000. *Animal Spaces, Beastly Places*. London: Routledge.

Pierce, Edgar F. 1994. "Exercise Dependence Syndrome in Runners." *Sports Medicine* 18(3):149–55.

Piper, Christine. 2000. "Historical Constructions of Childhood Innocence: Removing Sexuality." In *Of Innocence and Autonomy: Children, Sex and Human Rights*, edited by Eric Heinze, 26–46. Burlington, Vt.: Ashgate/Dartmouth.

Pivar, David. 1973. *Purity Crusade: Sexual Morality and Social Control, 1868–1900*. Westport, Conn.: Greenwood Press.

Plato. 1945. *The Republic of Plato*. New York: Oxford University Press.

Popiel, Jennifer. 2008. *Rousseau's Daughters: Domesticity, Education, and Autonomy in Modern France*. Lebanon: University of New Hampshire Press.

Powell, Aaron. 1886. "The Moral Elevation of Girls." *Philantropist* 1:5–6.

Prouty, Heather. 1998. "Iron Women: Portraits in Courage from One of the World's Toughest Triathlons." *Women's Sports and Fitness* 20(2):44–48.

"Putting Yourself to the Test. *OnHealth Reports*. http://about.onhealth.com/ch1/in-depth/item/item,56337_1_1.asp 10 .

Rail, Genevieve, editor. 1997. *Sport and Postmodern Times*. Albany:State University of New York Press.

Rasmussen, Claire, and Michael Brown. 2005. "Reviving a Dead Metaphor: The Body of Politics and Citizenship." *Citizenship Studies* 9(5):469–84.

Regan, Tom. 1983. *The Case for Animal Rights*. Berkeley: University of California Press.

Reinarman, Craig, and Ceres Duskin. 1992. "Dominant Ideology and Drugs in the Media." *International Journal on Drug Policy*. 3(1):6–15.

Reitan, Eric. 2001. "Rape as an Essentially Contested Concept." *Hypatia* 16(2):43–66.

Richards, David A. J. 1982. *Sex, Drugs, Death and the Law: An Essay on Human Rights and Overcriminalization*. Totowa, N.J.: Rowman and Littlefield.

Richmond, Winifred V. 1935. "Sex Problems in Adolescence." *Journal of Educational Sociology* 8(6):33–41.

Ritvo, Harriet. 1989. *The Animal Estate: The English and Other Creatures in the Victorian Age*. Cambridge, Mass.: Harvard University Press.

Roberston, Stephen. 2001. "Separating the Men from the Boys: Masculinity, Psychosexual Development and Sex Crime in the United States, 1930s–1960s." *Journal of the History of Medicine and Allied Sciences* 56(1):3–35.

———. 2002. "Age of Consent Law and the Making of Modern Childhood in New York City 1886–1921." *Journal of Social History* 35(4):781–98.

Roberts, Dorothy. 1997. *Killing the Black Body: Race, Reproduction and the Meaning of Liberty.* New York: Pantheon.

Robinson, Jerome, and James Jones. 2000. "Drug Testing in a Drug Court Environment: Common Issues to Address." *OJP Drug Court Clearinghouse and Technical Assistance Project.* Washington, D.C.: American University.

Rose, Nikolas. 1990. *Governing the Soul: The Shaping of the Private Self.* New York: Routledge.

———. 1992. "Governing the Enterprising Self." In *The Values of Enterprise Culture: A Moral Debate,* edited by Paul Heelas and Paul Morris. 141–64. New York: Routledge.

———. 1996. "Governing 'Advanced' Liberal Democracies." In *Foucault and Political Reason: Liberalism, Neo-Liberalism and Rationalities of Government,* edited by Andrew Barry, Thomas Osborne, and Nikolas Rose, 37–64. Chicago: University of Chicago Press.

———. 1999. *Powers of Freedom: Reframing Political Thought.* Cambridge: Cambridge University Press.

———. 2006. *The Politics of Life Itself: Biomedicine, Power, and subjectivity in the Twenty-First Century.* Princeton, N.J.: Princeton University Press.

Rosenbaum, Martha. 1997. "Women: Research and Policy." In *Substance Abuse: A Comprehensive Textbook,* edited by Joyce Lowinson, Pedro Ruiz, Robert Millman,and John Langrond, 654–65. Baltimore: Williams & Wilkins.

Rosenberg, Irene Merker. 1996. "Public School Drug Testing: The Impact of *Acton.*" *American Criminal Law Review* 33(2).

Rousseau, Jean-Jacques. 1911. *Émile.* London: Everyman.

———. 1992. *Second Discourse on the Origins of Inequality.* New York: Hackett.

———. 1997. *The Social Contract and Other Later Political Writings.* New York: Cambridge University Press.

———. 2000. *Confessions.* New York: Oxford University Press.

Ryan, Alan. 1998. *Liberal Anxieties and Liberal Education.* New York: Hill and Wang.

Salisbury, Joyce E. 1994. *The Beast Within: Animals in the Middle Ages*. New York: Routledge.

Sanchez-Eppeler, Karen. 2000. "Playing at Class." *ELH* 67:819–42.

Sayres, Sohnya. 1986–87. "Glory Mongering: Food and the Agon of Excess." *Social Text* 16:81–96.

Scales-Trent, Judy. 2001. "Racial Purity Laws in the United States and Nazi Germany: The Targeting Process." *Human Rights Quarterly* 23(2):260–307.

Scarry, Elaine. 1985. *The Body in Pain: The Making and Unmaking of the World*. New York: Oxford University Press.

Scheiner, Georgeanne. 2001. "Look at Me I'm Sandra Dee." *Frontiers: A Journal of Women's Studies* 22(2):87–106.

Schmottlach, Neil, and Jerre McManama. 1997. *Physical Education Handbook*. Boston: Allyn and Bacon.

Scholtmeijer, Maria. 1997. "What Is 'Human'? Metaphysics and Zoontology in Flaubert and Kafka." In *Animal Acts: Configuring the Human in Western History*, edited by Jennifer Ham and Matthew Senior, 145–64. New York: Routledge.

Sedgwick, Eve Kosovsky. 1992. "Epidemics of the Will." In *Incorporations*, edited by Jonathan Crary and Sanford Kwinter, 582–95. New York: Zone Books.

———.1993. *Tendencies*. Durham, N.C.: Duke University Press.

Seery, John. 1997. "Banana Republic: A Response to Goodin, Pateman and Pateman." *Political Theory* 25(5):850–55.

Silverstein, Helena. 1996. *Unleashing Rights: Law, Meaning and the Animal Rights Movement*. Ann Arbor: University of Michigan Press.

Simon, Jonathan. 1993. *Poor Discipline: Parole and the Social Control of the Underclass, 1890–1990*. Chicago: University of Chicago Press.

Singer, Peter. 1970. *Animal Liberation*. New York: Avon Books.

Smart, Barry, editor. 1994. *Michel Foucault: Critical Assessments*. New York: Routledge.

Smith, Anne Marie. 2002. "The Sexual Regulation Dimension of Contemporary Welfare Law: A Fifty State Overview." *Michigan Journal of Gender and Law* 8:121–240.

———. 2007. *Welfare Reform and Sexual Regulation*. Cambridge: Cambridge University Press.

Smith, D. K., B. D. Hale, and M. Collins. 1998. "Measurement of Exercise Dependence in Bodybuilders." *Journal of Sports Medicine and Physical Fitness* 39(1):66–74.

Smith, Rob Roy. 1999. "Standing on Their Own Four Legs: The Future of Animal Welfare Litigation after *Animal Welfare League Inc. v. Glickman.*" *Environmental Law* 29:989–1029.

Spivak, Gayatri Chakravorty. 1988. "Can the Subaltern Speak?" In *Marxism and the Interpretation of Culture,* edited by Cary Nelson and Lawrence Grossberg. Chicago: University of Illinois Press.

State of California Statutory Rape Vertical Prosecution Program. 2003. State of California.

Stephens, Sharon. 1995. "Children and the Politics of Culture in 'Late Capitalism.'" In *Children and the Politics of Culture,* edited by Sharon Stephens, 4–48. Princeton, N.J.: Princeton University Press.

Stoler, Ann Laura. 1995. *Race and the Education of Desire: Foucault's History of Sexuality and the Colonial Order of Things.* Durham, N.C.: Duke University Press.

Tannenbaum, J. 1995. "Animals and the Law: Property, Cruelty, Rights." *Social Research* 62(3):539–607.

Taylor, Angus. 1999. *Magpies, Monkeys and Morals: What Philosophers Say about Animal Liberation.* Orchard Park, N.Y.: Broadview.

Tester, Keith. 1991. *Animals and Society: The Humanity of Animal Rights.* New York: Routledge.

Thomas, Keith. 1983. *Man and the Natural World.* New York: Oxford University Press.

Towns, Ann. 2010. *Women and States: Norms and Hierarchies in International Society.* New York: Cambridge University Press.

Traffic. 2001. DVD. Dir. Steven Soderbergh. USA Films.

Trainspotting. 1996. DVD. Dir. Danny Boyle. Miramax.

Tully, James. 2000. "Struggles over Recognition and Distribution." *Constellations* 7(4):469–82.

Tunnell, Kenneth. 2004. *Pissing on Demand: Workplace Drug Testing and the Rise of the Detox Industry.* New York: New York University Press.

Turner, Bryan S. 1982. "The Government of the Body: Medical Regimens and Rationalization of Diet." *British Journal of Sociology* 33(2): 254–66.

U.S. Sentencing Commission. 1995. *Special Report to Congress: Cocaine and Federal Sentencing Policy.* Washington, D.C.: U.S. Sentencing Commission, February 1995, iii.

Verbrugge, Martha H. 1997. "Recreating the Body: Women's Physical Education and the Science of Sex Differences in America, 1900–1940." *Bulletin of the History of Medicine* 71(2):273–304.

Weinstein, Megan. 1998. "The Teenage Pregnancy Problem: Welfare Reform and the Personal Responsibility and Work Opportunity Reconciliation Act of 1996." *Berkeley Women's Law Journal* 13:117–53.

Weiss, Penny. 1993. *Gendered Community: Rousseau, Sex and Politics*. New York: New York University Press.

Williams, Patricia. 1991. *The Alchemy of Race and Rights*. Cambridge, Mass.: Harvard University Press.

Wingrove, Elizabeth. 2000. *Rousseau's Republican Romance*. Princeton, N.J.: Princeton University Press.

Wittgenstein, Ludwig. 1958. *Philosophical Investigations*. Englewood Cliffs, N.J.: Prentice Hall.

Wolch, Jennifer, and Jody Emel, editors. 1998. *Animal Geographies*. New York: Verso.

Wolfe, Cary. 2003a. *Animal Rites: American Culture, the Discourse of Species, and Posthumanist Theory*. Chicago: University of Chicago Press.

———, editor. 2003b. *Zoontologies: The Question of the Animal*. Minneapolis: University of Minnesota Press.

———. 2010. *What Is Posthumanism?* Minneapolis: University of Minnesota Press.

Wood, David. 2004. "Thinking with Cats." In *Animal Philosophy: Essential Readings in Continental Thought*, edited by Matthew Calarco and Peter Atterton. New York: Continuum.

Woodiwiss, M. 1998. "Reform, Racism and Rackets: Alcohol and Drug Prohibition in the United States." In *The Control of Drugs and Drug Users: Reason or Reaction?* edited by Ross Coomber, 13–30. Amsterdam: Harwood Academic Publishers.

Youngquist, Paul. 1999. "De Quincey's Crazy Body." *PMLA* 114(3):46–58.

Zerilli, Linda M. G. 1994. *Signifying Woman: Culture and Chaos in Rousseau, Burke, and Mill*. Ithaca, N.Y.: Cornell University Press.

———. 2002. "Castoriadis, Arendt, and the Problem of the New." *Constellations* 9:540–53.

Zorbaugh, Harvey W., and L. Virgil Payne. 1935. "Adolescence: Psychosis or Social Adjustment." *Journal of Educational Sociology* 8(6):71–77.

Index

abjection, 68–70

Adams, Carol, 124

addiction, 138, 141, 150–51, 158;
drugs and, 62–64, 67–70, 72, 77;
exercise and, 158–59, 165

adolescence, 25, 39, 43–44; girls
and, 41, 44–46, 48–57; invention of the category, 38, 172n7;
pregnancy and, 55–56; sex and,
34–35, 37–40, 49–57, 173n8

Agamben, Giorgio, 175n5

age of consent laws, 48–57, 174n18,
174n19

Alice in Wonderland, 128–29

animals (nonhuman): classification of, 101, 108, 114, 128,
133, 135, 179n4; the classification of humans and, 112–13,
179–180n8, 180n14, 181n19, 20;
ethical treatment of, 100, 128,
131–35; historical treatment
of, 110–12, 181n17, 181n18;
law and, 97–98, 102, 178–79n1;
othering and, 99–100, 103–4,
128–30; political movements
protecting, 111–13; political theory and, 102–8, 180n10, 180n11,
180n12, 180n15, 180n16; rights
and, 99, 101, 111–15, 119–20,
122, 125, 127, 179n7

Anslinger, Harry, 73

Arendt, Hannah, 12, 169

Aristotle, x, 103, 179n5

athletes, 84, 137–38, 141, 159–67

Aquinas, Thomas, 103

autonomy: compulsion and, 12, 16,
147; creativity and, 10–12, 58,
145, 152, 156–57, 169; democracy and, xi, 5, 7, 9, 11, 29, 40–42,
63, 78; vs. heteronomy, 10, 12,
50, 70, 87, 139, 168; history of
the concept x–xii; liberalism and,
xi, 8–9, 167–68, 171n6; management of the body and, 26, 29–30,
32, 40–42, 49, 57, 63–69, 85,
94, 140, 147–48, 150, 163, 166;
maturity and, 24–28, 33–35, 43,
58; the paradox of xiv–xv, 13, 18,
168–69; political exclusion and,
63, 70, 87–88, 95, 128; reason
and, 6; recognition and, 117; self
regulation and, xi, 2, 5–7, 14, 28,
65, 121, 140, 145, 149, 151, 154,
168; women and, 46–49, 57, 91

Baudrillard, Jean, 146, 151–52, 157

Bell, Vicki, 12, 167–68

Bell v. Wolfish, 441 U.S. 520 (1979),
86

Bentham, Jeremy, 118

Claire E. Rasmussen is associate professor of political science and international relations at the University of Delaware. Her work has been published in *Signs: A Journal of Women and Culture, Social and Cultural Geography, Society and Space,* and *Citizenship Studies.*